THE NAT HENTOFF READER

THE
NAT HENTOFF
READER

Nat Hentoff

DA CAPO PRESS

Designed by *Brent Wilcox*
Set in 12-point Weiss by Perseus Publishing Services

Cataloging-in-Publication data for this book is
available from the Library of Congress.

First Da Capo Press edition 2001
ISBN 0–306–81084–0

Published by Da Capo Press
A Member of the Perseus Books Group
http://www.dacapopress.com

Da Capo Press books are available at special discounts for
bulk purchases in the U.S. by corporations, institutions, and other
organizations. For more information, please contact the Special Markets
Department at the Perseus Books Group, 11 Cambridge Center,
Cambridge, MA 02142, or call (617) 252-5298.

1 2 3 4 5 6 7 8 9—05 04 03 02 01

To John Radziewicz—
who thought of, edited, and published this book.
In all his work, he keeps the First Amendment swinging.

That's one thing I like about jazz, kid. I don't know what's going to happen next. Do you?

—Bix Beiderbecke

Who is to determine which life is "meaningful," which life is not? Who is to have a right to the world's resouces, to food, to housing, to medical care? The prospects are frightening.

—John Cardinal O'Connor,
Harvard Law School Forum

CONTENTS

CONTENTS

INTRODUCTION

I was twenty, sitting at the bar in a struggling Boston jazz club, alongside Duke Ellington's longtime tenor saxophonist—the large, often volatile, Ben Webster. Now on his own, he often couldn't bring his regular rhythm section to out-of-town gigs because the club owners wouldn't pay what it cost. It was intermission. Ben had just finished a set with an earnest but stolid local rhythm section, and he had lifted them, as if in a huge fist, into a groove that at least approximated swinging.

"You see," Ben said, triumphant: "If the rhythm section ain't making it, go for yourself."

That principle of Ben's music and his life, which were the same, has stayed with me. If I'm to have a headstone, I'd like that to be on it.

A few years earlier, a Duke Ellington song had got me to thinking, or rather brooding. It was called "What Am I Here For?"

I was growing up in a Jewish neighborhood that was intensely, accusatorily ideological. The conservative majority were the Franklin D. Roosevelt Democrats, and they delivered Boston's Ward 12 for FDR handsomely at every opportunity.

But there were also insistent cadres of Communists, socialists and some anarchists. So far as I knew, the last group was non-violent, but certainly voluble.

At 15, having read Arthur Koestler's "Darkness At Noon"—about Stalin's Russia—a novel that foretold George Orwell's *1984*—I had innoculated myself against the Communists in my neighborhood. When my barber tried to recruit me for the Young Communist League, I mentioned "Darkness at Noon," and it was as if I had thrust a cross straight at Dracula. I never got a decent haircut at the shop after that, but it was otherwise a friendly place.

I still didn't know what I was here for. But I began to find out when, also at 15, I was among some kids recruited as apprentice journalists for a muckraking newspaper—actually a four-page mimeographed sheet—the *Boston City Reporter*. The only payment was that for me, it put a personal pulse, a rhythm, to Duke Ellington's song.

The publisher, editor and sole writer for the *Boston City Reporter* was a committed Catholic, Frances Sweeney, the only daughter of a saloon keeper. As Arthur Schlesinger, Jr. describes her in *A Life in the 20th Century: Innocent Beginnings, 1917–1950* (Houghton Mifflin):

"A fiery young Irish-American woman . . . she had reddish-blonde hair and flashing blue eyes, and she was afraid of nothing."

The paper was begun to expose corruption in Boston. While that was as easy as opening a window, it did require—for an editor so fiercely insistent on *facts*, not just opinions—a crew of volunteers who yearned for experience as reporters. That many of us were Jewish was due to the fact that Fran was also a ferocious enemy of anti-Semitism, which was pandemic in Boston during those years. Outside Catholic churches on Sundays, copies of Father Charles Coughlin's newspaper, *Social Justice*—which featured continual updates on *The Protocols of the Elders of Zion*—were distributed. After its contents were digested at dinner tables, young hooligans, avenging the crucifixion of Christ, would, during the rest of the week, descend on Jewish neighborhoods to bust heads and other parts of the body. I lost some teeth during one of those sanctified expeditions.

What infuriated Fran was the silence of the Boston archdiocese at these echoes of what was happening in Germany. In *The Boston City Reporter*, Fran cited and excoriated those of her fellow Catholics who encouraged—or said nothing—about this rampant anti-Semitism. And she called the autocratic, icy Cardinal William O'Connell to account.

The Cardinal was so incensed at her that he summoned Fran to his austere presence and threatened her with excommunication if she did not immediately and permanently censor herself. She would not.

Fran refused to take any advertisements for the paper. And in any case, she used to say, "Nobody can go past me to my boss." Gravely bowing to herself in the mirror, she would continue, "because *I* am my boss."

As I wrote about Fran in *Boston Boy* (Paul Dry Books), she didn't treat us cub reporters as kids: "You must understand how important you are, and how much damage you can do if you're careless, if your facts turn out to be lies. That's all our enemies will need to discredit the whole lot of us. You understand?"

We understood. And one day we learned, from her to our shame, a lot about ourselves that we hadn't suspected. A few days before, Fran surprised us by passing out sets of test papers. The questions had to do with what our attitudes were toward different racial, ethnic and religious groups in pluralistic America. On part of the test, we had to check off what we considered were the most dominant characteristics of these groups.

Still wondering what the point of all that was, we were summoned to *The Boston City Reporter* to get our grades. Fran strode into the room, those flashing blue eyes narrowed in scorn, and threw the test papers on a table.

"Most of you," she addressed her troops, "are Jewish, and I am happy to inform you that you are free of anti-Semitism." We started to laugh.

"You also," she said coldly, "turn out to be the scrimiest bunch of ignorant anti-Catholics I have ever had the penance of being associated with."

Underlining each of our stereotypes of her fellow religionists, she taught us a burning lesson that was not part of the curriculum of the nationally prestigious public school—the Boston Latin School, founded in 1635—that I was attending.

Fran had a heart condition. Her doctor kept warning her to slow down. She was not only putting out the paper, but also making speeches to largely Irish audiences, which either walked out on her or wanted to. And she had formed the Irish-American Defense Association to counter anti-Semitism, and isolationism in the time of Hitler, fueled by hatred of the British. In addition, she had set up a "Rumor Clinic" to expose the vicious stereotypes, lies and myths about "others" that were circulating ceaselessly around Boston.

Friends told Fran she was going to kill herself. Her answer— as reported in her obituary in the August 18, 1944, issue of *The*

Commonweal—"Well, then, I'll die fighting for what I believe, won't I?"

One rainy night in April, 1944, after she had put the paper to bed, Fran, alone, walking home on Beacon Street, one of Boston's most respectable thoroughfares, had a heart attack. She fell, still conscious, into the gutter. For hours, the rain falling on her, she could not move or speak as she heard passersby either ignoring her or muttering about the evils—so palpable at their feet—of liquor.

A cop finally thought to see if she were alive, Fran lived until June. She was 36 when she died. I was 19. I went home and put on recordings—not blues, but ballads by Ben Webster. Although he raged when he was drunk—his Ellington colleagues called him "the brute"—Ben, in ballads like "All Too Soon," could make you remember your most devastating and permanent losses.

To my mother's growing concern, I played Ben Webster recordings over and over for hours. In 1953, when I left Boston for New York to become an editor of the jazz magazine, *Down Beat*, Fran went with me. And she has never left.

—*Nat Hentoff*

PART **1**

THE CONDITION
OF LIBERTY

FAIR-WEATHER FRIENDS
OF THE FIRST AMENDMENT

Of all the Supreme Court justices, William O. Douglas was the most passionate and unequivocal defender of the First Amendment. In 1951, he said: "Very few Americans have ever actually been willing to grant [First Amendment] freedoms respecting either political or aesthetic matters that they dislike or believe fraught with danger to the general welfare."

So it has always been from the time of the Alien and Sedition Acts of 1798 to the present. In recent months at Cornell University, black students have twice stolen copies of *The Cornell Review*, a conservative campus paper, and burned them in public celebrations.

The dean of students told me approvingly that those actions were, after all, simply the exercise of free expression by students critical of the paper. But, somehow, the Framers of the Constitution neglected to include theft and arson as protected speech under the First Amendment.

Meanwhile, there is rising censorship of high school newspapers by principals and school boards—as documented regularly in the *Student Press Law Center Report* (1101 Wilson Blvd., Suite 1910, Arlington, VA 22209). The Center provides free legal advice to beleaguered student editors, and calls have increased by a third in the past year—coming from all fifty states. In Texas, school administrators "pulled a story about the formation of a gay and lesbian support group for students on campus from the front page of the school's student newspaper in May 1998," the *Report* notes.

There is also a continuing, very often successful attempt to remove books from classes and libraries in public schools. *Huckleberry Finn* is the most frequent target because the word "nigger" appears in many parts of the book. Mark Twain used the word to illuminate the pervasiveness of racism in the time and place of his novel. Except for Huck, the only person of integrity in the novel is a black man, Jim.

There is good news, however. The clearest and strongest federal court opinion protecting the First Amendment rights of teachers to assign controversial books has just come down from the Ninth Circuit Court of Appeals.

Writing for the three-judge panel that heard a case involving censorship of *Huckleberry Finn*, Judge Stephen Reinhardt first made an essential point that is often overlooked in all kinds of censorship cases: "The right to receive information is a corollary of the rights of free speech and press because the right to distribute information protects the right to receive it." When Justice William Brennan made the same point years ago, he was mocked by some of his brethren (no women were on the court then) who claimed the First Amendment says nothing about the right to receive information.

In the current case, *Kathy Monteiro v. The Tempe Union (Arizona) High School District*, Justice Reinhardt went on to emphasize "the students' rights to receive a broad range of information so that they can freely form their own thoughts. . . . It is important for young people to . . . discover both the good and the bad in our history. . . . It is simply not the role of the courts to serve as literary censors or to make judgments as to whether reading particular books does students more harm than good."

In years of visiting high schools around the country, I have found that just about the only students who have a clear and ardent understanding of the First Amendment are the high school journalists who have fought for their free press rights. Mark Goodman, director of the Student Press Law Center, emphasizes: "For most high school journalists, their attitude about the media and the importance we place on press freedom will be fundamentally shaped by experiences that end the day they graduate from high school."

Having also taught in a number of colleges, I can attest that far too many college students are ignorant of the scope and depth of the First Amendment.

Only recently has a book been published that documents how pervasively and cynically the Bill of Rights, including the First Amendment, has been subverted on college campuses—including at the most prestigious schools.

This documented indictment is *The Shadow University*, by Alan Charles Kors and Harvey Silverglate (The Free Press). Included in the book is a memorandum to all faculty at the University of Minnesota suggesting that a "Classroom Climate

Adviser be invited to scrutinize those classes where a student feels that a classroom discussion about race or gender was disrespectful or insulting."

George Orwell lives!

The right to be offensive—in any of the limitless meanings of that term—continues to be in danger also on the Internet. Although the Supreme Court unanimously rejected the Communications Decency Act in 1996 as an assault on the First Amendment, Congress has now passed the Child On-Line Protection Act, which Bill Clinton signed into law.

The Communications Decency Act was struck down because it would have lowered the permissible standard of expression on the Internet to material suitable—that is, not "indecent"—for children. The new law makes it a crime—as the American Booksellers Foundation for Free Expression points out—"for any commercial web site to distribute to a minor material that is 'harmful to minors.'" Since any material that is posted on the web can be accessed by minors, this means that an on-line bookstore could be prosecuted for merely displaying a book excerpt—or pictures of a book jacket—that could be judged "harmful to minors."

If former Surgeon General C. Everett Koop's specific recommendations for preventing AIDS were placed on the Internet under the new law, those responsible could be fined up to $50,000 for each day of violation and sent to prison for up to six months for "knowingly" communicating for "commercial purposes" material judged "harmful to minors."

Although Congress is so often a visible enemy of free expression, a new array of more subtle devaluers of the First Amendment has been emerging in recent years. Floyd Abrams, a leading paladin of free expression in arguments before the Supreme Court, cited some of them in an article in a 1997 issue of the *Columbia Journalism Review*, "Look Who's Trashing the First Amendment."

Abrams cited Yale Law School professor Owen Fiss as one of the more prominent trimmers of the First Amendment among teachers of the Constitution: "To serve the ultimate purpose of the First Amendment, Professor Fiss has written, 'we may sometimes find it necessary to restrict speech of some elements of our society in order to enhance the relative voice of others.'"

Fiss was talking about the need to restrict expenditures in political campaigns, but consider the slippery slope his recommendation invites.

It is the power of government to regulate speech, after all, that the First Amendment protects us against.

Another law professor who appears frequently in *The New Republic*, *The New York Times*, and other nonconservative publications as an advocate of reducing the power of the First Amendment is Cass Sunstein of the University of Chicago. Floyd Abrams notes with alarm that according to this much-respected constitutional expert, "The government should . . . be permitted to require the news media to provide a 'right to reply to dissenting views . . . and to impose in public universities significant limitations on "hate speech" on campus.'"

If there is a mandated right to reply to the press, who will administer that right? The government, of course. So the governmental decision to tell an editor what to print—an action hitherto forbidden by the First Amendment—could well be a political decision to favor the incumbent government.

Similarly, many liberals have been urging that television networks give free time during political campaigns to reduce the huge percentage of campaign expenditures that goes to television. There again, however, it would be the government determining what goes on the air by implementing the "free time" provisions.

As William O. Douglas foresaw, once the camel gets its nose under the tent (his expression) there will be more government edicts against television programs. There already are some—none of which could be imposed on the print press. But since there isn't a hamlet in the United States that doesn't have more television channels than newspapers, the old "scarcity doctrine"—which allowed government restrictions on television—no longer applies. Newspapers, alas, are now scarcer than television channels.

The First Amendment should protect the independence of television, which should not be forced to provide free time for political candidates.

I expect that if a poll were taken on whether there should be a legal right to reply to newspapers or television, a large majority of the population would agree. The concept of free television during political campaigns would also enjoy popular support. What this reveals is how little most Americans understand about the fundamental necessity of keeping government out of the business of regulating expression.

It was Chief Justice Warren Burger—hardly a noted champion of the First Amendment—who made clear in *Miami Herald v. Tornillo* (1974) that the First Amendment forbids government "intrusion into the function of editors."

And it was Justice William Brennan—who for years wrote majority opinions, however narrow, saying that "obscenity" was not protected speech—who finally said he could no longer discern a rationale for keeping so subjective a concept as "obscenity" outside the pale of the First Amendment.

As William O. Douglas put it, "There are as many definitions of obscenity as there are men, and they are as unique to the individual as his dreams. . . . Any test that turns on what is offensive to the community's standards is too loose, too capricious, too destructive of freedom of expression to be squared with the First Amendment."

How many Americans agree with William O. Douglas? Do you?

In liberal college communities—like Cornell—there was no protest from the left or from the faculty when conservative student papers were stolen and destroyed. Meanwhile, elsewhere in the country, there are continuous calls from the right for censoring schoolbooks and books in public libraries. Brothers and sisters under the skin.

Justice William Brennan was essentially an optimist, basing his faith in an evolving Constitution. Accordingly, for instance, he was sure that eventually we would become sufficiently civilized to put an end to the death penalty.

He was worried, however, about the extent to which the First Amendment was part of most people's true beliefs. Or, as he said to me one day, "For how many Americans do the words of the First Amendment come off the page and into their lives?"

Think of the people you know. How many do agree, as Oliver Wendell Holmes said, that the only useful test of whether someone believes in the First Amendment is whether he or she would vigorously protect the views of the people they hate?

Would you?

1999

THE DIMINISHING
FIRST AMENDMENT

On Oct. 23, 1999, at Foley Square in New York City, more than 6,000 protesters gathered to curse and snarl at 18 hooded Ku Klux Klan men rallying to express their First Amendment right to assemble. Many of those protesting the Klan's presence had brought their children to witness the bigots exercising their democratic right in the heart of New York's courthouse area. Among this crowd was a woman who commented, "This is America. They have a right to speak." At hearing this, the mob surrounded her and, being patriots, beat her on the head with American flags. After some 15 punches she fell, but then police took her into a city building.

The right to assemble. Freedom of speech. They are two of the five freedoms guaranteed by the First Amendment to the U.S. Constitution. According to the First Amendment Center's *State of the First Amendment* 2000 survey, "Most respondents were able to name only a single freedom contained in the First Amendment"—usually freedom of speech. Even though it has a vested interest in explaining and championing the First

Amendment, the press does little to address this dangerous ignorance of the five freedoms from which, in the words of the late U.S. Supreme Court Justice William Brennan, "all our other freedoms flow."

According to Floyd Abrams, a longtime defender of the press's First Amendment rights, too many journalists focus almost entirely on the part of the First Amendment that prohibits abridging freedom of the press. Having worked for a wide range of newspapers as well as in television and radio, I can say that in my experience reporters and editors fail to sufficiently understand the other four freedoms. A vivid illustration is that only John Kifner of *The New York Times* reported the events that occurred in Foley Square on that October day. The incident slipped past the other news organizations, and there were no editorials addressing it.

Similarly, the press, with very few exceptions, ignored the most draconian restraint of the First Amendment in U.S. judicial history. In *Aguilar vs. Avis Rent a Car System, Inc.*, a bitterly divided Supreme Court of California ruled that "any derogatory racial or ethnic epithets directed at, or descriptive of, Hispanic/Latino employees of Avis" be forbidden in the workplace forevermore—even if spoken outside the presence of those employed, and, as a dissenting justice noted, "even if welcome or overtly permitted." In sum, no matter what the context, such speech was prohibited. Furthermore, the court ordered the trial judge to include a specific list of forbidden words. This was a first in the history of the First Amendment. Except for light coverage on the West Coast, the media ignored the story and the implications of this gargantuan gag rule. And the American Civil Liberties Union celebrated the decision.

When the Supreme Court denied review, only one justice—routinely described by the press as an inveterate right-winger—Clarence Thomas, vigorously objected in a long dissent: "A theory deeply etched in our law is that a free society prefers to punish the few who abuse rights of speech after they break the law than to throttle them and all others beforehand. . . . We must remember that we deal here with a claim at the core of the First Amendment."

The press—having failed to realize that this unprecedented threat to the First Amendment could eventually be used in "hostile work environment" lawsuits directed at newsrooms—ignored the Clarence Thomas dissent.

Meanwhile, another of the five freedoms of the First Amendment is beleaguered. In an increasing number of states, the courts are involved in the highly contentious issue of vouchers—that is, the legality of providing tax money for vouchers that parents may use in sending children to private, religious schools. Without actually taking sides on the issue, much of the press's emphasis has been on the voucher opponents' argument that such diversion of public funds would weaken public schools.

But the U.S. Supreme Court will eventually decide on the *constitutional* issue of whether vouchers violate the part of the First Amendment that prohibits "an establishment of religion." That clause has been interpreted many ways, but the key Supreme Court precedent so far disallows "the entanglement of church and state." The court has not overturned the reigning decision, *Committee for Public Education and Religious Liberty vs. Nyquist*, which states, "The Establishment Clause is violated whether or not the actual (public) dollars given eventually find their way directly into the sectarian institutions" including schools.

Despite the clear import of this 1973 decision, the general media have scarcely mentioned the entangling mission statements of religious schools in Milwaukee and Cleveland that currently are getting tax-funded vouchers from parents. Some of these mission statements surely will be before the U.S. Supreme Court when it finally hears a voucher case, possibly this term. A characteristic mission statement given to parents using vouchers for Milwaukee's Lutheran Chapel of the Cross School says unequivocally: "Religion is not only taught as a subject, but our teachers have been trained to integrate God's Word across the curriculum." Other mission statements make it clear that the school's religious values must be supported in the home, even if the families are not adherents of that particular religion. The press can fully report the story about school vouchers only by including these mission statements as well as, on the other side, the views of justices Clarence Thomas and Antonin Scalia in favor of tax-funded vouchers.

The State of the First Amendment 2000 survey makes other dismaying points concerning the public's lack of knowledge about the First Amendment. For example, one respondent in five said that freedom of worship "was never meant to apply to religious groups that the majority of the people consider extreme or on the fringe." How many news stories focus on "fringe" groups' actual constitutional religious rights?

As for freedom of the press, 51 percent agreed that "the press has too much freedom to do what it wants." With regard to freedom of speech, a whopping 67 percent said that public remarks offensive to racial groups should not be allowed. Thirty-six percent would support a law that banned such speech. These results correlate with the finding that 65 percent of those polled said America's schools do only a fair or poor job of teaching students about First Amendment freedoms.

The year-earlier *State of the First Amendment 1999* survey asked a different question: "To the best of your recollection, have you ever taken classes in either school or college that dealt with the First Amendment?" Forty-seven percent said no. Having visited many secondary schools and colleges, I can attest that most of the courses that are given are brief, cursory and superficial. David Broder, reporting in *The Washington Post* in July 2000, cited a finding by the National Assessment of Educational Progress that "fully 57 percent of the high school seniors failed to demonstrate a basic level of understanding of American history and institutions—the lowest category in the test."

Kenneth A. Paulson, executive director of the First Amendment Center, has noted in the center's Legal Watch that the press ought to report news stories on the First Amendment more aggressively. But, he adds, there are editors who don't because they "believe that writing about the First Amendment is 'inside baseball,'" and therefore feel the press would have a conflict of interest in doing First Amendment stories.

However, says Paulson, "the First Amendment belongs to all Americans, not just the press." So does the rest of the Bill of Rights. And not nearly enough reporting is also done "inside the Constitution."

But the press does little to dispel this dangerous ignorance. Although many editors assign stories that highlight the inadequate teaching of various subjects and skills, very few articles examine students' knowledge of the Bill of Rights, the rest of the Constitution and the struggles throughout history to secure our fundamental freedoms.

More reporting is needed on the Bill of Rights and the Constitution generally. Most Americans, for example, have little or no knowledge of the oldest English-speaking right firmly embedded in the body of the Constitution: *habeas corpus*. In the Antiterrorism and Effective Death Penalty Act of 1996, Congress and President Clinton eviscerated this right of all defendants, including those in death-penalty cases, to find a federal judge to review the fairness of their conviction and sentencing. There was scant mention in the press of this reduction of one year, with very limited exceptions, for a defendant to get a writ of habeas corpus. Sen. Daniel Patrick Moynihan, D-N.Y., tried to alert his colleagues to this assault on so basic a right but could muster fewer than 20 votes. Shortly thereafter he asked me, "Where the hell was the press?"

The press also is largely ignorant of a key reason its own First Amendment rights are called into question by a majority of the populace. How many reporters and editors are aware of a crucial comma in the First Amendment: "Congress shall make no law . . . abridging the freedom of speech, or of the press"? As already noted, the *State of the First Amendment* 2000 survey found more support for freedom of speech than for freedom of the press. The comma may tell you why. Paul K. McMasters, First Amendment ombudsman for The Freedom Forum, says, "The disparity may be attributable to a perception that freedom of the press belongs to the press while freedom of speech belongs to every individual." McMasters goes on to say that if indeed "individuals view speech as a very personal freedom, that may explain why some are inconsistent about extending it to others, especially to those they dislike or with whom they disagree."

Justice Oliver Wendell Holmes stated the clearest and most powerful need for the perennial protection of the First Amendment: "If there is any principle of the Constitution that more imperatively calls for attachment than any other, it is the principle of free thought—not free thought for those who agree with us but freedom for the thought that we hate." Because this reverberating principle of Americanism is hardly taught in the schools or in the legislatures or spoken of in courts, shouldn't the press bring Holmes' warning into the conversation?

George Orwell pointed out that, "If large numbers of people believe in freedom of speech, there will be freedom of speech, even if the law forbids it. But if public opinion is sluggish, inconvenient minorities will be persecuted, even if laws exist to protect them." The press has some responsibility for public opinion, the least of which is to make sure it does not become sluggish with regard to free speech. All the more so now when, as Sen. Patrick Leahy, D-Vt., told *The New York Times* in July 2000, "Everybody is in favor of the First Amendment. But we'd have a hell of a time ratifying it today."

2000

THIS "LIBERTY STUFF"

Of all the experiences I've had with students in trying to bring the words of the Constitution off the page, the most illuminating took place in Charleston, West Virginia, on a crisp October day in 1981. It was so striking that I can relive it, in detail, at will. And I often do.

The West Virginia Civil Liberties Union, a Charleston minister, and several unaffiliated friends of the Constitution had decided to hold a Bill of Rights Day for high school students—beginning early in the morning and lasting until evening.

For a week before the designated day, the high school students were assigned readings and engaged in class discussions of freedom of speech and press; the tangled relationship between the free-exercise-of-religion and the establishment clauses; cruel and unusual punishment; the occasional collisions between the demands of the free press and a fair trial; and other dilemmas of liberty. But these preliminaries were far less important than what happened on the day itself as the students plunged into specific issues involving the Constitution.

As the sun rose, the youngsters—150 of them—came to a large central site. They came from the city itself and from the rural enclaves within the steep hills outside Charleston. They were separated into twelve groups, each led by a teacher or by various outside workers in the constitutional vineyards. I was one of them.

Each group of youngsters was given both actual case histories and hypothetical situations. And the students took different roles, as participants do in Fred Friendly's Public Broadcasting System series on the Constitution and other subjects.

During the course of the day, some students imagined themselves cops confronted by deliberately provocative demonstrators advocating—but not engaging in—violence. Others became parents insisting that certain books must be removed from the schools because they were flagrantly obscene, unpatriotic, blasphemous, or contemptuous of the family. Still other students turned into librarians trying to point out that *if* library books were purchased solely according to the majority vote of the community, the kids would be growing up pathetically ignorant in a good many vital areas.

In the group I was working with, the main focus was on a real case—whether a group of utterly repellent American Nazis should have been allowed to demonstrate in Skokie, Illinois, where many Jews lived, including survivors of the Holocaust. The exchanges among the students were continually intense, not only during the group discussions but also during the breaks for soft drinks and sandwiches. Looking around, I saw much the same level of intellectual and emotional energy crackling in the other groups scattered around the meeting place.

By late afternoon, our group, having worn itself out, put the question to a vote. By a thin margin, the vote sustained Oliver Wendell Holmes. It was decided that the Nazis' placards and insignia, hateful as they were, fell under the protection of the very First Amendment those Nazis would destroy if they ever came to power.

Elsewhere in the room, some of the other units were still trying to make sense out of the Constitution and each other. I walked over to one. The students there were being told by a teacher leading the discussion that a bunch of West Virginians, members of a Communist splinter group, had decided to march up and down the streets of Charleston, brandishing red flags. They were going to carry inflammatory signs denouncing and insulting the President, the First Lady, the Constitution, and calling for the overthrow of the government.

The question was then posed by the teacher: Do these Communists, even under the First Amendment, have the right to so grievously offend decent people, including children, on the streets of Charleston? And since they will be calling for the overthrow of the government, was the Constitution intended to be a suicide pact? Was it intended to give the sworn enemies of our liberties the freedom to gain converts who would help destroy that liberty?

Furthermore, if the march were allowed, some of these Communists—as had actually happened during an aborted demonstration by the Communist Workers Party in Charleston a year before—would surely be beaten up. With the high probability of violence, including violence likely to spill over onto innocent bystanders, is it not more crucial to protect the public peace by prohibiting the march than to allow it?

The students argued long and loudly. I was particularly watching a slight young women, looking like a young Sissy Spacek, with thin brown hair, maybe seventeen, who had not yet said a word during this explosive discussion. As she listened, she was biting her lip and suddenly, in a soft voice— which somehow silenced all the others—she started speaking, very slowly, more to herself than to the rest of us.

"Well," she said, rubbing her nose, "I was there last year when they beat up those Communists. I didn't think much about it, one way or another." She bit her lip again. "If I had, I guess I would have done some beating up myself. But now"— she screwed up her face—"well, now, after all I've been hearing and thinking today, well, maybe, they do have a right to go out there and march."

She paused, and then said, even more slowly, "And I guess they got a right not to get beat up doing it. No matter what they say. No matter what their signs say." She shook her head. "It's hard. But I guess I don't see no other way."

The young woman slipped into the background as another student, shaking his head in vigorous disagreement, shouted, "No, I don't see that at all! Communists have no rights. They want to take away our rights. It's just plain stupid to let them go around doing that. What I say is, let them go back where they came from!"

"But they're all West Virginians, remember?" said the teacher who was leading the discussion.

The student frowned and countered, "Well, let's kick them out of West Virginia. Send them to New York or some place like that."

The debate grew more fiery until finally there was a vote. A majority of the unit sided with the hard conclusion of the shy young woman who had not said another word.

I was standing next to a woman who lived in Charleston and had helped organize the Bill of Rights Day. "You see," she told me, "if you just give kids a chance to think about these things and work them out inside their heads, this liberty stuff comes alive for them. Of course, one day isn't enough, but you start any way you can. Why isn't this, or something like it, going on all over the country? Why isn't it a regular series on television?"

Why indeed? This "liberty stuff" will never come alive for most of the young if the Constitution continues to have as much personal meaning to them as the average annual rainfall in Wichita. And if the Bill of Rights does not become of passionate interest to them—and to their children—it will eventually dissolve into a charming legend of the early years of the Republic when individual liberty—rather than the will of the majority in all things—was actually considered the core of democracy.

1992

INDIVIDUALS OF CONSCIENCE
AGAINST THE STATE

One of our most insistent and lucid champions of American liberties was Supreme Court justice Louis Brandeis. Before he was confirmed as the first Jewish justice on the Supreme Court, Brandeis suffered a four-month-long confirmation process in the Senate that was marked by blatant anti-Semitism.

When he arrived at the Court, Brandeis found more prejudice. The custom, then and now, is for the justices to shake hands with one another before they begin their initial deliberations on the cases they have just heard. One of the justices, James McReynolds, would never shake hands with Brandeis because he was a Jew.

Brandeis ignored the insult. He just did his work on the Court, producing some of the most powerful opinions concerning free speech, privacy, and other civil liberties in the Court's history. For example, the following words are from *Whitney v. California* (1927): "Those who won our independence . . . valued liberty both as an end and as a means. They believed liberty to be the secret of happiness, and courage to be the secret of liberty. . . . They believed that it is hazardous to discourage thought, hope and imagination; that fear breeds repression; that repression breeds hate. . . . Those who won our independence by revolution were not cowards. They did not fear political change. They did not exalt order at the cost of liberty."

The Americans portrayed in this chapter had views that were decidedly unpopular in their communities, which ranged from Grand Saline, a small town in Texas, to the national community of basketball fans in the case of Mahmoud Abdul-Rauf, a star of the game. What happened to them illustrates the fear of James Madison, the architect of our Bill of Rights, that the majority in any community is often willing to violate individual rights and liberties—and often does.

Sometimes a dissenter ultimately triumphs, but others are defeated, at least temporarily. Rarely, a member of Congress—Nancy Pelosi here—has the courage to speak publicly against her party and her president. And it is not often that a college or university president—such as Belinda Wilson in California, who figures in this chapter—resists strong pressures from the left and the right to bar an incendiary speaker from appearing at the university.

In their diverse ways, everyone featured in this chapter lives the Bill of Rights and has been attacked for being faithful to the Constitution. Two resounding illustrations are the stories of a Georgia high school teacher, Sherry Hearn, and of a high school student in a small Tennessee town, Kathryn Sinclair.

At the June graduation exercises of Riverdale High School in Murfreesboro, Tennessee, eighteen-year-old Kathryn Sinclair was one of four valedictorians. In addition to her 4.0 average, she had been accepted in the honors program in premed studies at East Tennessee State University with a full scholarship.

Yet when she finished her speech, there was silence—in contrast to the applause for the other valedictorians. Indeed, some of the students had planned to turn their backs on her and sing the school's alma mater while she spoke, but a degree of reluctant civility had prevailed. In case of a disturbance, however, two teachers and a plainclothes county policeman were assigned to keep an eye on Kathryn and her family.

In her speech, Sinclair quoted from the First Amendment and from one of her favorite songs: "You've Got to Stand for Something or You'll Fall for Anything" by country singer Aaron Tippin. To her mostly sullen classmates, she said, "My challenge to you is not to be afraid to stand up for what you believe. If no one else supports you, know that you can support yourself."

In recent months, Kathryn Sinclair had shown how to do that. In April, she was told that as a valedictorian, she would have to submit her speech to school officials for approval. It had to meet their standards. (No other public schools in the immediate area have such a policy.)

The other three valedictorians dutifully obeyed the rule, but Sinclair objected. She had no intention, she said, of saying anything negative, but she had a First Amendment right not to subject herself to prior restraint of the content of her speech. The principal, Hulon Watson, told reporter Amy Sutton of the Murfreesboro *Daily News Journal* that his standards did not call for changing the content. But he insisted that he had a right to "make sure it's not vulgar, racist, or derogatory to other people." In addition, he said, "we would certainly not allow things in bad taste to be done." The latter term was not defined, nor was the principal's definition of censorship.

Kathryn Sinclair eventually did read her speech to the principal beforehand, but she told him that she would not permit any change in its content if he found anything "negative" in it. Supporting her was an unexpected ecumenical alliance of the Tennessee ACLU and the Virginia-based American Center for Law and Justice, founded by Pat Robertson. Both groups said they would defend her if she took legal action.

The principal finally decided that despite Sinclair's defiance of his stated power to change the speech if he wanted to, she would be permitted to deliver it as written. Meanwhile, Sinclair was so ostracized in school for her rebellion that she finished her senior year at home. Before she left the school, some students had worn armbands reading K.K.O. (for "Kick Kathryn Out").

"They don't realize," she told me, "that they're doing exactly what I'm fighting for. They are utilizing their freedom of speech."

At her home, there were hostile letters—at one point, five or six in a day. One afternoon, reporter Amy Sutton told me over the phone that Dan Sinclair, Kathryn's father, had just told her he had received a threat to firebomb their home. Kathryn heard from students that someone might stab her at the graduation.

The students were angry at her particularly because they were afraid she would spoil their graduation by saying something negative about the school. "And no one on the faculty," Kathryn Sinclair said, "has come out in my support." A number of faculty members said she was making the school look bad.

"There were threats that I'd be beaten up if I went back to school," Kathryn said. "When I did [go back] for an awards ceremony, before graduation, I was kicked during the assembly."

At graduation, after her speech, one brave student broke the silence. He rose and applauded Kathryn Sinclair.

Afterward, she tried to get at the root of what had happened: "One of the main things they should be teaching is who we are as Americans. In four years, we had to memorize the preamble of the Constitution for extra credit, but a study of the Bill of Rights was never required. We did not cover the First Amendment or any of the other amendments."

It was not surprising, she added, that the principal of Riverdale High School never told the students during the furor that they—and Kathryn—have First Amendment rights. But in his way of teaching Americanism, this principal is far from alone among the nation's educators.

The following is a true story about a teacher accused of satanism in Grand Saline, a town of twenty-six hundred in northwest Texas. In addition to the eerie light it sheds on ideological terrorism, the story is valuable because it shows that the involvement of a Christian Right *organization* is not necessary to "expose an infectious sinner." No one can be sure of the extent to which these purely local autos-da-fé take place, because many are unreported. I first found out about the pursuit of evil in Grand Saline as a result of People for the American Way's annual state-by-state report, *Attacks on the Freedom to Learn.*

The credo of most parents of schoolchildren in town is, as one of them put it, "We don't like our children being separated from the values we've given them."

At the center of the story is a teacher, Jackie Haskew, who refused to hand over her integrity. A fourth-grade teacher with a child of her own, she began to be accused of assigning books containing satanic imagery. (For example, someone might point to the goat head in an African folktale called "Brother to the Wind.")

It was no wonder, then, that her "true reason" for being a teacher was found out at Christmastime. There, on her classroom door, was a large drawing of Santa Claus with a big bag of gift books. That drawing, once some parents saw its significance, had to be taken off the classroom door. Why? Look carefully at the letters in Santa, they said. Could it be an anagram hiding its actual meaning? Could it stand for—SATAN?

At home, Jackie Haskew began receiving anonymous calls from people accusing her of teaching devil worship and of being an atheist. As it happens, for all the good it did her in Grand Saline, Jackie Haskew is a Christian, a churchgoing Methodist.

A town meeting was held to discuss this strange woman. (Cotton Mather did not attend.) As Jackie Haskew sat there, amazed that this was happening to her, a woman came over and took her hand. At last, a comforter. The woman told the teacher to be of cheer because something good would come of all this.

You see, the woman said, these recent events had awakened many people in Grand Saline to realize that the Antichrist is present in the town, and to realize that the Antichrist must be destroyed. The comforter then said to Jackie Haskew with a knowing nod that she, the teacher, was the Antichrist.

I doubt that there is a course in any teachers college that tells a teacher how to respond to that.

Haskew was getting very angry. Her seven-year-old daughter, who also attended the eventful Grand Saline elementary school, asked her mother one day what a devil worshiper is. When one hears one's mother called that, it helps to know what it means. To add to Jackie Haskew's frustration as a teacher, a parent firmly informed her that it is not safe for children to read fairy tales.

At last, Haskew fought back. She filed a defamation suit against a number of her more wildly imaginative critics. And she told the *Houston Chronicle,* "I don't know how it's going to come out, but I'm not going to give up. I think the children are worth it. I think all children are worth it."

But she did give up. When Jackie Haskew heard that the school board was going to fire her, she and her daughter left town. I called people in Grand Saline and in Houston who knew her, but they have no idea where she is now.

While she was still teaching in the Athens of Texas, Jackie Haskew heard some parents tell her point-blank, "Don't teach my child to think." And one day she was confronted by a parent who sternly lectured her that she did not want her child to read anything concerned with "death, abuse, divorce, religion—or any other issue."

Jackie Haskew is a classic example of a teacher who believes that one of her responsibilities is to nurture the imagination of her students and to create a classroom that is as wide as the world, enabling kids to learn about cultures and ideas they never dreamed of.

The parents of Grand Saline haven't the slightest idea of how much their children have lost. Nor will the children themselves know, except for those who may eventually leave Grand Saline and discover how much there is to know and dream of.

A couple of months after I tried—and failed—to reach Jackie Haskew, I was watching *CBS Evening News* and saw a segment about, of all places, Grand Saline.

There was no mention of Jackie Haskew or the bearded, red-suited fat man from Hell. The focus of the reporting piece was on the fact that Grand Saline is all white. Not a person of color lived within the town limits. Moreover, as several proud citizens emphasized, Grand Saline always has been free of blacks and always will be.

Said one contented woman, "We're not used to being around black people. If any of them moved here, I don't know that they would stay."

After sundown.

While I was looking into the Jackie Haskew story, I talked to one of the journalists in Grand Saline. The town has only one paper, a weekly. The journalist wasn't all that eager to speak to me. Outside reporters, she said, kept distorting what went on in Grand Saline, blowing things out of proportion or making things up, like that story about Santa Claus being taken off the classroom door. I told her that Ann Tartelton of the International Reading Association verified that story for me, as she did for People for the American Way.

There was no response. "Bad press," the journalist in Grand Saline said. "We always get bad press."

For a very long time, Satan has had the same complaint.

During the national firestorm over the refusal of Mahmoud Abdul-Rauf to stand for the national anthem, I remembered an incident from when I was in the fifth grade of the William Lloyd Garrison public school in Boston. For several weeks before Christmas, all of us had to sing Christmas carols, including those citing Jesus as our Savior.

He was not my savior, but it never occurred to me to ask to be excused. My immigrant parents had sent me to public school to be assimilated, to become an American. Anyway, students had no rights then. The Supreme Court was otherwise occupied.

When lyrics affronted my conscience, I mumbled irreverent Yiddish substitutes. I didn't have the courage to declare my protest so it could be heard. The principal, who could have posed for an illustration in a Dickens novel, had a rattan in her office that she applied vigorously to the hands of any child who needed civilizing. I had felt the sting and didn't want to return.

Abdul-Rauf, a Muslim, did not hide his dissent, and some patriotic sportswriters and talk-show hosts told him he could either love this country or leave it. The state commander of the American Legion in Colorado characterized this member of the Denver Nuggets as having committed "treason." Rooting for Abdul-Rauf, I agreed with the admirably lucid statement of Alex English of the Players Association: "We support Mahmoud Abdul-Rauf, and we support the American flag, which symbolizes Mahmoud's right to precisely the action he is taking."

Years before, Supreme Court Justice Jackson had emphasized that a free society means the freedom to differ. He added that "freedom to differ is not limited to things that do not matter much. That would be a mere shadow of freedom. The test of its substance is the right to differ as to things that touch the heart of the existing order."

During the uproar over Abdul-Rauf's exercise of *his* right to differ, I wondered if any public school teacher in the land dared to bring the words of Justice Jackson into a class discussion of the controversy, if there was any class discussion at all.

Abdul-Rauf's objections to taking part in compulsory patriotism were not a First Amendment issue. That arises only where there is action by the government—federal, state, or local. But there is also, or should be, the spirit of the First Amendment: a respect for the freedom to differ even when the rules are imposed by a private organization such as the National Basketball Association. I suggest that in a future contract, the Players Association include an "act of conscience" clause.

Abdul-Rauf finally compromised, although he says he hasn't. Now, as the anthem of liberty reverberates, he stands and prays, but not to the Stars and Stripes. He used to say he would not stand for "any nationalist ideology" or a flag that is "a symbol of oppression." However, as noted by Steven Shapiro, the legal director of the American Civil Liberties Union, this accommodation shows "the enormous pressure people come under when they stand up for their personal beliefs in the face of enormous public opposition."

At least Abdul-Rauf did openly hold to his beliefs for a while, which is more than I did in the fifth grade. This "Star-Spangled Coercion," as the *New York Times* called it in an editorial, is quite a civics lesson for America's schoolchildren.

Ron Rappoport, National Public Radio's sports reporter, said: "A man stands up for his beliefs! What's this country coming to?"

Diogenes searched with a lantern, in daylight, for an honest man. He figured he needed the extra illumination even before dark because honest folk would be so hard to find.

For some thirty years, I have been searching, around the country, for teachers who have the knowledge and passion to make the words of the Constitution, including the Bill of Rights, leap off the page and into the lives of their students.

I have found very few of those teachers. Most of the kids I've talked to—in middle schools and high schools and, for that matter, colleges—are as ignorant of the Constitution as are the majority of voters and Bill Clinton. In the last presidential election, the most fundamental issue—Bill Clinton's dangerous weakening of constitutional rights—was utterly ignored by nearly all newspapers and the broadcast press. This evisceration of basic liberties included limiting habeas corpus to one year, thus condemning prisoners on death row who will not have time to prove their innocence. Clinton also pushed for limiting the Internet to material suitable only for children. In addition, he enabled people to be deported without their—or their lawyers'—ability to see the evidence against them.

The voters, having been deprived during their schooling of the most vital information an American should have, were as ignorant of Clinton's betrayal of their rights as were the journalists "covering" the election. And they were kept ignorant by these journalists. Moreover, Jim Lehrer, host of the only news hour on public television, failed even to mention the subject during the presidential debates he moderated.

Undaunted, I keep searching for educators who help at least some youngsters to understand what their liberties and right are. One of the most impressive teachers of constitutional freedoms I've found is Sherry Hearn in Savannah, Georgia. I first talked to her after she was fired last year for her knowledge of—and dedication to—the Constitution.

The story of her termination begins with one of the frequent, massive random raids on students at Windsor Forest High School, where she had been teaching for more than twenty years. The raids were described as follows by Bill Osinski in the *Atlanta Constitution*: "Without warning, teams of armed county and school-system officers would periodically come into the schools, order everyone into the hallways, use dogs to sniff the students' book bags and purses, and scan the students' bodies with metal detectors." The students were imprisoned in their classrooms for two to three hours.

Although the Supreme Court has set a lower standard for searching students in schools than when they are stopped on the street, the Court has not approved random searches of *all* students in a school without reasonable suspicion that *any* of them may have violated the law. The way it comes down in Savannah and a number of other cities and counties, every student during these dragnet raids is presumed guilty of possessing drugs or weapons—unless exonerated by a drug dog.

A massive police detention and search of students, without any particularized information about anyone's possession or use of drugs, is a serious invasion of constitutional rights. It is in contempt of the Fourth Amendment of the Bill of Rights, which presumably secures us all against limitless invasion of our privacy by law-enforcement officers.

Sherry Hearn had taught the Fourth Amendment for years. She was outraged by these unconstitutional SWAT team invasions of her classroom—and the whole school. Accordingly, whenever there was a random police search, Sherry Hearn protested—to the principal, to the school board, and to cops she accused of being unduly rough with students during the sweep searches.

During a November 1995 lockdown, as the cops called these raids, one of her students asked Hearn why she was so angry. Said Hearn, "Because I teach the Constitution!"

She is much admired by students who have been in her classes over the years, and she has turned some of them away from drugs. In April 1994, she was named Teacher of the Year in Chatham County.

One of Hearn's caustic comments about the lockdown was overheard by a cop. He reported her to the principal, thereby showing his respect for Hearn's freedom of speech. The cop also told the principal that because Hearn had an "attitude" problem, she ought to be detained or restrained during the next surprise raid.

The police had now marked Hearn—and her family. During a subsequent sweep, her son was the only student out of fifteen hundred to be searched with special care.

In April 1996 there was another lockdown at Windsor Forest High School, and in addition to searching students in the classroom, the cops and canine brigades were assigned to search the cars in the parking lot. Under school policy, however, no teacher's car could be searched without the teacher's consent.

Sherry Hearn's car had a large white faculty identification card on the dashboard. Nobody asked her consent to the search, but the police dog jumped in and found—what do you know?—half a hand-rolled marijuana cigarette.

School authorities later conceded that Sherry Hearn had absolutely no record of drug use. So how did that marijuana cigarette get into her car? Surely no cop would have planted it?

For months in Georgia, particularly in Atlanta and Savannah, the letters columns in the newspapers were filled with praise or scorn for a teacher, Sherry Hearn. She was fired because she had, at first, refused to take a drug test after the half of a marijuana cigarette had been found.

The school administration and the school board said they had initially suspended her because her refusal to take the test violated school policy. She, on the other hand, pointed out that as a passionate teacher of the Constitution she had told her students that they did not have to go along with unconstitutional orders. In recent years, she had particularly criticized the kind of SWAT team search—with drug dogs—that reached into all the classrooms and the parking lot, without even reasonable suspicion that *any* student had drugs.

When she was ordered to take the drug test, she said, although she was only three years short of retirement, "How could I face my students? To do what I genuinely believed to be an unconstitutional act out of fear was a kind of public shaming I could not face."

Moreover, ever since she had complained about the unconstitutional drug searches, the police had marked her as a possible troublemaker. It was noted that she had left open the doors and windows of her car, an old Oldsmobile, when she parked it. Also, the school board and the superintendent stated unequivocally that she had no previous record of drug use. So who could have put the marijuana cigarette in her car? Satan?

After she refused to go for the drug test, Sherry Hearn, with great reluctance, decided to take one the next day. Her lawyer had persuaded her that she might need that test as medical evidence if she ever had to sue the school board. She passed the test, but the school superintendent refused even to look at the results because she had not taken the test *he* had ordered.

After a long hearing by the school board, Sherry Hearn was fired. It was not because of any suspicion of drug use but for insubordination—for not taking the test when she was ordered to.

After she was fired, I called the superintendent of schools, Patrick Russo, who is the very model of an unyielding bureaucrat. I had found out, beforehand, that he did not have to fire her. He had the options of reprimanding or suspending Sherry

Hearn. So why fire her, especially because Russo regards her as "a wonderful teacher"?

Russo answered, without hesitation, "Because she failed to uphold the integrity of the school system's drug policy." She didn't jump when he told her to jump into the test.

Because of the school district policy that no teacher's car can be searched without his or her permission and because the search dog, and its uniformed companion, did not have Sherry Hearn's permission to search her car, I asked Patrick Russo if any action had been taken against the officer who prowled through her car without asking her first and therefore violated the school's drug policy.

"No action has been taken," Russo said.

The *Atlanta Constitution* made this comment in an editorial: "This is not about drugs. This is about the fundamental freedoms guaranteed by the U.S. Constitution."

Since being fired in the spring of 1996, Hearn has not been able to find a full-time teaching job; she told me that "most public systems are fearful of anyone involved in a lawsuit." Our right to file a lawsuit for redress of injustice can keep us unemployed.

On the other hand, Sherry Hearn was honored by the Georgia Civil Liberties Union. She was pleased to get the award, but she would be more delighted to be back in school enabling kids to discover their liberties and rights under the Constitution.

Her ordeal—beginning with her protest against the warrantless SWAT team's contempt for the Fourth Amendment—climaxed with the violation of her own privacy rights. This brought to mind a fiery eighteenth-century Boston lawyer,

James Otis, whose fierce arguments before the king's judges in Massachusetts set the stage for the eventual inclusion of the Fourth Amendment in the Constitution.

Like the SWAT teams in the public schools now, British troops in the colonies were ransacking places and people at will, searching for contraband goods. The colonists had no protections against these brazen invasions of their privacy.

In 1761, in a Boston courtroom, Otis established the American case against British tyranny. As Justice William O. Douglas admiringly summarized Otis's speech, Otis reminded the judges that "the freedom of one's house is an essential liberty and that any law which violates that privacy is an instrument of slavery and villainy."

Otis also delivered a not too subtle warning to the king of England, recalling that it wasn't so long ago that a recent king of England had lost his head and another his throne because he authorized the kind of arbitrary power that now, in the colonies, encouraged the king's troops to search without restraint the properties and bodies of the colonists.

Listening intently in the courtroom was a young lawyer, John Adams, who was to become the second president of the United States. "Then and there," he wrote in his notebook that night, "was the first scene of the first act of opposition to the arbitrary claims of Great Britain. Then and there the child Independence was born."

But not yet in the Georgia public school system.

It was a landmark Supreme Court decision. In *West Virginia Board of Education v. Barnette*, Justice Robert Jackson, writing for the Court, ruled that no public school student can be suspended, expelled, or otherwise punished for refusing to salute the flag for reasons of conscience, religious or secular.

The West Virginia Board of Education had expelled the children of Jehovah's Witnesses, forbidden by their religion to bow to any "images," and refused to let them return to school until they obeyed the state's command to be properly patriotic. If they did not, their parents could then be prosecuted for complicity in that delinquency.

Justice Jackson, in the most illuminating definition of Americanism in the history of the Court—or anywhere else—said this: "If there is any fixed star in our constitutional constellation, it is that no official, high or petty, can prescribe what shall be orthodox politics, nationalism, religion, or any other matters of opinion, or *force citizens to confess by word or act their faith therein*" (emphasis added).

Justice Jackson's decision came down in 1943, and since then there has been a series of utterly clear federal court rulings that no public school student can be punished in any way for refusing to salute the flag or refusing to stand for the Pledge of Allegiance. It has been further ruled that if a student remains in his or her seat during the Pledge of Allegiance, he or she cannot be removed from that room and exiled in the principal's office. This is wholly settled law.

One would think that in public schools, the principal would know Supreme Court law as it affects his or her responsibilities. However, throughout the country there are principals who know—but ignore—certain Supreme Court decisions and instead bow to the desires of conservative religious parents. For example, official prayers in a public school are unconstitutional—being a violation of the separation of church and state—yet in some public schools the day begins with a prayer, often recited over the public address system.

It takes a brave parent, willing to be ostracized in her community, to go to court and have the principal overruled. In some towns, no parents are that brave.

I was surprised to learn that in Connecticut—a state not known to be backward in these matters—Waterbury school officials have for years been penalizing Tisha Byars, a black student. She has never participated in the Pledge of Allegiance because she does not believe there is "liberty and justice" for African Americans in this country.

Tisha Byars went to federal court through the Connecticut Civil Liberties Union (*Byars v. City of Waterbury*). As the record shows, from the first grade on, she remained seated during the Pledge. Initially, her refusal was on the instruction of her father, Dennis, who is convinced that the wording of the Pledge is unconnected with black reality in the United States.

Predictably, this First Amendment lawsuit, based on her First Amendment freedom of belief, has been condemned by some war veterans and others to whom the flag is more sacred than someone's freedom of conscience. One angry protester couldn't resist a touch of bigotry, urging that the Byars family move to Africa. When Tisha's picture appeared on the front page of a local newspaper, several business owners threatened to remove their ads. Joe McCarthy is not quite dead.

Part of Tisha Byars's court action concerned school officials' refusal to qualify her for the National Honor Society, although she had the credentials. Their ostensible reason was an incident of misconduct: Tisha once was eating corn chips in class and wouldn't stop right away when told to by the teacher.

Her case was heard in New Haven by Chief Federal Judge Peter Dorsey. During oral arguments he told one of the school officials, "I think you're dead wrong." As his ultimate ruling showed, the judge didn't believe any of the alleged educators, principals or faculty.

Judge Dorsey declared flatly that it was a violation of the First Amendment to banish Tisha Byars from her homeroom and segregate her in the principal's office during the Pledge of Allegiance. It must stop, he said.

As for her crime of eating corn chips in class, Judge Dorsey noted there was no other misconduct on her record. She had, moreover, apologized to the teacher, and no further action had been taken. The judge added pointedly that the school officials' decision to keep her out of the National Honor Society had nothing to do with corn chips but rather with her refusal to stand for the Pledge of Allegiance.

In his ruling, the judge mentioned another instance of misconduct by the school officials. Another student, Ira Sykes had also been denied admission to the National Honor Society because of what school officials called an "intemperate" essay he had written while serving an in-school suspension for refusing to stand for the Pledge of Allegiance. That "intemperate" essay, Judge Dorsey noted sardonically, was the young man's analysis of his constitutional right to stay seated while refusing to give the Pledge of Allegiance.

In his decision, Judge Dorsey, of course, cited Justice Robert Jackson's decision in *West Virginia School Board of Education v. Barnette.* And his own decision mirrored Jackson's declaration: "To believe that patriotism will not flourish if patriotic ceremonies are voluntary and spontaneous instead of a compulsory routine is to make an unflattering estimate of the appeal of our institutions to free minds."

Waterbury's school authorities—anticipating Judge Dorsey's ruling, decided that students would no longer be removed from their homerooms if they refused to pledge allegiance to the flag. Indeed, Waterbury students will no longer be required to pledge allegiance at all.

Tisha Byars should be honored by the Waterbury school system—and the state department of education—for being Connecticut's leading educator of the year. Meanwhile, the court has awarded her $60,000 in damages plus legal costs.

The faculty of California State University at Northridge was divided about whether former Ku Klux Klan grand wizard David Duke should come to the campus for a debate on affirmative action. Journalism professor Cynthia Rawitch, a member of the faculty senate, pointed out during debate that "we'd look foolish if we were the only part of the university that failed to support free speech, since the students and the university president have already supported Duke's coming."

When she sat down, a young professor leaned forward and instructed her, "There is such a thing as too much free speech, you know."

"As a matter of fact," Rawitch told him, "there isn't. That's the point."

Rawitch's point was largely lost during preparations for the debate. A good many newspaper editors and columnists deplored the university's decision to have Duke come. (Duke is "beyond the pale of legitimate political discussion," said an editorial in the *San Francisco Examiner.*) However, the *Los Angeles*

Times, in an editorial, noted that "free speech is not the exclusive province of excellent messengers or even decent ones."

The subject of the debate was Proposition 209, which was on the state's ballot in November 1997. It would prevent California from granting "preferential treatment to any individual or group on the basis of race, sex, color, ethnicity or national origin in the operation of public employment, public education, or public contracting."

Ward Connerly, chairman of the Proposition 209 campaign and a member of the state's board of regents, wrote to Blenda Wilson, president of Northridge, saying he would accept a previous invitation to participate in the debate provided she instructed Duke not to come "unless it is your choice to dishonor your university."

Wilson, former chancellor of the University of Michigan, Dearborn, and Northridge's first black president, made it clear she finds Duke's views repellent. She told Connerly that it was up to the students who invited Duke, not her, to rescind the invitation. But she emphasized that since Northridge is "a public, taxpayer-supported institution, it must always be an open place where all ideas are explored. If only one view is heard, there is no learning."

Later, Wilson said to me, "This debate about the debate is what I call 'a teaching moment.' I think the students will learn a lot about free speech."

California governor Pete Wilson emphatically disagreed. He insisted, as did Ward Connerly, that bringing Duke was a setup to discredit Proposition 209. Meanwhile, opponents of 209 were just as furious, predicting Duke would arouse the kinds of racial prejudices that might militate for Proposition 209.

Blenda Wilson remained calm and firm. "You know," she told me, "there is a twenty-two-year-old black student who says he wants Duke to come because 'I've never heard a white racist out loud.' Also wanting to hear and challenge Duke were leaders of some of the minority groups on campus, including the Black Student Union and the American Indian Student Association.

At last, on September 25, the debate took place despite efforts of Proposition 209 officials to get a court to stop the dreaded arrival of David Duke. Opposing Duke in the debate was Joe Hicks, director of the Los Angeles Multicultural Collaborative. Some eight hundred diverse spectators peacefully listened to, and some participated in, the exchange of views. Outside, however, there were confrontations, some briefly violent but controlled by police.

Prominent among the two hundred fifty protesters outside were members of a Berkeley-based group, BAMN, who are dedicated to opposing Proposition 209 "by any means necessary." They were at Northridge to disrupt the debate, but they failed, and few Northridge students joined them.

Also on hand, as reported by Sarah Lubman of the *San Jose Mercury News*, was Susan Scheer, "one of 15 self-proclaimed communists." She shouted, "No free speech for racists!"—and presumably felt good. Ward Connerly, exercising his own free speech, held a counterrally nearby.

During the melee in front of the student union while the debate was going on, an aging member of the Jewish Defense League was dressed in Klan-like white robes to express his acute distate for David Duke. It had not occurred to him that others who shared his view would not recognize that he was in disguise. As he was being attacked by haters of the former grand wizard, the Jewish protester was rescued by members of the Nation of Islam, who had come to observe the goings-on. That was a true multicultural teaching moment.

In 1989 the world watched in horror as Chinese troops massacred large numbers of unarmed pro-democracy students in Tiananmen Square. Some of the students held up, as long as they could, a replica of the Statue of Liberty. The chief of staff of the People's Liberation Army at the time was General Chi Haotian. It was under his orders that the brutal, bloody suppression of dissent was carried out. Since then, he has been promoted to defense minister.

On December 9, 1996, Chi Haotian and his entourage arrived in Washington on an official visit, the highest-level Chinese military delegation ever to be welcomed by the Defense Department—and to meet the president of the United States.

As Vicky O'Hara reported on National Public Radio, General Chi was received "with flags flying, anthems playing, and cannon firing over the Potomac." It was a disgusting, disgraceful spectacle, all the more repellent because it bore the approval of the president of the United States. Clinton's imprimatur was not surprising. He has no democratic principles to betray because he has no principles to start with.

Neither do the loyalists around him. In November of 1996 Secretary of State Warren Christopher, soon to depart, said in Shanghai about the monster of Tiananmen Square that his government and ours have "common hopes and interests."

The following is from the *Human Rights Watch World Report 1997*: "Torture of China's detainees and prisoners continues.

. . . Medical treatment continued to be denied to political and religious prisoners. . . . [Chinese] security forces in Tibet used forms of torture which leave no marks against those suspected of major pro-independence activism."

I wonder if Bill Clinton, after just a month in a Chinese prison, would still consider trade with China more important than the broken bodies of its political prisoners. The protesting Chinese students once hoped that the United States, the fount of democracy, would at least publicly condemn a government that so viciously and persistently violates the most basic human rights. Instead, General Chi Haotian is a highly honored guest in this cradle of democracy. An old-fashioned political cartoonist might have shown the Statue of Liberty with a tear in her eye.

There was some concern among Washington apparatchiks that the general's visit might be marred by vigorous demonstrations that could sour relationships between China and the United States, thereby causing loss of trade. But there was little protest against the presence of the general. Chris Smith, the conservative, pro-life New Jersey Republican, did attack Clinton for honoring "the butcher of Beijing" and for giving a "stamp of approval to the continuing reign of terror in China."

Where, however, were the liberal Democrats in Congress? A breakfast reception for the general on Capitol Hill was boycotted by all Republicans but one. Democrats loyally attended. Nancy Pelosi was the only publicly dissenting congressional Democrat. She *is* a Democrat, but she considers human rights in China a far greater priority than loyalty to the president, the alleged leader of the free world. *Human Rights*

Watch called her "the conscience of the Congress on China and human rights."

Pelosi, who also continually attacked George Bush's dismaying record on human rights in China, including Tiananmen Square, gives no quarter to Clinton. On the day the butcher of Beijing arrived to the flying flags and cannonades, Pelosi expressed her vehement objection "to our country giving full military honors to the person who was in operational command over the Tiananmen Square massacre. . . . Those civilians honored our ideals, and now we honor those who crushed them.

"At the same time that President Clinton will not meet with any of the Chinese dissidents or have an official meeting with . . . the Dalai Lama of Tibet, he has an official meeting with the person who continues to crush dissent in China and Tibet. With its actions, the Clinton administration has given great face to the hardliners in the Chinese regime."

Pelosi angrily called attention to the October 25, 1996, "unclassified biography of General Chi Haotian prepared by the CIA for members of Congress and other officials. It makes no mention of the 1989 Tiananmen Square massacre. . . . This is indicative of the policy of the Clinton administration to make this visit appear as benign as possible."

The most grotesque event during this "benign" visit was a statement by General Chi at the National Defense University. A navy officer asked the general if he had any regrets about the use of military force against civilians in Tiananmen Square. Said Chi: "Here I can tell you in a responsible and serious manner that at the time *not a single person lost his life in Tiananmen Square* (emphasis added).

In his report on that astonishing piece of revisionist history, John Diamond of the *Washington Post* pointed out that "hundreds, perhaps thousands of student demonstrators and civilian bystanders were killed by forces of the People's Liberation Army sent into Beijing by Chi to quell the demonstration."

If there were a Joseph Goebbels Big Lie Prize, General Chi would win it hands down. It should be noted that the general made his speech washing all the blood from Tiananmen Square on International Human Rights Day.

In the *Washington Times*, Bill Gertz reported that Marc Theissen, a spokesperson for Senate Foreign Relations Committee chairman Jesse Helms, said that General Chi's remarks about Tiananmen were appalling and compared them to Joseph Stalin's denials of killing millions of people under Soviet rule.

Why was no Democratic member of Congress as appalled as Nancy Pelosi? Bill Clinton has turned the Democratic Party into a mirror image of his slippery self—and Al Gore will be no better.

This celebratory visit by General Chi is one of the low points in American history, and there have been more than a few. William Triplett, a specialist on China and former chief Republican counsel to the Senate Foreign Relations Committee, said of Chi's pretending there was no massacre of the Chinese students: "He is an unreconstructed killer."

This killer of Chinese students who so desired democracy has been honored by the president of the United States—as the torture continues in Chinese prisons of others guilty of wanting to be free.

I asked Pelosi about her reaction to a dismaying, disheartening Oval Office photograph of a smiling Clinton and the smug general. "Oh, my God," she said. "I thought I would never see the day. The president won't see the Dalai Lama, he won't see the pro-democracy dissidents, he won't see Harry Wu, but he did see this thug. It's absolutely appalling."

Pelosi criticized Clinton "with great regret because I think he is capable of some good things." She did not enumerate what these are. But Clinton's policy of placing trade with China over criticism of its abysmal human rights record has, said Pelosi, "led to crackdowns in China. You would be hard put to find a dissident to talk to in China. They're all in prison, in labor camps, or in exile. Their families have been silenced. It's heartbreaking."

She told me of a characteristic Clinton turnaround: In 1995, at the United Nations anniversary session in San Francisco, he actually said in his speech, "We will not limit our enthusiasm for human rights just because of the almighty dollar."

"I was sitting in the box with Tony Lake (then the National Security Adviser), and I said, 'How can he possibly say that?'"

I asked her what Lake said. "Nothing," said Nancy Pelosi.

It is not only Clinton and his administration that anger Pelosi. She spoke of the "huge amounts of money" being spent to legitimize the trade-over-human-rights policy. "Corporations allowed to do business with China make presentations in Washington, lobby and schmooze with members of Congress and journalists. Money is the biggest enemy of those of us on the other side. All we have been asking is that the Clinton administration does for human beings in China what it does for American intellectual property rights."

A corollary obstacle to helping China's prisoners of conscience is, as Pelosi put it, the revolving door by which lobbyists become administration policymakers. "Sandy Berger," she noted, "was the point person at the Hogan & Hartson law firm for the trade office of the Chinese government. He was a lawyer-lobbyist. When he went into the Clinton administration he was second to Tony Lake, and now he is Clinton's National Security Adviser."

When the president of China, Jiang Zemin, came to Washington on a state visit in October 1997, Nancy Pelosi was protesting at a rally outside the White House: "It is shameful for the United States to give a state dinner and a twenty-one-gun salute to the leader of a regime that crushed Tiananmen Square. It's the best welcome money can buy for a regime that tortures political prisoners, uses prison labor, forces women to have abortions, and restricts freedom of speech and religion."

1998

FIRST FRIEND

To the incremental surprise and perhaps discomfiture of some of his critics, Justice Clarence Thomas is growing harder to stereotype. It's become the conventional wisdom to say that he should *not* be dubbed Justice Antonin Scalia's "twin." And this term, he has written as boldly and uncompromisingly in celebration of the First Amendment as did Justices William O. Douglas and William Brennan Jr. in days of yore.

It was not always thus.

His first term with the high court, Justice Thomas handed those who questioned his commitment to individual rights a very large club—his 1992 dissent in *Hudson v. McMillian*. Two guards had beaten Keith Hudson, an inmate at the Angola State Penitentiary in Louisiana, so brutally that his face was swollen, his teeth were loosened, and his partial dental plate was cracked. One guard had held him while the other kicked and punched him. Their supervisor, watching approvingly, had warned them "not to have too much fun."

Seven members of the Supreme Court had no trouble finding this to be cruel and unusual punishment. But Thomas said that Hudson had only suffered "minor injuries" and, more to the constitutional point, the protections of the Eighth Amendment did not apply to prison inmates. The justice's ardent detractors have been citing this case ever since.

Still, Thomas continues to be seen by many as primarily and stubbornly implanted on the far right wing of the Court. Many blacks regard him as a traitor to his race. The late A. Leon Higginbotham Jr., a widely admired federal appellate judge, once furiously urged a black bar association to rescind a speaking invitation to Thomas.

But, maybe, those defenders of individual rights need to take a closer look. At least when it comes to free speech—the quintessential right of all Americans—Clarence Thomas understands the Constitution. Just look at the record.

An unprecedented gag rule came before the Court for review in *Avis Rent A Car System v. Aguilar.* In this hostile-work-environment case, the California Supreme Court had narrowly affirmed a permanent prior restraint on speech. Prohibited was a list of "offensive, discriminatory words." (The plaintiff employees had also won $135,000 in damages under the California Fair Employment & Housing Act.) As I noted in my April 3 column ("Don't Say a Single Word," Page 74), these particular words were forbidden even if they were spoken outside the presence of those employees and even, as dissenting state Justice Stanley Mosk wrote, "if the words were welcome or overtly permitted."

Moreover, for the first time in American jurisprudence, an appeals court had instructed a trial judge to promulgate a list of specific words that could no longer be uttered in a particular workplace, regardless of context. This pernicious example was already being followed: In San Mateo County, Calif., the *Avis* decision was cited in placing a prior restraint on an entire police department after a jury found that a cop had made a racist remark.

In a long dissent, Justice Thomas was the *only* member of the U.S. Supreme Court to protest its denial of review in *Avis*. Not even Justice John Paul Stevens seems sufficiently troubled by this unprecedentedly broad prior restraint of speech.

Teaching basic First Amendment law to his silent brothers and sisters, Thomas wrote: "A theory deeply etched in our law [is that] a free society prefers to punish the few who abuse rights of speech *after* they break the law than to throttle them and all others beforehand. It is always difficult to know in advance what an individual will say, and the line between legitimate and illegitimate speech is often so finely drawn that the risks of freewheeling censorship are formidable. . . . We must remember that we deal here with a claim at the core of the First Amendment."

That's the kind of First Amendment thinking that William O. Douglas would have joined. Though Douglas and Thomas would have disagreed in many cases, the two are similar in their vigorous clarity on the matter of free speech.

In another case this term that the Supreme Court did hear, the issue was the requirement of §505 of the Telecommunications Act of 1996 that cable television channels must protect children by scrambling or blocking sexually oriented but nonobscene programming. Alternatively, cable channels could choose to limit sexually oriented programs to late-night hours.

Thomas provided the swing vote in the 5–4 decision in *United States v. Playboy Entertainment Group*, written by Justice Anthony Kennedy, that struck down this provision. In opposition was a coalition of Chief Justice William Rehnquist and Justices Scalia, Sandra Day O'Connor, and Stephen Breyer.

This was the first time that the Court applied the highest standard of First Amendment protection—"strict scrutiny"—to cable programming. In his concurring opinion, Thomas aimed at the core of the Clinton Justice Department's frequent discounting of the First Amendment—as in the department's fortunately unsuccessful support of other Telecommunications Act provisions aimed at "indecent" or "offensive" speech in *Reno v. American Civil Liberties Union* (1997).

Thomas wrote: "We have no factual finding that any of the materials at issue are, in fact, obscene [and thus unprotected speech]. . . . The Government does not challenge that characterization in this Court, but asks this Court to ratify the statute on the assumption that this is protected speech. . . . I am unwilling to corrupt the First Amendment to reach this result. The 'starch' in our constitutional standards cannot be sacrificed to accommodate the enforcement choices of the Government."

'Relied on Anonymity'

Don't think that Justice Thomas' faith in free speech is new this term. In an earlier 1995 decision often overlooked by his critics, *McIntyre v. Ohio Elections Commission*, Thomas concurred in a 7–2 decision upholding the core First Amendment right to anonymous political speech. The dissenters were Rehnquist and Scalia.

A state statute prohibiting the distribution of anonymous campaign literature had been upheld by the Ohio Supreme Court. In an extended opinion—actually an absorbing foot-noted lesson in early American history—Thomas reminded us (me, anyway) that John Peter Zenger became an icon of the free press not because of what he wrote, but because he re-fused to disclose the anonymous authors of attacks on the governor of New York that he printed. "The large quantity of newspapers and pamphlets the Framers produced during the various crises of their generation show the remarkable extent to which the Framers relied on anonymity," wrote Thomas.

Scalia, with customary scorn, said of the majority that they were ignoring "the considered judgment of the American peo-ple's elected representatives from coast to coast [who had left this issue to the states]." The Court, snapped Scalia, "had dis-covered a hitherto unknown right-to-be-unknown while en-gaging in electoral politics."

Thomas, so long regarded as a Scalia subsidiary, countered: "While, like Justice Scalia, I am loath to overturn a century of practice shared by almost all of the States, I believe the histor-ical evidence from the framing outweighs recent tradition. When interpreting other provisions of the Constitution, this Court has believed itself bound by the text of the Constitution and by the intent of those who drafted and ratified it." The premier originalist on the Court was thus rebuked by his al-leged acolyte.

Scott Douglas Gerber, in his illuminating book, *First Princi-ples: The Jurisprudence of Clarence Thomas* (New York University Press, 1999), makes a good point: "People judge Justice Thomas, as they judged nominee Thomas, in almost purely partisan terms. . . . This is not scholarship or journalism. This is advocacy."

During his confirmation hearings—apart, if that's possible, from Anita Hill's accusations—Thomas was mocked by many scholars and journalists for what they considered his weak grasp of the Constitution. Many of his views are certainly arguable (by me, at least). And he can be fiercely stubborn at the wrong times (as when he recently refused to grant Gary Graham a deserved stay of execution and joined Scalia's futile denial of the constitutional justification for the *Miranda* warnings).

But give him his due: Justice Clarence Thomas has revealed a considerable intelligence and a powerful understanding of the First Amendment.

2000

THE FIRST STATE TO
ABOLISH OBSCENITY

Whatever obscenity is, it is immeasurable as a crime and delineable only as a sin. As a sin, it is present only in the minds of some and not in the minds of others. It is entirely too subjective for legal sanction. There are as many different definitions of obscenity as there are men [and women]; and they are as unique to the individual as his [or her] dreams.

—Supreme Court Justice William O. Douglas

I f it were possible for the Framers of the Constitution to return for its 200th birthday, they would, of course, be astonished at many of the changes that have taken place. The nearly total evisceration of the Fourth Amendment, for instance, through wiretaps, bugs, and undercover operatives who are not required to get a warrant before they slither into your lives. After being under the rough thumb of the British, the first Americans greatly valued privacy. We have largely given up the expectation of privacy.

The Framers would also have been surprised, and mightily amused, at how afraid of words—"dirty words"—so many of our officials have become. Senator William Armstrong of Colorado, for example, has devoted much of his energies in recent months to urging the President to remove "sexually explicit" material from federal buildings and military stores. As Senate Republican Policy Committee chairman, Armstrong is going to try to make the presence of *Playboy* and *Penthouse* in such places a crucial issue in the Presidential campaign. (In addition to taking a drug test, each candidate may yet be asked to disclose the full list of magazines to which he or she subscribes.)

And the FCC chose this Bicentennial year to go well beyond the seven prohibited dirty words of the 1978 George Carlin–WBAI Supreme Court decision. More of this in a later column because no one has yet gone back to William Brennan's 1978 dissent—a deeply, angrily illuminating probe of a dominant culture's attempt to impose its moral standards of language on a pluralistic nation. It's an opinion that should be passed out to schoolkids this year and every year.

One aspect of the current FCC action which might particularly dismay the Framers is that the new extended censorship will be enforced against amateur as well as professional broadcasters.

The Framers greatly valued the "lonely pamphleteer," the amateur maker of broadsides, for such patriots helped create the Revolution. They were not "professional" communicators. They were Americans whose rough forthrightness led to our Constitutional guarantees of freedom of speech. (The First Amendment does not say: "except for patently offensive speech concerning sexual or excretory activities or organs.")

Indeed, when all kinds of folks, from the Attorney General to acres of professors, are digging this year into the "original intent" of the Framers of the Constitution, let's look at how they felt about dirty words and images and allusions. Would they have agreed with Kay Gardella of the *Daily News* (April 24) that to talk about the First Amendment protections of a Howard Stern or a Don Imus is to support their "right to poison their listeners and drag them down into the gutter with them"?

To begin with, as William O. Douglas noted, "The First Amendment was the product of a robust, not a prudish age." James Madison, the principal architect of the First Amendment, was also known for his store of Rabelaisian anecdotes. Not only the Framers but many of the other colonists were well versed in erotic literature, and among the books in their libraries were John Cleland's *Memoirs of A Woman of Pleasure*, Ovid's *Art of Love*, Henry Fielding's *Tom Jones*, volumes of Rabelais, and a highly regarded work written by Ben Franklin, who was described by Madison as "an ornament of human nature."

The work by Ben Franklin was *Advice to a Young Man on Choosing a Mistress*. (He also wrote *The Speech of Polly Baker*, which might cause Edwin Meese to blush.) Both these books, said Federal Appellate Judge Jerome Frank during an opinion in 1957, could have led—had they been sent through the mails—to Franklin being busted for obscenity. Not at the time he lived but in a later more "civilized" America when the First Amendment had been diluted to the refined taste of far less robust citizens.

Herewith, an excerpt from *Advice to a Young Man on Choosing a Mistress*, in which Franklin lists the advantages of selecting older rather than younger women:

". . . Because in every animal that walks upright, the deficiency of the fluids that fill the muscles appears first in the highest part. The face first grows lank and wrinkled; then the neck; then the breast and arms; the lower parts continuing to the last as plump as ever; so that covering all above with a basket, and regarding only what is below the girdle, it is impossible of two women to know an old one from a young one."

That and other passages by Franklin could not be safely read on the air—even during a celebration of our Founders—under the new FCC rulings.

Not even when kids aren't listening? The FCC says it used to think kids went to bed by ten o'clock, but it's been informed that this is not so anymore. So the Commission can't tell a broadcaster when he or she can put on something the FCC doesn't want kids to hear. You have to take a chance and see what happens. Maybe at three in the morning it might possibly, just possibly, be okay for Howard Stern and his sidekick, Robin Quivers, to read such stuff. Antiphonally—he'd do the Ben Franklin and she'd read Molly Bloom's soliloquy from Joyce's *Ulysses*.

In the America of 1987, the Government does not trust its people to operate their own radios without moral aid. There must be a prior restraint by the FCC on "patently offensive" material. Offensive to whom? To officials who will save us from our baser selves. Isn't that what Government is for?

The American colonists didn't think so.

In his book, *American Constitutional Law*, Harvard law professor Laurence Tribe points out that in the colonies at the time of the revolution, "only one state [Massachusetts] had any . . .

law" punishing obscenity. And the Massachusetts statute concerned sacrilegious, not secular, speech. While there were obscenity laws and court cases during the 19th century, it was not until 1957 (*Roth* v. *United States*) that the Supreme Court directly ruled that "obscenity is not within the area of Constitutionally protected speech or press."

The Justice who wrote that was William Brennan, then in his first year on the Court. He came, as we shall see in another column, to bitterly regret the damage he had done to the First Amendment.

On the other hand, it has been Brennan in recent years who keeps reminding us that the Supreme Court does not necessarily have the ultimate word on freedom of expression. There are state constitutions that provide more protection than current Supreme Court decisions, and, Brennan emphasizes, lawyers and judges ought to make use of those protections in the individual states.

The United States Supreme Court sets down the *minimum* Constitutional protections for all of us. The state courts cannot go below that minimum. They can't rule, for instance— as 28 states did earlier in this century—that Red flags cannot be public displayed. But the state constitutions and courts can go *above* the minimum Constitutional protections, and that, in a historic decision, is what the Supreme Court of Oregon did on January 21 in this year of the Bicentennial of the Constitution.

Obscenity has been abolished in the state of Oregon.

It started as an ordinary bust in an "adult" bookstore in Redmond, Oregon. The owner, Earl Henry, was charged with breaking a law of the state by possessing and disseminating obscene materials. Eventually, Henry and his obscene materials were examined by the state's highest court and in January 1987, in a unanimous decision—written by the most conservative member of the court, Robert E. Jones—the judges pointed to what Article I, Section 8 of the Oregon state constitution says:

"No law shall be passed restraining the free expression of opinion, or restricting the right to speak, write, or print freely on any subject whatever."

Therefore, said this clear-eyed state court, "We hold that characterizing expression as 'obscenity' under any definition [including that set by the U.S. Supreme Court] does not deprive it of protection under the Oregon constitution. Obscene speech, writing, or equivalent forms of communication are 'speech' nonetheless."

The court's opinion went back 200 years and found, as I've noted, that only one of the 13 colonies had any anti-obscenity statute at all, and that concerned only anti-religious speech. Edwin Meese, that indefatigable searcher for the "original intent" of the Framers of the Constitution, must surely have congratulated the Oregon Supreme Court for this decision, but somehow I have seen no notice of such a tribute.

The Oregon Supreme Court then looked to the history of its own state and found that "most members of the [Oregon] Constitutional Convention of 1857 were rugged and robust individuals dedicated to founding a free society unfettered by the governmental imposition of some people's views of morality on the free expression of others."

But what if an "adult" bookstore is planted smack in the middle of a residential section that doesn't want it? Or what about a town in Oregon that wants to keep kids under 12, let's say, from stores that show movies of the real thing topped with bananas, yams, and blue cheese?

There can be regulations, says the Oregon Supreme Court, "in the interest of unwilling viewers . . . minors, and beleaguered neighbors." However, *"No law can prohibit or censor the communication itself."* (Emphasis added.)

That is, the "adult" bookstore in the middle of a residential neighborhood may be forced to move, but the proprietor cannot be busted for possessing or disseminating obscene materials because there is no such thing as obscenity any more in Oregon.

On the other hand, there are states moving in the opposite direction. Inspired by the Meese Commission "Report on Pornography"—and its recommendations to state legislatures—a number of those legislatures are acting to make it a lot easier to arrest dirty books and movies and their dirty disseminators.

The Office of Intellectual Freedom of the American Library Association—the First Amendment's most alert protector in these and many other matters—has sent an urgent memorandum to its state intellectual freedom committees.

The memorandum warns that in four states, the drive in the legislatures is to redefine "community standards." Under the Federal criteria of obscenity (as fuzzily defined by the United States Supreme Court in the 1973 case, *Miller v. California*), a work is obscene if:

(1) By community standards, it appeals to the prurient interest; (2) it depicts patently offensive sexual conduct; or (3) it lacks serious literary, artistic, political, or scientific value.

That means there is no national First Amendment anymore so far as obscenity is concerned. What can't be successfully prosecuted in New York can send a bookseller in Mason City, Iowa, to prison. But some states at least have statewide standards. The new move in some of those state legislatures is to let each town and hamlet decide what's criminally dirty. Imagine what that's going to mean to a librarian in a college town who's involved in an inter-library loan with a librarian in a rural community that doesn't even let *National Geographic* on its newsstands.

If Ben Franklin came back, the only state in which he could surely be safe would be Oregon—the only state which recognizes that there is no way to reconcile censorship and a free society.

1987

MULTICULTURAL CONTEMPT
FOR FREE SPEECH

"W̶e don't put as many restrictions on freedom of speech as we should," Canetta Ivy told her fellow students in 1989. Ivy, an African-American leader of student government at Stanford University and a major in African-American studies, was planning to apply to law school.

In the years since then, it has become clear that Canetta Ivy was not alone in her desire to discipline free expression. On campuses throughout the nation, a significant number of students have shown active contempt for speech they find offensive. And they have often done so in the high-minded language of "tolerance," of "diversity," of stamping out "hate speech."

At Penn State, for example, copies of the conservative student newspaper, *Lionhearted*, were stolen and trashed. It turned out that two feminists had done away with them because they felt the newspaper displayed "incorrect" attitudes toward women. Both thieves, recently graduated, had been journalism majors.

At Boston College, feminists jeered at some of the women on the staff of the conservative biweekly, the *Boston College Observer*. The mocking critics told the women on the paper that since they were conservatives, they had no right to call themselves women. Apparently, the slope was slippery: From no right to speak, there was no right to be what you are.

As reported by Thor Halvorssen in the *Wall Street Journal*, "That night, student vandals stole thousands of copies of the *Boston College Observer*. Two thousand copies were found in a recycling bin, many of them torn in half."

At Amherst College, a conservative paper, the *Spectator*, offended both feminists and gays. The controversial issue was publicly burned.

The largest theft and mutilation of the student press took place in 1993 at the University of Pennsylvania. The *Daily Pennsylvanian* had a range of columnists, but some black students took particular, vehement objection to a conservative columnist. Accordingly, they stole 14,000 copies of one issue of the paper. The then president of the university, Sheldon Hackney, never condemned the attackers of the free press.

The only person punished by the administration was a university museum officer who tried to stop a group of enraged black students, their hands full of stolen papers, from running away. The guard was charged with "overreaction." The perpetrators, declared a *Philadelphia Inquirer* editorial, were acting "in the best tradition of book-burners. . . The point of free expression is: You get to decide what to read and think—not some Puritan, religious zealot, or redneck judge."

Another prestigious university, Cornell, practically encourages reckless disregard for a free press. The target there is the

Cornell Review, a conservative student paper. It reprinted a cartoon by nationally syndicated cartoonist Chuck Asay titled "Which One of These Kills More Blacks?" The panel included a Ku Klux Klan murder of a black man by fire and a doctor about to perform an abortion in front of a sign, "Planned Parenthood Abortion Clinic." The politically correct arsonists gave warning. Signs appeared on the day of the bonfire: "The *Cornell Review* has gone too far! Copies will be burned at 11:30!"

This was not the first auto-da-fé at Cornell. A few months before, copies of the *Cornell Review* containing a parody of ebonics were stolen and burned. This time, in front of the main dining hall, some five hundred copies of the offending issue were set on fire.

Presiding over the purification of bad ideas from the university community was a student, Shaka Davis. Adding a note of unintended parody, Davis is a communications major. His intent, he said, was to raise "awareness" of the communication sins of the *Cornell Review.*

Had none of Shaka Davis's professors ever shown him photographs of the burning of subversive books by acolytes of Hitler, who also wanted to raise awareness? Probably not. No Cornell faculty members had publicly protested the previous theft on campus and the subsequent burning. As for the administration, the dean of students, John Ford, was standing right there at the fire, and he was not protesting.

At Cornell, and at most of the universities where there is contempt for free expression, the administrators speak as if they had stepped out of a George Orwell essay. Jacqueline Powers, a spokeswoman for the university, told the *Chronicle of Higher Education:* "It would not have been appropriate to prevent this symbolic burning. We support the right of newspapers to publish and the right of people to protest what newspapers publish."

The right to protest with matches?

This is not the only instance of such Orwellian ingenuity: Another party line among Cornell administrators—and their counterparts in some other colleges—is that free papers (which most college newspapers are) cannot be stolen because they are free. Therefore, students can take as many copies as they want and do what they will with them.

However, the Student Press Law Center in Arlington, Virginia, notes that student plunderers of papers at the University of Texas's *Daily Texan,* the University of North Carolina's *Daily Tarheel* and the University of Kentucky's *Kentucky Kernel* have been prosecuted for what Cornell calls "symbolic acts." In another case, criminal charges were filed against four University of Florida students for stealing free issues of the *Florida Review.* They have been sentenced to six months of unsupervised probation, community service and court costs.

During both acts of student arson at Cornell, I contacted Barbara Kause, Cornell's judicial administrator (a sort of appellate judge). Both times, she told me, "There was no violation of the Code of Conduct."

Well, I studied the extensive Code of Conduct, and it states: "The right to free expression . . . requires respect for the rights of others."

Theft and arson on campuses are a logical outgrowth of student speech codes which, though found to be an unconstitutional violation of the First Amendment in Michigan and Wisconsin federal courts, still exist on a good many campuses. These days they tend to be enfolded in student codes of conduct in the hope that judges won't find them there.

Pressure to censor offensive student language—and, in some places, professors' speech—is strong and often unrelenting. At Stanford, a particularly eloquent objector to speech codes was Gerald Gunther, a renowned constitutional scholar. He pointed out during the campus debate that he received his elementary school education in a very small town in Nazi Germany. There his teacher, classmates and other townspeople would address him as *Judensau* (Jew pig). That, he recalled, was one of the milder ways in which they used to make his day.

Knowing what constant vilification feels like, professor Gunther learned in Nazi Germany and in his life in America that "it's necessary to denounce the bigots' hateful ideas with all my power yet at the same time challenge any community's attempt to suppress hateful ideas by force of law. The way to deal with bad speech is with more speech, with better speech, with repudiation and contempt."

As I have gone to various campuses, sometimes as a speaker against speech codes (and quoting Gerald Gunther), I have been struck by the intensity of the students, most of them liberal, who insisted on the urgency of punishing "bad" language. Some of them "exposed" professors whose language was sometimes ironic and whose wit was sharp. Students were also bitterly intolerant of views they themselves did not hold.

A law student at New York University told me that he had become a pariah among his colleagues because he had said in class that blacks from middle- and upper-class families should not be entitled to affirmative action. In other colleges, pro-life students have been mocked and scorned.

As Harvard law professor Alan Dershowitz said, "I am appalled at the intolerance of many who share some of the views I myself hold. And I worry about the impact of politically correct intolerance on the generation of leaders we are currently educating." Among them will be the lawyers, judges, educators, legislators and Supreme Court justices of the future. The mind-set of too many of these graduates seems to be: Some censorship is okay, provided that the motivations of the censors are okay.

Of all the stories I came across during this epidemic of suppression of speech, the most poignant and enraging case was that of Murray Dolfman, a part-time lecturer in the legal studies department at the Wharton School, University of Pennsylvania.

A practicing lawyer in Philadelphia, Dolfman taught because he enjoyed teaching. He was very popular, and his classes were usually oversubscribed. Yet he was condemned by the university's committee on academic freedom for impermissible behavior, and there were furious demonstrations against him by distinguished black professors as well as black students.

This was Dolfman's crime: One day, lecturing about personal service contracts, he told the students that the Constitution forbade anyone being forced to work against his or her will, even if a contract had been signed. A court may prevent you, said Dolfman, from working for someone so long as the contract you signed is in effect. But, he emphasized, "There can be nothing that smacks of involuntary servitude."

"So," said Dolfman, "where does this concept come from in American law?"

Tentatively, a student answered, "The Constitution."

"Where in the Constitution?"

No one knew.

Dolfman told them: "The Thirteenth Amendment."

"What does the amendment say?"

No one knew.

"We will lose our freedoms," Dolfman told the class, "if we don't know what they are. As a Jew, and as an ex-slave, I and other Jews begin Passover every year by celebrating the release of Jews from bondage under Pharaoh."

Dolfman looked around the room:

"We have ex-slaves in this class, and they should know about—and celebrate—the Thirteenth Amendment."

Later, after he had become a pariah, Dolfman told me, "I used that approach because I wanted them to think about that amendment and know its history. You're better equipped to fight racism if you know all about those post–Civil War amendments and civil rights laws."

On that fateful day in class, Dolfman started asking the black students if they knew what is in the Thirteenth Amendment. None of them did.

"This amendment," he explained, "provides that 'neither slavery nor involuntary servitude . . . shall exist within the United States."

At that point, he asked a black student to stand and read the amendment and repeat it. A few days later, four black students complained to the administration that Dolfman had hurt and humiliated them. They had resented being called "ex-slaves," even though Dolfman had said that he too was an ex-slave. Furthermore, the black students asked what reason should they have to be grateful for an amendment that gave them rights that should not have been denied them—and that gave them little else.

They had not made any of those points in the class.

Dolfman said he had been unaware that they had been offended, and apologized to them. The black students did not accept his apology.

Official charges of serious misbehavior were filed against Dolfman, and there was an investigation. The probers found out that Dolfman had always taught that way—challenging the students. He did that with all students, black and white.

Meanwhile, one of Dolfman's classes was disrupted by students decrying his "racism." And ten days later, there was a mass rally at which Houston Baker, professor of human relations and director of the Center for the Study of Black Literature and Culture, declared, "We have people here who are unqualified to teach dogs, let alone students, and they should be instantly fired."

One rally wasn't enough. Four days later, a vigil and rally took place in front of the home of university president Sheldon Hackney. There, Professor Baker roared: "Some asshole decided that his classroom is going to be turned into a cesspool . . . this administration is bullshit." Also present—via recordings—were speeches by Martin Luther King and Malcolm X.

Dolfman's ordeal continued. The Black Student League categorized him as "a racist." They added that they would not be satisfied until "such actions as those undertaken by Senior Lecturer Dolfman will NEVER, NEVER take place again in this university."

University president Sheldon Hackney did not come to the defense of academic integrity or free inquiry on campus. He joined the chorus condemning Dolfman. If he wanted to ever come back and teach at the university, Dolfman had to make a public apology to the entire university. He was also forced to attend a "sensitivity and racial awareness" session.

There was more punishment. Dolfman was exiled from the university for a year. But many members of the faculty were frustrated. They wanted him fired. I was able to find only two faculty members who believed no punishment was necessary.

There had been one other charge against Dolfman by the Academic Freedom and Responsibility Committee. He had told a black student to change his pronunciation of "de" to "the." It was somehow demeaning, it was said, to correct speech patterns of black students. Yet Dolfman had also corrected the speech of white students and told them to get their hands out of their pockets when they spoke.

After a year off the campus, Dolfman came back to teach and took his students to hear oral arguments at the Supreme Court of Pennsylvania. On that day, the diction of one of the lawyers was so bad, full of "deses" and "doses," that the students found it difficult to concentrate on his argument. When they left, Dolfman told the students, "Now you see why I stress the need to speak well."

The "dese" and "dose" lawyer was white.

In exuberant, encouraging contrast to the multicultural slandering of Murray Dolfman, there is the way four young black women at Arizona State University handled deeply offensive expression directed against them and all other blacks. Nichet Smith, a junior majoring in justice studies, was going with three friends to visit a student in the Cholla Apartments on campus. The women, all of them black, stopped suddenly in front of the door of one of the rooms. On it was a flyer:

- WORK APPLICATION (*Simplified form for Minority Applicants*).

The next line said:

- BLACK APPLICANTS—*It is not necessary to send photos since you all look alike.*

Among the questions on the form were:

- NUMBER OF CHILDREN CLAIMED FOR WELFARE
- NUMBER OF LEGITIMATE CHILDREN (if any)
- LIST APPROXIMATE ESTIMATE OF INCOME AND INDICATE SOURCE: THEFT, WELFARE, UNEMPLOYMENT
- MARITAL STATUS: COMMON LAW, SHACKED UP, OTHER.

"Seeing that hurt big time," Nichet Smith said. "I wonder how many people actually feel that way about us."

Along with hurt there was rage. But the women did not turn to the administration to "protect" them. They did not invoke Arizona State's antiharassment speech code. The code is as deeply suspicious of free speech as all of its many equivalents around the country. Rather, Smith and her friends went to the resident adviser at Cholla and said they intended to confront the students who had put that poster on the door.

They knocked at the door of the apartment and found one of its inhabitants. He hastily assured them that he'd had nothing to do with putting up that flyer. And yes, he understood why they were so furious and yes, yes, he would take it down right away.

It didn't end there. The four women spread the word and were the main force in organizing and leading an open meeting the next evening at the Cholla Apartments. About fifty students, half of whom were white, showed up. One of the whites on hand, Tami Trawbells, said, "The poster was offensive for me as a white person because it looks like all white people feel that way."

Also present was Charles Calleros, the assistant dean of the law school and a professor there. Some of the students were wondering why the hell the administration had not ordered the poster taken down, rather than letting the four women do it.

Arizona State, however, is a public university, and so the First Amendment protects even such hateful expression as the poster. Calleros carefully explained that to the students. Furthermore, the rules of the Cholla Apartments made it clear that students living there can post whatever they like on their doors. There was no constitutional way, therefore, for officials of Arizona State to rip that flyer from the door. The four black women, however, were not agents of the state, and so they got it done, by drawing on their own inner strength and moral resources.

Professor Calleros pointed out, as the women had already demonstrated, that the First Amendment did not prevent anyone infuriated by the poster from telling the offending students and anyone else how they felt about it. The four women delivered that message very clearly and repeatedly. They and other black students organized a rally and a press conference, together with an evening program at Cholla on African-American history.

Rather than rhetoric, the evening was focused on a compelling public-broadcasting program about the black lawyers, headed by Charles Houston of Howard University Law School, who fought against great odds to end segregated schools during the twenty years preceding *Brown v. Board of Education* (which finally declared segregated public schools to be unconstitutional).

There were also a march and a rally, as well as a session organized by student members of the NAACP at which race relations at Arizona State were forcefully discussed before a hundred or so students. A strong thread through all these discussions was the need for more multicultural education at Arizona State. Not insular multicultural disdain of opposing opinions, but honest, robust exchange of ideas and views.

As for the four black women, according to Charles Calleros, "They expressed pride in being identified not just as persons but also as black women. Yet they demanded that others recognize that each of them is unique rather than a collection of stereotypical physical and emotional characteristics."

An obligato to these events on campus, sparked by the racist poster, was a stream, sometimes a torrent, of letters in the college paper, the *State Press*.

One of the letters ("names withheld upon request") read: "We would like to extend our sincerest and deepest apologies to anyone and everyone who was offended by the tasteless flyer that was displayed on our front door . . .

"We did not realize the hurt that would come of this flyer. We now know that we caused great distress among many different people, and we would again like to apologize to whomever was offended."

Around the same time, the Arizona State chapter of the NAACP presented its annual Image Awards to these four black women "who exhibited positivity where negativity once prevailed."

"At first we felt like victims," reflected Smith, "but then we learned how to be empowered."

1992

MY MAN OF THE CENTURY

I n June 1789, James Madison presented to Congress his
draft of those amendments to the Constitution that would,
in part, become the Bill of Rights.

"The most valuable in the whole list," he told Congress, was:
"No state shall violate the equal rights of conscience, or the
freedom of the press, or the trial by jury in criminal cases."

It was not enough, he insisted, to provide protections of individual liberties against violations by the federal government.
Individual states had indeed adopted declarations of rights,
but, Madison pointed out, "repeated violations of these parch-
ment barriers have been committed in every State.

"The greatest danger to liberty," he added, "was not found in
either the executive or legislative departments of government,
but in the body of the people, operating by the majority
against the minority."

The House adopted that clause, but Madison failed to get
the necessary two-thirds majority in the Senate.

It wasn't until the 14th Amendment was ratified in 1868 that a key was provided to protect individuals from the states as well as the federal government. Section 1:

"Nor shall any State deprive any person of life, liberty, or property, without due process of law; nor deny to any person within its jurisdiction the equal protection of the laws."

Nonetheless, for many years after the amendment's passage, the Supreme Court ruled that the Bill of Rights limited only the federal government. Accordingly, each state had its own definitions of those rights.

Incrementally, the Supreme Court began to follow Madison's desires in the early part of the 20th century. After a few provisions of the Bill of Rights had been applied, in 1937—as Linda Monk writes in her valuable "The Bill of Rights: A User's Guide"—Justice Benjamin Cardozo, in *Palko v. Connecticut*, proposed the test for whether a section of the Bill of Rights should be applied to the states. To qualify, that particular right had to be "fundamental" and essential to "a scheme of ordered liberty."

The one justice who passionately kept trying to persuade his colleagues that the *entire* Bill of Rights be incorporated into state laws was Hugo Black.

In his dissent in *Adamson v. California* (1947)—concerning the Fifth Amendment's right against self-incrimination in a trial—Black spoke of the "human evils that have emerged from century to century wherever excessive power is sought by the few at the expense of the many. In my judgment, no nation can lose their liberty so long as a Bill of Rights like ours survives."

Therefore, he continued, "I would follow what I believe was the original purpose of the 14th Amendment—to extend to all the people of the nation the complete protection of the Bill of Rights" through due process of law.

As for only selective incorporation, Black—emphatically, as was his custom—said: "To hold that the Court can determine what, if any, provisions of the Bill of Rights will be enforced, and if so to what degree, is to frustrate the great design of a written Constitution."

James Madison would have been greatly pleased.

With Black pushing the court, the First Amendment's Establishment Clause was incorporated (in a majority decision by Black earlier in 1947), followed by the right to a public trial; protection from unreasonable searches and seizures; and the exclusionary rule (which states that illegally obtained evidence cannot be admitted at a trial).

Also, prohibition of cruel and unusual punishment; the right to counsel in non-capital felonies and then imprisonable misdemeanor cases; the right against self-incrimination; the right to an impartial jury and a speedy trial; the right to trial by jury in non-petty criminal cases; and the right against being placed in double jeopardy.

Not yet applied to the states is the right to a trial by jury in civil cases; the right to a grand jury indictment; and the prohibition of excessive bail and fines. And, under the Third Amendment to the Bill of Rights, the government can still quarter troops in your home.

Justice Black was never without a blue paperback copy of the Constitution. When a liberty was threatened, he would slam the Constitution on his desk and—quoting the first line of the Bill of Rights, "There shall be no law"—he would thunder: "No law means no law!"

A portrait of Hugo Black ought to be hung in every legislative, executive and judicial office in the land. And in newspaper offices.

2000

PART **2**

THE PASSION OF
CREATION

LENNY BRUCE:
THE CRUCIFIXION OF A
TRUE BELIEVER

Dizzy Gillespie, the great jazz trumpeter, once said of Louis Armstrong, "If it hadn't been for him, there wouldn't have been none of us. I want to thank Louis Armstrong for my livelihood."

In similar fashion, a long and growing list of comedians— actually, social satirists—owe a great thanks to Lenny Bruce. These include Richard Pryor (who came closest to meeting Lenny's standards), George Carlin, Eddie Murphy, Chris Rock and an emerging number of young black and Hispanic fearless, funny commentators. Bruce opened the doors not only on the way we live, but also on the way we often cover it up.

For Lenny Bruce, however, this was a pyrrhic and posthumous victory. His many arrests around the country for alleged obscenity culminated in a trial in New York City. Before the trial started, Lenny told me, "If this bust holds, my working life is over because if you're convicted in New York, club own-

ers everywhere else are not going to take the chance of booking me."

Although Lenny *was* convicted in 1962, he never relin-
quished his faith—his obsessive faith—in the First Amendment. He was certain that a higher court would liberate him
from the police and prosecutors who pursued him like an army
of Inspector Javerts.

In his room at the no-star Hotel Marlton in Greenwich Village, I could hardly move without stepping on the legal briefs
and constitutional law books on the floor. Others were on the
table and chairs. And in the few gigs he did get after his New
York conviction, his "act" was his First Amendment case. He
got a lot of laughs from reading and commenting on the tran-
script of his trial. But as those marginal engagements faded
away, Lenny became more depressed and bewildered. Could
the Constitution have let him down?

In the months before he died on August 3, 1966, he had no
jobs and spent his time writing about his case. On the day he
died of an overdose on morphine, he had found out that he
was going to lose his home. Ralph Gleason, a San Francisco
journalist who first told other writers, including me, about
Lenny, was convinced that the overdose was not deliberate.
"Lenny kept insisting," Ralph said, "that he and the First
Amendment would win." And they did. A mid-level New York
state court reversed Lenny's obscenity conviction in February
1968, and the state's highest tribunal, the State Court of Appeals, confirmed that reversal in January 1970.

In the years since, books on Lenny and such documentary
films as the Oscar-nominated *Lenny Bruce: Swear to Tell the Truth*
by Robert Wade have established Lenny Bruce as not only a

paladin of free speech but also a still-penetrating, woundingly hilarious speaker of truth to the powerful and the complacent. In my view, he is the equal of Mark Twain.

As Ralph Gleason wrote, "Lenny utterly changed the world of comedy." But not only comedy. He was an ethicist, an increasingly rare phenomenon among public figures in any field. Lenny, who was Jewish, would ask an audience how a Jew could mourn the murdered in the concentration camps while having no sense of personal guilt at all about those human beings killed by America, long distance in Hiroshima. Lenny wanted to open all the doors. Or, as Pope John XXIII said of the Catholic Church when he took office, "Open the windows!" Lenny believed that if people didn't use language to conceal from themselves what they actually do, and want to do, life would be a lot more open and flowing. And there would be considerably more pleasure—even for those for whom that word was so hedged with restrictions that its transformation into experience was guardedly limited.

What first attracted the alarmed attention of the whited sepulchers in authority was Lenny's use of such words as "tits and ass," "fuck" and "cocksucker." Like Mark Twain, though more boldly, he used the language as it was actually spoken in private. When he was busted in San Francisco for using "cocksucker" in a skit, the arresting police sergeant said to him, "I can't see any way how you can say this word in public. Our society is not geared to it." Lenny looked at the sergeant and explained, "You break it down by talking about it."

One night, at the Village Vanguard in New York where he often worked until his fateful arrest at another club in the city, Lenny came on the stand and looked at the audience—which was more multicultural than was the norm in those days with regard to race, gender, sexual practice and ethnicity. Suddenly Lenny said, "Any niggers here tonight? Any spics? Any kikes?" The audience froze. What dybbuk had gotten into him? "Why do you let words paralyze you?" he asked. Then he began to merrily dissect those—and other unpardonable—words as to their origins and use to deny individuality.

My favorite Lenny Bruce number began with Christ and Moses returning to earth. They were standing in the back of imposing St. Patrick's Cathedral on Fifth Avenue in New York, watching then Cardinal Francis Spellman—a fierce foe of "obscenity" and the lead strikebearer in an action by cemetery workers at a Catholic cemetery. The Cardinal dug the first spadeful for a new grave. Christ says to Moses, "My visit took me to Spanish Harlem where there were forty Puerto Ricans living in one room. What were they doing there when this man"—Lenny pointed to the Cardinal—"has a ring on worth $10,000?"

This observation infuriated the city's District Attorney, Frank Hogan, much revered by the populace and most of the city's judges. A devout Catholic, Hogan began to inquire about assaults that this heathen had made on the standards of the good, God-fearing members of the community. Hogan then decided to prosecute, but some members of the staff dared to decline. Another, Gerald Harris, tried unsuccessfully to persuade Hogan to drop the case. Harris then presented it to the grand jury, which, to Harris' dismay, voted to file charges. He went to Hogan and said he could not, in good conscience, go on with the case.

But Richard Kuh, an ambitious assistant D.A., was eager to take on Lenny Bruce. The chief witness against Bruce was Herbert Ruhe, an inspector for the city's licensing division and a former C.I.A. agent. At the Café Au Go Go in Greenwich Village, Ruhe took notes on Lenny's performance, which he read from at the trial. (By the way, Ruhe told me later that he was just doing his job, that he had nothing against Lenny.)

Lenny was in a state of desperate frustration. He begged— he literally begged—presiding judge John Murtagh for permission to do *his own act* and not have it dismembered by an agent of the prosecutor.

"This guy is bumbling," Lenny told me, "and I'm going to jail. He's not only getting it all wrong, but now he thinks *he's* a comic. I'm going to be judged on *his* bad timing, *his* ego and *his* garbled language."

An unusual witness for Lenny was the syndicated columnist Dorothy Kilgallen, an active Catholic and political conservative. But she had a keen sense of humor and had attended some of Lenny's club gigs in New York. In taking the stand, she was treated with great respect by the judges and court attendants. Kuh, the Torquemada-like prosecutor, had put together—out of any context—all of Lenny's "dirty words" from the tape of the Café Au Go Go performance, which Bruce was not permitted to give to the court in his own way.

Kilgallen, demurely dressed, wearing white gloves, sat coolly on the witness chair as Kuh circled her and then, in a loud, accusatory voice, roared a barrage of "dirty words" at her. Pouncing, he shouted: "You say that Mr. Bruce is an artist of social value. What is your reaction, Miss Kilgallen, to these words—*these words*—he used in his act?" Dorothy Kilgallen looked at her gloves, looked up at Kuh and then, with precise constitutional logic, said: "They are words, Mr. Kuh. Words, words, words."

I was another witness for Lenny. But I was not wearing white gloves. I had a beard and was known as a writer for the "alternative," left-leaning, decidedly counter-cultural *Village Voice.* As Kuh approached me with menacing disdain, I tried to moderate my acute distate for him. "Is it not true," he thundered "that you have written a book praising a man who advocates draft resistance and other forms of civil disobedience? Is it not true that this lawbreaker has been arrested and imprisoned? Is it not true that his name is A. J. Muste?"

My publisher had done no promotion for my book, *Peace Agitator: The Story of A. J. Muste,* so I was delighted to confess my authorship and give the title to members of the press in the courtroom and the jurors. Muste, a minister, was a pacifist who was much influenced by Mohandas Gandhi. Dr. Martin Luther King, Jr. had told me that while he was in theological school, a visit to his class by Muste had persuaded him of the power of nonviolence. Muste was an adviser to King in the civil rights movement and was a key strategist in the campaign to get the United States out of the Vietnam War. As Kuh glowered, I said that I indeed much admired A. J. Muste.

In the course of the interrogation, Kuh asked me: "What would be your major field of reputation, *such as it is?*" (emphasis added). He was to find out later that I had some credibility as an investigative journalist.

During the years after the trial and Bruce's conviction, Kuh's reputation became somewhat damaged as Lenny's—posthumously—grew. When Frank Hogan, much gratified by Lenny's initial conviction, died, Kuh expected, with reason, to succeed him in the next election for that position.

I began writing a series in the *Village Voice* on Kuh's qualifications for that office. I interviewed former and present colleagues of his in the district attorney's office and other members of the legal community. After the third article had appeared, I got a telephone call from a much-respected former United States Attorney, Robert Morgenthau, whom I had never met. He asked me if I could vouch for the highly critical facts about Kuh in the series. I told him I'd be glad to send him my backup material and notes. Morgenthau said he had not intended to run for District Attorney but now he was thinking of going against Kuh in the race. Morgenthau did, he won and is still in office. On the night the returns came in, I said to my wife Margot: "This one's for Lenny!"

The effect of Bruce's prosecutions—even before the New York trial—was international. He was becoming known in other countries as a social critic and an illuminator of the mores, pretensions and evasions of a considerable section of American society, particularly its enforcers and interpreters of the law. As Ralph Gleason noted, "He tried to perform in Australia but was evicted before he could perform. He was invited to the Edinburgh International Drama Festival, but the British government refused to let Lenny enter the country."

Lenny could not understand why he had become an international pariah as well as a criminal at home. "What I wanted people to dig," Lenny used to say, "is the lie. Certain words were suppressed to keep the lie going. But," Lenny insisted, "if you do them, you should be able to say the words."

For example, he would add, "An out-of-town buyer checks into a hotel, goes up to his room and decides he wants a hundred-dollar prostitute. He makes the call, and a few minutes later there's a knock on the door and a bearded writer comes into the room."

Occasionally, a friend who was concerned about what was happening to Lenny—his decline in health and his despair at not being able to work at his calling—advised him to use his considerable comedic skills in a less controversial, less threatening way. Said Lenny: "You don't know anything about anybody but you. Just live in that thing. You always live alone. You're always in there, even with your wife. That's why I can't sell out. That is, so long as I stay honest with myself. And that's why I'm somebody different each time out. I keep changing. I'm not bragging about this but—well, it exists, that's all I'm telling you."

At Lenny's sentencing, Assistant District Attorney Kuh, speaking in the name of *The People v. Lenny Bruce*, said to the court:

First, as to the defendant Bruce:

I'm here at the direction of the District Attorney, Frank S. Hogan, and ask on behalf of the people of this county that the defendant Lenny Bruce's sentence be one of imprisonment.

May I say in support of that request, if it please the court, that apart from the defendant Bruce's conduct prior to the trial, the defendant Bruce—throughout the trial and since the trial—has shown by his conduct *complete lack of any remorse whatsoever.*

In a letter to the editor of *The New York Times* published on October 10, 1990, Lester Block wrote: "It was tragic to see arguably the most brilliant comedian of our time destroyed by the society whose freedom he was vainly trying to protect."

It was not entirely in vain, though, as you can hear in his disciples on television, in clubs and in movies. "The crime I committed," Lenny said, "was pulling the covers of 'respectability,' which means 'under the covers.'"

Lenny's mother, Sally Marr, a forthright believer in pulling the covers off, remembered this conversation with her son:

Lenny said, "You don't understand, I'm not a comedian." I said, "Oh, you're not?" He said, "Do comedians get arrested? All the time?"

Lenny once got a note from an Episcopalian minister: Thank you for caring so much about life." And that, of course, as Lenny knew, was what did him in.

2001

Jazz:
Music Beyond
Time and Nations

A t Gestapo headquarters in Paris, Charles Delaunay, under suspicion of being a member of the Maquis, was brought in for questioning. Delaunay, an expert on jazz, was the author of the first definitive jazz discography—listings of full personnel on jazz labels.

As the interrogation began, the first thing the German officer said to Delaunay was, "You have the wrong personnel on the 1928 Fletcher Henderson recording." They argued the point for a while, and Delaunay was eventually released after routine questioning. "There are jazz aficionados everywhere," Delaunay, who had a quick sense of irony, told me years later.

In Nazi Germany, jazz was forbidden as a mongrel black-and-Jewish music, but recordings were still played behind closed doors. And in Russia, under the Communists, jazz was declared an enemy of the people, but there too it could not be entirely suppressed. Some of my liner notes for a John

Coltrane recording were surreptitiously distributed to jazz lovers in Moscow as *samizdats*.

What is it that makes this music a common language throughout the world—as it so transcends popular fads that recordings made seventy years ago are played again and again, continually beyond the ordinary boundaries of time?

A vivid sense of the jazz experience is a 1998 New York play, *Side Man*, by Warren Leight. This is a key scene, described by Peter Marks in the *New York Times*: "Three musicians . . . sit around a cassette player listening to the tape of a fervent, wrenching trumpet solo. The jazz man on the tape is dead, but his instrument remains feverishly alive."

The essential attraction of jazz throughout time is its "sound of surprise"—a term invented by *The New Yorker's* critic Whitney Balliett. Because the music is largely improvised, the listener is often startled by a sound, a phrasing, a turn of rhythm that is so deeply emotional that he or she may shout aloud in pleasure.

I was eleven when I first heard jazz. Walking down a street in Boston, I was stopped by the sound coming out of a public address system attached to a record store. I was so exhilarated that I yelled in delight—something I had never done before on the proper streets of Boston. The music was Artie Shaw's "Nightmare."

I was soon working in a candy store and expanded my jazz horizons by buying recordings of Duke Ellington, Billie Holiday, Lester Young, Bessie Smith and blues singer Peetie Wheatstraw ("the Devil's son-in-law").

A few years later, I came upon the very essence of jazz. It was late on a winter afternoon when I walked past the Savoy

Cafe, in a black neighborhood of Boston. The club was closed, but the blues coming from inside stopped me. I looked through the glass in the door and saw, as in a fantasy, several of the legends of jazz. Sitting in a chair that was leaning back against a table was a saxophonist with a huge, swaggering sound. It was Coleman Hawkins, who had invented the jazz tenor saxophone. The pianist was Count Basie, whose bands were the very definition of swinging, and he had created a precisely economical way of improvising. Each of his notes was surely placed to give the big tenor a further lift. And on the drums was Jo Jones, whom his colleagues in the Basie band described as "the man who plays like the wind." Uncommonly subtle, his eyes darting from player to player, Jo's brushes were dancing on the drumhead, punctuated by an occasionally deep sigh from a cymbal.

Every night, in many clubs in many countries throughout the world, this ceaselessly intriguing interplay between improvising musicians creates new patterns of melody, harmony and rhythm for an audience that knows no generational divide. Youngsters are drawn to the depth of feeling that can't be found in popular music and older listeners relive their own musical adventures while learning more about the further dimensions of this music.

There is also the spirit of the jazz musician that attracts lay enthusiasts. Since the music is largely improvised and risk-taking, those qualities also usually define jazz musicians off the stand. They tend to be self-confident, irreverent and unflinchingly independent.

An incandescent illustration of that spirit was Dizzy Gillespie. On one of his trips for the U.S. State Department, he had been scheduled to play at a lawn party in Ankara, arranged by the American ambassador to Turkey. The climax was to be a Jam session with Dizzy in charge.

"While I was signing autographs," Dizzy recalled, "I happened to look at the fence surrounding the grounds. A lot of street kids were pressed against the fence. They wanted to come in and hear the music. One of them actually climbed over the fence and a guard threw him right back over it. "I asked what was going on. 'Why did they do that?' And some said, 'This party is for select people—local dignitaries and important Americans in the city.' I said, 'Select people! We're not over here for no select people! We're over here to show these people that Americans are all kinds of people!' I had a girl in the band, and almost as many whites as blacks. We had a good mix." "The ambassador comes over and asks, 'Are you going to play?' I say, 'No! I saw that guard throw a little kid over the fence. Those are the people we're trying to get close to—the people outside the fence.' So the ambassador said, 'Let them in, let them all in!'" That is the spirit of jazz.

Dizzy Gillespie was an original, and so are—and have been—many other conjugators of the forms and feelings of the music. Part of the originality of the music consists of how players have expanded the capacities of their instruments—from the gypsy guitarist Django Reinhardt to the first full-scale and never entirely surpassed jazz soloist, Louis Armstrong.

In the early 1930s, a delegation of the leading brass players in the Boston Symphony Orchestra made a journey to Louis Armstrong's dressing room in a theater in the city. They had heard of his almost unbelievable technique and range and asked him to play a passage they had heard in his act. Arm-

strong picked up his horn and obliged, performing the re-
quested passage and then improvising a dazzling stream of
variations. Shaking their heads, these "legitimate" trumpet
players left the room, one of them saying, "I watched his fingers and I still don't know how he does it. I also don't know
how it is that, playing there all by himself, he sounded as if a
whole orchestra was behind him. I never heard a musician like
this, and I thought he was just a colored entertainer."

The older players, though very serious about their musician-
ship and the quality of their instruments, were also entertainers.
In the years before there was a reasonably sizable number of
jazz admirers, the players worked before all kinds of audiences,
and so they had to entertain them between improvisations.

In time, younger musicians, playing by then before musically
sophisticated listeners, declined to entertain in the traditional
sense. And their music began to reflect their interests outside of
music. Max Roach and Julian "Cannonball" Adderley, for instance, composed pieces dealing with the Civil Rights Movement. Duke Ellington, of course, had been writing about black
music and culture long before the Civil Rights Movement had
begun ("Black Beauty," "Black, Brown and Beige," et al.).

Revealingly, in one of the more dramatic events in jazz history, Louis Armstrong also inserted himself into the struggle
for black equality. Before then he hadn't done this explicitly in
his music, and there were younger musicians who, accordingly, called him an "Uncle Tom." Armstrong proved them decidedly wrong when, in the 1950s, Governor Orville Faubus
of Arkansas defied the orders of the Supreme Court of the
United States to integrate the public schools of Little Rock.
When then President Dwight Eisenhower delayed and de-

layed intervening, Armstrong declared: "The way they are treating my people in the South, the government can go to hell! The president has no guts."

In 1965, when Martin Luther King's march on Selma, Alabama, was brutally attacked by local and state police, Armstrong told the nation: "They would beat Jesus if he was black and marched."

At one point Armstrong's manager, the powerful and forceful Joe Glaser, sent an emissary to find Armstrong on the road and order him to stop saying such controversial things, for they would cause him to lose bookings. Louis Armstrong threw Glaser's emissary out of his dressing room. That, too, is the spirit of jazz!

It is unavoidably personal music. John Coltrane, who created new ways of hearing as well as playing jazz, told me, "The music is the whole question of life itself." Other players have also emphasized that what you live—and how you live—becomes an integral part of what you play each night. Jazz, then, is a continual autobiography, or, rather, a continuum of intersecting autobiographies—one's own and those of the musicians with whom one plays. As the prodigious bassist and bold composer Charles Mingus told me: "I'm trying to play the truth of what I am. The reason it's difficult is because I'm changing all the time."

Then there was Charlie "Bird" Parker, who changed music fundamentally, as Louis Armstrong had before him. Describing Parker, as he evolved into a dominant musician of his time, bassist Gene Ramey was also describing the acute sensitivity of other jazz players to the sounds all around them: "Everything had a musical significance for Bird—the swish of a car speeding down a highway, the hum of the wind as it goes through the leaves. If he heard a dog bark, he would say the dog was speaking . . . And maybe some girl would walk past on the dance floor while he was playing, and something she might do, or an expression on her face, would give him an idea for something to play on his solo."

And Duke Ellington would tell me how, at a dance, a sigh of pleasure from a dancer would float back to the bandstand and enter into the music. One of his sidemen told me how, after a long, wearying bus trip, the musicians would be regenerated by the dancers: "You're giving them something to move by, but you're giving them something back. You can tell whether you're really cooking by how they move on the floor, and when they groove, they make you groove more."

It's harder for these physical and emotional messages to be sent and received in a concert hall, where more and more jazz is played. But the interactions between musicians and listeners take place there too, because jazz is a music in which both the player and the audience are continually in conversation.

I once asked the flawless pianist Hank Jones whether he agreed with Dizzy Gillespie that music is so vast that no one can get more than a small piece of it. "That's exactly right," Jones said. "That's why every night, I begin again."

Duke Ellington resisted the very idea of ending. Trumpeter Clark Terry said of him, "He wants life and music to be always in a state of becoming. He doesn't even like to write definitive endings to a piece. He always likes to make the end of a song sound as if it's still going somewhere."

And that's the story of jazz.

1998

Lester Young:
President of the Blues

Wearing his customary porkpie hat and long black coat, Lester Young, or "Prez"—as tenor saxophonists called him because he had influenced so many of them—was standing at the back of Birdland one night in the mid-1950s. On the stand was Paul Quinichette, a tenor saxophonist whose Prez-like sound and phrasing made Young say softly about his clone, "They don't leave anything anymore for Prez himself to play."

The lament was more ironic than true because Young, a very lonely, very shy man who once said his horn was his life, tried, through the years, "to play different because this is later, that was then." But Prez was well aware of having shaped the playing and thereby the careers of scores of jazzmen—among them Stan Getz, Zoot Sims, Paul Desmond, Gerry Mulligan, John Coltrane and Charlie Parker.

Recalling his formative years, Parker once said, "I was crazy about Lester. He played so clean and beautiful." Unlike another reigning influence on the tenor, Coleman Hawkins, whose style could be as aggressive as a thunderstorm—with torrential chordal improvisations—Lester was light, graceful, witty, unerringly swinging and full of subtle surprises. As Prez put it, "I'm always loose in space, lying out there somewhere."

However, before he became widely known with Count Basie in the mid-1930s, Young was regarded as tonally defective by many of his contemporaries. Billie Holiday, his friend and supporter—the respect was mutual—recalled, "When he first started everyone thought his tone was too thin. And I told Lester, 'It doesn't matter because you have a beautiful tone, and you watch, after a while, everybody's going to be copying *you*.'"

Lady Day, as Lester named her, was very pleased that her prophecy was so accurate. And she was the one who first called him Prez, before it was the thing to do.

In his playing, Prez always, as drummer Jo Jones said, "told a story." He was not in the least interested in technical displays. And to get inside each song, he once said to me, "a musician should know the lyrics of the songs he plays. A lot of musicians nowadays don't. That way they're just playing the chord changes. Most of the time I spend in listening to records is listening to singers and picking up the words right from there." His favorite vocalist by far was Frank Sinatra.

He surprised me one afternoon when he told me that a key early influence on his playing had been Frank Trumbauer, the limpid white alto saxophonist most often heard with Bix Beiderbecke. "He always told a little story," Lester explained.

For Prez, it was never the same story. "In my mind," he said, "the way I play, I try not to be a repeater pencil, you dig?"

Lester could be genial and funny, but often he was alone, even when he was with someone. His own feelings were easily bruised and so he was careful of the sensibilities of others. The result was that sometimes he figured it was safer to keep quiet.

Off the stand, as well as on, Prez's credo was: "It's got to be sweetness, man. Sweetness can be funky, filthy or anything. But not loud."

Prez generally did not read jazz critics. They got his playing wrong, he said to jazz historian Bob Perlongo, so why should he depend on their accuracy in describing other musicians. "They keep saying I'm a cool jazz tenor or be bopper or something. But I play swing tenor."

Although he did selectively incorporate in his playing what he liked in modern jazz, Prez was the embodiment of the way of swinging that delighted in melodic improvisation.

In his later years—Prez was 49 when he died in 1959—his dependence on gin got worse and he had great difficulty eating. Still, there were some nights when he told gently compelling stories on his horn that were far more intimate, I suspect, than he had put into words for many years.

Recently, an illuminating array of Lester Young recordings have been reissued. "The Complete Lester Young" (Mercury) is not complete, but it includes all the crisply exuberant Kansas City Seven sides—with Count Basie, Buck Clayton and Jo Jones.

"Prez & Sweets" (Verve) is the very essence of jazz as conversation. Young is joined by trumpeter Harry Edison.

"The Jazz Giants" (Verve) is a dream band—using the terminology of basketball players and defense attorneys. With Prez are trumpeter Roy Eldridge and trombonist Vic Dickenson (a blithe humorist on the order of Lester Young).

Also worth having are "Prez and Teddy Wilson" (Verve); "The President Plays With the Oscar Peterson Trio" (Verve); and "The Lester Young Trio" with Nat "King" Cole and Buddy Rich (Verve).

The last time I saw Prez was two years before he died, in a CBS television studio on West 57th Street where "The Sound of Jazz" was soon to go on "live." There was a starkly furnished room off the studio with white walls and black-and-white tile on the floor. It could have been a setting for Vermeer, except that the Dutch painter might not have known what to make of the man, alone, in a porkpie hat and long black coat seated on a chair very close to the leather case holding his horn.

Prez was sick and weak and either didn't have the energy—or the desire—to join the musicians next door swapping stories of past gigs.

Young just sat there, waiting for his cue. Later, on the show, he blew the cleanest, most beautiful and deepest blues I had ever heard. I looked for him after we had gone off the air, but he had disappeared.

1995

"The Deepest Blues
We Ever Heard"

*B*lues Review, a handsomely produced magazine published
in Salem, W. Va., has an international audience, because
the blues know no boundaries. In April, 1998, a domes-
tic reader of the Review, Steve Salter, reported in a letter to
the editor that blues giant Otis Spann was in Burr Oak Cemetery on Chicago's South Side, but his grave was unmarked.

Readers sent in more than $2,000, and in June, 1999—
during the Chicago Blues Festival—a headstone was dedicated with an inscription by blues-harmonica virtuoso Charlie
Musselwhite:

"Otis played the deepest blues we ever heard. He'll play for-
ever in our hearts."

Spann was as penetrating a pianist as he was a singer. In the
brochure given to those attending the dedication of the headstone, Muddy Waters—with whom Spann played for years—
was quoted: "There's a man raised singing the blues . . .
There's no one left like him who plays real solid bottom blues
like he does."

Born in Jackson, Miss., on March 21, 1930, Spann played in juke joints and house parties as a teenager. (When he was eight, he earned his first pay—a $25 first prize at a Jackson blues contest.)

He went on to Chicago and at 17 was hired by Muddy Waters. He also recorded as a sideman with Howlin' Wolf, Chuck Berry and other blues bards.

Spann made his first solo album in August, 1960, and I was the A&R man, the guy responsible for Spann's relationship with the record company on this particular session. I'd heard him often with Muddy Waters, and he was on my list of people I wanted to record when, for a short time, I was able to actually live a jazz fan's fantasy by having the freedom to record anybody I wanted to.

Archie Bleyer, owner of a successful pop music label, Cadence, said he wanted to do something for jazz and asked me to start a new label for him, Candid Records. When the sales of Cadence releases diminished, Candid was shut down. It has had a number of owners since, and the sets are still selling in many countries. I only got paid for the sessions I did. No royalties, then or since.

The first album I did with Spann, "Otis Spann Is the Blues," has recently been released here on Artists Only! Records (212-941-9900, also generally available in record stores).

Of all the Candid sessions—with Charles Mingus, Max Roach, Coleman Hawkins, Pee Wee Russell, Cecil Taylor, et al.—the Otis Spann date was the most spontaneous. Two albums were recorded in one afternoon. My only role was to send out for sandwiches and, for one number, "Otis in the Dark," to turn out the lights. He wanted it that way.

Spann just sat down at the piano and told his stories. As I remember, nearly every number was done in one take. His four vocals in the set included memories of hardscrabble years, but the stories were told with the resounding triumph of a man who had always known what he was in this world to do.

The "cry" of the blues was in his voice, but also a mellowness, sometimes wistful, always sure of what his basic audience wanted to hear—and how.

"Most of the people who come to hear us," he told me, "work hard during the day. What they want from us are stories. The blues for them is something like a book. They want to hear stories out of their own experiences, and that's the kind we tell."

His solo piano was powerfully, exultantly compelling. "People were wondering at first," he said, "about what I could do because I have short fingers. They figured I couldn't physically play that much piano. But the piano is made for both hands, and you can make an instrument do what you want it to do."

There are two tracks of the Spann piano alone, and the rest of the album has four numbers by Robert Lockwood Jr., a blues singer Spann had brought to the date. Lockwood worked with the best Chicago bluesmen. He had been taught guitar by the legendary Mississippi blues force, Robert Johnson. Murdered at the age of 22, Johnson continues to influence generations of blues players.

In the September 1999 issue of Blues Review, Moses Glidden, a white blues enthusiast, wrote a memoir of his friendship with Otis Spann, starting when Spann stayed at Mr. Glidden's home when he used to play the college town of Madison, Wis.

"Spann would play his amplified keyboard on the porch," Mr. Glidden writes. "I don't know what all the white adult neighbors thought about the music, but as the afternoon progressed, a mob of kids from two years to 12 appeared and grew just below the porch, dancing in the grass."

Every time Spann and Mr. Glidden would see each other in the years afterward, Spann would say, "You remember those kids, all dancing down there on the grass?"

"At times," Mr. Glidden writes, "Otis definitely could get the blues, but he also had an ocean of joy in him that poured out in his music and in his life."

Among other available Otis Spann CDs, two are on Testament, a division of High-tone Records in Oakland, California (510-763-8500). Their titles: "Otis Spann's Chicago Blues" and "Otis Spann with Muddy Waters and His Band/Live the Life." In his notes for the latter set, Dick Shurman makes the cogent point that Spann's life work is a "reminder that great blues is as much about 'take your time, son!' and giving the music and beat a chance to breathe as it is about in-your-face high energy."

The second Otis Spann session we did on that August afternoon 40 years ago, "Walking The Blues," will be out later this year on the Artists Only! Label. (All the Candid releases are now owned by Alan Bates's Black Lion Records in London, and most will eventually be released here.)

Otis Spann died in Chicago on April 24, 1970. He had just reached the age of 40. He'd had three previous heart attacks. "Please tell my mother I'm gone," he used to sing. "Everybody's gonna miss me when I'm gone."

2000

A CLARINETIST OF SWING
AND SWEET SORROW

Guitarist Danny Barker used to tell of how "a bunch of kids," playing in the streets of New Orleans in the 1910s, "would suddenly hear sounds of musicians. That music could come on you any time like that. The city was full of the sounds of music."

Before the term "jazz" was current, those sounds were of marching bands. In his book "Louis Armstrong, in His Own Words" (Oxford), Armstrong wrote that as a child, "I would stay at the parade and listen to them blow all day. They'd come along with blue serge coats, white pants, and band hats. They just knocked me out." Later, playing second trumpet in the Tuxedo Brass Band, Louis "thought I was in heaven. They had some funeral marches that would touch your heart, they were so beautiful."

Another musician who found his calling in those sounds of both sorrow and jubilation was the late clarinetist George Lewis, born in New Orleans in 1900. When he was seven, his mother gave him 25 cents to buy a toy violin, but they were all gone, so he took home a fife instead. Nine years later, he got a clarinet for four dollars.

"I never had a music lesson in my life," Lewis often said. Nor did he ever learn to read music. But as a child, living across the street from Hope's, a dance hall, he heard such eventual trumpet legends as Freddie Keppard and Bunk Johnson.

By the 1920s, he was leading bands in parades and at dance halls with such sidemen as trumpet player Henry "Red" Allen. This classic jazz was essentially ensemble improvisation. There were solos, but the hometown style was formed and firm before Louis Armstrong—in Chicago and then New York—created what became the next era of the music, virtuoso solos emerging from written arrangements.

In an interview with jazz writer Tom Bethel, George Lewis described the music that nurtured him and that he preferred all his life: "It shouldn't be just one chorus of ensemble and then everybody takes a solo. It's a conversation. If you've got six men playing together, then you've got a full band. . . . When I play music, I like people around me, especially people dancing. Then you don't think too much."

Clear but subtly surprising melodies and pure emotion characterized his playing—conversing in the ensembles, and in his solos. It was as if he were singing. His sound was often poignant but determined—speaking of sorrow and loneliness, but never yielding to bathos. And always, at all tempos, he had what was later called swing.

A small, wiry man, weighing less than a hundred pounds, Lewis was resilient and competitive. Riding on horse-drawn trucks in parades, the bands would try to wear their rivals out.

Lewis's band did that one day to Buddy Petit's—a trumpet player Lewis greatly admired. But they came upon each other the next Sunday, and Lewis recalled: "Somebody sneaked around and chained the wheel of our truck to theirs so we couldn't get away, and that day they really wore us out!"

The robust spirit of the George Lewis Band was particularly well recorded in "George Lewis: HELLO CENTRAL . . . give me doctor jazz," reissued on the Chicago-based Delmark label. Delmark has an extensive catalog of blues and jazz in most manifestations. Its owner, Bob Koester, bought the masters of this and other sessions that Lewis had recorded in 1953. The songs are part of the New Orleans jazz canon: "Just A Closer Walk With Thee," "Doctor Jazz," "Dippermouth Blues" and "Ain't Gonna Give Nobody None of My Jelly Roll."

George Lewis's colleagues on this, as on many of his other recordings, were among the vintage masters of these flowing conversations—more easeful than the insistent inflection of the later, largely white Dixieland and Chicago jazz styles. They included the lusty trombonist, Jim Robinson ("If everyone is in a frisky spirit the spirit gets to me and I can make my trombone sing"); trumpeter Kid Howard; banjo player Laurence Marrero; bassist Alcide "Slow Drag" Pavageau; drummer Joe Watkins; and Alton Purnell, whose barrelhouse piano is akin to the honky tonk pianists in old-time country-music bands.

Most veteran New Orleans musicians had day jobs to supplement their gigs in dance halls, taverns and parades. George Lewis worked as a stevedore for a long time. He especially needed that job during the 1930s, when, as he said, "everyone was saxophone crazy."

But in the 1940s, there was a surge of interest in pristine New Orleans jazz, due primarily to recordings of Bunk Johnson, George Lewis and other survivors by historian-researcher and producer William Russell for his American Music label. This led to a demand for the George Lewis Band in New York, San Francisco, Los Angeles and on college campuses.

Lewis also became a late-rising star in England, where, as Bob Koester writes in his notes to this CD, the Lewis Band was "an early influence on the British rock movement," which had its own beginnings in "Skiffle (blues played on guitar, washtub bass, perhaps harmonica or jug.)" This blues revival, spurred by the presence of the New Orleans improvisers and American blues visitors, influenced the Beatles, Rolling Stones and other British acolytes.

It was in Japan, however, that the joys of New Orleans jazz created the most rapturous reactions George Lewis and his companions had ever received. As William Carter writes in "Preservation Hall" (Cassell): "Having been warned the Japanese rarely showed emotion, the musicians were astonished by an outpouring that included stamping, jumping on the stage, shouting requests, and clapping even for spoken instructions to the tunes. The musicians were mobbed for autographs and attention wherever they went."

Back in New Orleans, George Lewis appeared regularly at Preservation Hall. After his death, in 1968, Woody Allen, whose clarinet playing had been shaped by Lewis, came to Preservation Hall to record the sound track for his film, "Sleeper." As William Carter writes, Jim Robinson asked Mr.

Allen: "Did anyone ever tell you you sound like my old friend, George Lewis? What's your name, again?"

George Lewis's sound was so compellingly personal that listeners familiar with his playing can hear it just by saying his name.

2001

DIZZY IN THE SUNLIGHT, I

Cheraw, in northeastern South Carolina, figured briefly in the history of the Civil War. There was a Confederate supply depot there, which was captured by General William Tecumseh Sherman during his scorched-earth march through the South.

Cheraw is much better known now as the birthplace of John Birks Gillespie. There's a Dizzy Gillespie Drive there. He used to go back from time to time, and one afternoon a couple of years ago, I asked him if the place had changed much when it came to Jim Crow.

"There are nice people down there," Dizzy said, "but you have to be careful because you're still colored." And he told me about going down for a day not long before.

"I was on my way to the mayor's house—I knew all the mayors over the years, most of them from when they were kids. He was giving a cocktail party for his sister who lived in San Francisco. I asked if I could bring a couple of my cousins, and he said to bring whomever I wanted.

"So everything was cool. I needed a haircut. There were two black barbershops. We stopped the car before each of them, but they were all filled up with people waiting, so I told my cousin to take me to the white barbershop. He say, '*What!*' I say, 'Take me to the white barbershop, and let's see what they say.'

"We walked in the door. Only the barber was in there. No customers. He didn't look up. I said, 'I'd like a haircut, please.' Then he looked up for a second and said, 'I'm sorry, we don't cut colored hair.'

"I figure I'm going to show my class by just turning around and walking out. Here I am in the South Carolina Hall of Fame, and the year I won that, there were two others who got in—General William Westmoreland and Father Joseph Bernardin, who became a cardinal. So, me being in that Hall of Fame with the military and religion, I thought I was ready for something. At least a haircut.

"As I turned to go, the barber takes another look and says, 'I know you.' I just walked out, and when I told the mayor, he said, '*What!*'"

Dizzy smiled. "It got in the papers."

We were talking about Charlie Parker. I asked Dizzy what he found so different about Bird's music when he first heard him. "His phrasing," Dizzy said. "And his bluesiness. He played blues better than anybody. I mean, he played blues like T-Bone Walker would sing, and then Bird would put some little extra things in there. He was the most fantastic musician I ever heard."

I may have missed it, but I don't recall any of the obituaries having mentioned that Dizzy himself was a hell of a blues player. He was very conscious and proud of his roots in the music. That's why one day when I casually talked about the revolution in the music created by him, Bird, Thelonious Monk, and others, Dizzy corrected me: *"Evolution,"* he said, "not revolution."

Another time, I mentioned that the day after Charlie Parker died, Art Blakey said that the second tragedy was that young people in America—black as well as white—didn't know who Charlie Parker was.

"Yeah," Dizzy said. "As a kid, I didn't get taught my heritage. I went to a segregated school, the Robert Smalls School. In that public school, I never heard of Robert Smalls. I wondered where this name had come from. But later, I found this guy was black, one of the great Americans."

In the new paperback edition of *There Is a River: The Black Struggle for Freedom in America* (Harcourt Brace Jovanovich), Vincent Harding tells of an event in South Carolina during the Civil War: "One audacious group of [black] families under the leadership of a skilled black harbor pilot, Robert Smalls, actually commandeered and sailed the *Planter,* a Confederate coastal supply ship, past the unwitting Southern keepers of the Charleston harbor batteries, and delivered it—and themselves—into Union hands."

On one of his trips to Africa—in Benin, West Africa—Dizzy was made a chief. "They made me both an artist and a chief. Double respect, man. My great-grandmother was the daughter of a chief.

"When I went to Nigeria, I saw my family there. I saw in the faces there my brother, my mother, my father."

Art Taylor, one of the continually inventive jazz drummers, compiled an illuminating book of conversations with musicians, *Notes and Tones* (Perigree Books, published by Putnam). In his conversation with Dizzy Gillespie, Taylor asked him about his religion. Said Dizzy: "I belong to the Baha'i faith. Baha'i means follower of Baha'u'llah'. Baha'u'llah means 'glory of God' in Persian. The one principle that holds true in the Baha'i faith is the unity of mankind. Everything you do is designed to bring about the unity of mankind. So that's what I'm about now."

In one of our conversations, I also asked about the Baha'i faith, many of whose adherents have been murdered during the 150 years of the religion's existence—especially in Iran, where the religion began. The rulers of that nation, who maintain that their religion is the holiest of all, are still executing Baha'is.

The faith, Dizzy told me, "teaches that God has had a special plan for mankind on earth for all these billions of years, and that plan has been moving, moving, moving. Each period in our spiritual development, he sends a manifestation of himself. He picks somebody out from the people here on earth, and he tells him what to say to the people about the way to live with your fellow man. The message changes as we get more knowledge.

"So he sent these guys—Abraham, Moses, Jesus, Muhammad, Buddha, Krishna, Zoroaster. And each of them would start a religion, an evolving religion. Eventually, mankind will become unified, when there is a world government and everybody belongs to it and you don't need a passport. There'll be an international language taught in all the schools, and all your important papers will be in that language.

"This should take another one thousand or two thousand years. But on the way we get little pinches of unification. The

League of Nations was another little pinch. So was the United Nations."

"And jazz?" I asked.

"Yeah, yeah. That really is a pinch of unification. It makes me feel really good to belong to jazz, to that part of society."

I knew Dizzy for some forty years, and he did evolve into a spiritual person. That's a phrase I almost never use because many of the people who call themselves spiritual would kill for their faith. But Dizzy reached an inner strength and discipline that total pacifists call "soul force."

He always had a vivid presence. Like they used to say of Fats Waller, whenever Dizzy came into a room, he filled it. He made people feel good, and he was the sound of surprise, even when his horn was in its case.

But in later years there was also a peaceableness in Dizzy. There was nothing passive about it. It was his soul force that resolved tensions.

For example, in the 1980s, there was to be a concert at Lincoln Center honoring Dizzy. He and a big band were, of course, to be at the center of the celebration. A few days before, I went to a rehearsal. Everyone was there but Dizzy.

No music was being played. The only sounds were a bitter argument between Max Roach and Gerry Mulligan. Each had some compositions on the program, and at the start the argument was about who was to have more of his pieces played. Then it became very personal and poisonous.

The other musicians, all of them renowned, either looked down at their music in embarrassment or found a place on the ceiling in order to avoid, God forbid, meeting the eyes of the combatants. The tension in the room got fiercer and fiercer.

In the back, Dizzy, who had not moved, was watching. Then he strode to the front of the band, spread out a score, and said, "Letter B, we'll start at letter B."

He had filled the room with reasonableness without getting involved in the battle. Most of the leaders I've known through the years would have scolded the antagonists for wasting valuable rehearsal time and acting like children. But Dizzy, by his very presence, had broken the tension.

Of course he had, for so many years, earned the respect of the musicians, but so had other leaders, who would have added to the tension. Softly, being able to relax now, an alto saxophonist blew the rest of the bad feelings out the door, as he played "I'll Always Be in Love with You." Even Max and Gerry laughed.

Dizzy used to say that of all the awards he'd received, he was most proud of the Paul Robeson Award from the Institute of Jazz Studies at Rutgers.

"I was a great fan of Paul Robeson," he told me.

"What made him one of your heroes?"

"He wouldn't capitulate. He wouldn't back down. And he wouldn't be corrupted by money or by anything else."

Paul Robeson was a classic victim of McCarthyism except that—as Dizzy emphasized—he refused to play the victim. Robeson was denounced as a Communist by the right-wing press, which was in abundance. He lost work and for years couldn't accept engagements overseas because the State Department denied him a passport.

"He was so great at so many things," Dizzy said. "A great sports figure, a lawyer, an actor, a singer. So many things. I don't see how he had the time to develop all those qualities.

"He heard us play at the Apollo. He wrote me a note and said he'd enjoyed it so much. And then he said that he would have liked to come backstage and tell me personally how much he'd liked the performance. But he didn't want to cause any trouble."

"You mean he was afraid that being there would cause you trouble with the FBI as someone who knew him?"

"Yeah, something like that. I called him up, and I said, 'Paul, for you to come backstage and tell me you liked the performance, I'd be willing to go to jail.'"

1995

DIZZY IN THE SUNLIGHT, II

When I first heard Charlie Parker, I said, "That's how our music should be played . . ." I'd never heard anything like him. It was scary! After we got it together, yeah, I knew we were making something new. It was magic. Nobody on the planet was playing like that but us.

—Dizzy Gillespie, San Francisco Chronicle, May 25, 1991

All of the music is out there in the first place, all of it. From the beginning of time the music was there. All you have to do is try to get a little piece of it. I don't care how great you are, you only get a little piece of it.

—Dizzy Gillespie, in a conversation with this writer, 1983

Dizzy was talking about Bird. He had always given Charlie Parker great credit, the major part of the credit, for the invention of modern jazz. But Dizzy made far-ranging original harmonic and rhythmic contributions—and continued to long after Bird died. Dizzy, however, saw Bird as the primary source.

Duke Ellington told Dizzy, by the way, that the biggest mistake Dizzy had made was to let people, namely critics, call that music bebop. "From the time they name something," said Duke, "it's dated."

As Duke predicted, some of bebop has become dated. But not the music of the originators. A few months ago I put on a Charlie Parker record for the first time in quite a while. I was stunned once again by the torrent of ideas—fresh, original, brilliant ideas—and the depth of his time. Bird is no more dated than Duke or Lester Young. But Duke was right about the name.

"Charlie Parker was brilliant," Dizzy said one afternoon. "And not only in his music. He was a very serious guy. He knew a lot about politics and other things besides music."

"You could tell that sometimes," I said, "but at other times, he was a wholly different person. There were many Charlie Parkers."

Dizzy nodded. I told him about an interview I'd had with Bird on a radio station in Boston. His answers were only grunts as he flipped through *The New Yorker*. A few months later, also on the radio, Bird wouldn't stop talking. He told me about a session he was planning with woodwinds, a choral group, a harp, and a rhythm section. "Something," he said, "on the line of Hindesmith's *Kleine Kammermusik*. Not a copy or anything like that. I don't want ever to copy." He also gave an incisive analysis of Bartók's Second Piano Concerto.

"He was just a phenomenon," Dizzy said, shaking his head. "Nobody knew where he got what he had." And nobody knew how to keep him from destroying himself. During one of his last nights anywhere, Bird ran into Dizzy. "Save me! Save me!" he said. By then, Dizzy didn't know how.

"Would things have been different for Charlie Parker," I asked Dizzy, "if he'd had a Lorraine?"

At his death, Dizzy had been married to Lorraine for fifty-two years. And for fifty-two years he had carried their marriage certificate in his pocket. Dizzy dedicated his remarkably candid, multivoiced, essential book, *To Be Or Not to Bop* (Da Capo paperback) to Lorraine: "Her love, help, humor, and wisdom. Her unselfish and unswerving devotion made me the man and musician I wanted to be."

It was clear from the start of Dizzy's courtship with the former dancer that "if I wanted to marry her, I would have to walk the straight line." Dizzy kept walking that line while some other musicians lost control of themselves and lost everything else.

Another thing about being married to Lorraine, Dizzy told me, was that "she does not want to be wrong. So I just let her be right all the time. That's a harmony that works—you just be wrong all the time." Dizzy laughed.

"But could it have made a difference with Bird—if he'd had a Lorraine?"

"I guess that would have depended on him. If he'd have been willing to do what I did for her—walk the straight line."

There are many stories about Dizzy, but the one that most graphically captures a particular dimension of Dizzy's way of throwing bigots off balance is in *Jazz Anecdotes* (Oxford University Press) by Bill Crow, a first-rate bassist who is also an invaluable chronicler of the jazz life.

"In 1958," Crow writes, "George Wein arranged to stage a jazz festival at French Lick in southern Indiana. He demanded and received assurances that there would be no discourtesies shown the black musicians and fans who would be visiting this former lily-white resort. . . . When the Gerry Mulligan Quartet arrived there, however, Art Farmer and Dave Bailey expressed doubts about using the swimming pool. They wanted to avoid any ugly scenes.

From the lobby the blue water of the pool looked inviting, and Art and Dave had just about decided to get into their swimsuits when Dizzy Gillespie stepped out of the elevator. He was wearing bathing trunks from the French Riviera, an embroidered skullcap from Greece, and embroidered slippers with curled-up toes that he'd picked up in Turkey.

A Sheraton bath towel draped over his shoulders like a cape was fastened at the neck with a jade scarab pin from Egypt. With a Chinese ivory cigarette holder in his left hand and a powerful German multiband portable radio in his right, he beamed cheerfully through a pair of Italian sunglasses.

"I've come to integrate the pool!" he announced. He led the way to the poolside beach chairs, enthroning himself in one with plenipotentitary panache. After he had the attention of everyone at the poolside, he grabbed Jimmy McPartland, who had also come down for a swim. Arm in arm, the two trumpet players marched to the diving board and jumped in together, and the last barrier to integration at Frenck Lick was down.

Dizzy integrated all kinds of scenes. On a State Department tour, the band was in Karachi, Pakistan, and Dizzy was fascinated to see a snake charmer in the park. "I had my horn there, and I saw him playing and the snake moving, moving. So he say to me, 'Come on, come on.' I went and got next to him, and he say, 'Go on, go on, play something.' I started playing "Groovin' High," and the snake was going and going, and the snake charmer say, 'Move your horn a bit.' I must have put that horn too close. The next thing I hear was ,'ssshhhhllllick!' And the snake was *moving*. I broke the record for the backwards jump. I must have jumped back nineteen feet."

Dizzy still wanted to learn more about that powerfully moving music. He invited the snake charmer and his companion up to his hotel room.

The hotel manager was aghast. Not at the snake, but at the fact—he vigorously pointed out—that the snake charmer was of a decidedly lower caste than the establishment's clientele. Dizzy, who could be the stubbornest man on the planet, insisted. "The man's a musician, isn't he?" he told the manager. And so, in that hotel room, duets were played before an audience of one suspicious, ever-vigilant snake.

Dizzy liked to tell another story about one of his missions for the State Department. ("I used to do a lot of apologizing for what the State Department had done.") This happened in Ankara, Turkey, where a lawn party had been arranged at the American embassy. The climax was to be a jam session presided over by Dizzy. "While I was signing autographs," he recalled, "I happened to look at this fence surrounding the grounds. A lot of street kids were pressed against the fence. They wanted to come in and hear the music. One of them actually climbed over the fence, and a guard threw him right back over it.

"I asked what was going on. Why did they do that? And some official said, 'This party is for select people. Local dignitaries and important Americans in the city.'

"I said, 'Select people! We're not over here for no select people! We're over her to show these people that Americans are all kinds of people.' I had a girl in that band, and almost as many whites as blacks. We had a good mix.

"The ambassador comes over and asks, 'Are you going to play?' I say, 'No! I saw that guard throw a little kid over the fence. Those are the people we're trying to get close to—the people *outside* the fence.'

"So the ambassador said, 'Let them in, let them all in.'"

And that is how John Birks Gillespie brought democracy to the American embassy in Ankara.

In all the years I knew Dizzy, I rarely heard him put anybody down. But there were exceptions. In Arthur Taylor's book *Notes and Tones*, Dizzy said, "History will either off you or make you valid. History has wiped Stan Kenton out completely. They thought he was a master, they thought he was greater than Duke Ellington, and that motherfucker couldn't even keep time."

Most of the time Dizzy had a lot of fun and was fun. But as he would tell you, he was very serious about his music. He was continually looking for and finding new ways of shaping and coloring sounds, and he was continually teaching what he found to musicians—of all ages. At the funeral service for Dizzy at Saint Peter's Lutheran Church, Hank Jones—a truly master pianist who himself is always searching—told of how Dizzy, through the years, would show him "chord inversions I hadn't even thought of."

Seeing Dizzy, however casually, was like coming into sunlight. By the warmth of his greeting, his natural considerateness, and the keenness of his intelligence—which made his wit so sharp—he was a delight to be with. And he was a delight to himself when he was all alone.

In *Waiting for Dizzy* (Oxford University Press), Gene Lees tells of arranging to meet Dizzy in a small park in Minneapolis so that his photographer could take some pictures. As Lees and the photographer approached, they saw Dizzy, who did not see them.

"Lost in some musical thought, Dizzy was softly dancing, all alone there in the sunlight."

1995

WHITE LINE FEVER

It is a game played by children of all ages. Depending on the alleged sophistication of the participants, the creepy questions can range from "Which would you rather lose, an arm or a leg?" to "Which would you rather be—impotent for the rest of your life or the Elephant Man?" (Ah, but who knows what horny compassion lurks in all manner of sensitive women?) The most common version is: "If you had to choose between being blind and deaf, which would it be?"

I played the game in elementary school, and I played it a couple of months ago, when I answered without hesitation: "Blind." There was hooting incredulity. I am so compulsive a reader that I read while walking in the street, including at night, by flashlight. Nonetheless, I tried to explain, for me music is a much, much deeper need. Like, if I have to go without it for a few days, I get to feeling hollow. But I can go for weeks without reading the First Amendment.

The reason this comes to mind has to do with my being at the bar of the Lone Star Cafe on lower Fifth Avenue one late afternoon in 1980. On the stand, going through a sound test and a lighting test, were Merle Haggard and the Strangers, ten weathered-looking klezmorim of quite varied ages. They'd been playing together so long that they were swinging with powerfully relaxed ease from note one. In the front line, a tall, bearded, impassive man in his early middle years took a swig from a bottle of beer, picked up an alto saxophone, and cut through the band, cut through the years, with a lean, hot, jumping solo that brought Pete Brown, Don Stovall, and other startling jazz ghosts into my head. I hadn't felt so satisfied in a long time.

But this was a white cat, Don Markham of Bakersfield, California, and this was a country band. Yeah, but there's a hell of a lot more to country than most trendy city folk think. Especially with Haggard and his obsession with roots, all kinds of roots. There's nobody playing country now who *knows* as much as Haggard. He's a practicing expert on Jimmie Rodgers, Bob Wills's western swing, Lefty Frizzell, and Hank Williams. And Haggard himself is, except for Bill Monroe, the only singer/musician/writer left whose own body of work makes him fit right into that company of lasting originals. It's like Kris Kristofferson said a couple of years ago: "When we speak of Haggard, we aren't speaking about how he's going to come out on the Country Music Association Awards this year; we're talking about posterity."

At that moment in the Lone Star, however, Haggard was very much into the present. He started going over some songs he must have played hundreds of times, but he wasn't satisfied. As it used to be in Duke Ellington's band, Haggard's arrangements are constantly subject to editing. Wearing a railroad cap, jeans, workshirt, a white nylon windbreaker, and western boots, the wiry Okie was tinkering with the tempo of "I'm a

Lonesome Fugitive," a song that is not his but that years ago, he says, "gave me a direction for writing. I mean, it was a true song." It was then he decided he could write about his own true life, including his time in prison. If it hadn't been for "Fugitive," he might have tried to hide his past, which, to his astonishment, turned out to be "one of the most interesting things about me."

Haggard, with as much controlled intensity as if he were playing to a packed room rather than to us strays at the bar, started "Fugitive" again ("Down every road there's always one more city/I'm on the run, the highway is my home"). Lead guitarist Roy Nichols—no household name but revered by guitarists all over the world—lined out a biting, crackling commentary. But suddenly Haggard gestured it all into silence and worked for a while with the band on getting different guitar/violin/horn voicings. "And," he looked up at one of his two drummers, "not so strong. It's got to be lighter."

The one woman on the stand, Bonnie Owens, stepped off and came over to the bar, where I cleared a seat for her by removing various newspapers of mine that had no business being there anyway. She has reddish-brown hair and an extraordinarily clear, open look. Introducing herself rather diffidently as "the harmony singer with Merle Haggard," she insisted on buying me a beer for my courtesy; and as the musicians moved into another song, Bonnie said, "We have the best band in the country, you know." And paused. "The best singer too."

I agreed, adding that I have all of Haggard's albums.

She was surprised hearing this from someone who was manifestly not a good old boy. A good old Yossele Rosenblatt boy, maybe, but where does this stranger come to "White Line

Fever"? "I know a lot of people," Bonnie told me, "who would *kill* for all his albums."

Bonnie, now forty-eight but looking some ten years younger, used to be more than a harmony singer. In the mid-sixties, while featured with her then-husband, Merle Haggard, she won the Academy of Country & Western Music's Top Female Vocalist award. But she spent more and more of her energy taking care of Merle's business and even retired from performing in 1975. For a while. I'd last seen her several years ago, in an auditorium. By then Bonnie was one of several backup singers for Haggard. That night she was banging a tambourine as well and having one hell of a problem keeping it and herself in time. Merle finally came over to her and in front of all those people, took the tambourine, and plopped it on her head. He didn't seem to be funning.

They were divorced a couple of years ago, and when Merle remarried, Bonnie was the bridesmaid. (If you want to read about how that happened, look at Peter Guralnick's chapter on Merle in his indispensable book *Lost Highway*, published by Godine. It's as if Chekhov had filed a report from Harrah's in Lake Tahoe.)

Bonnie stayed with the band and is now the *only* harmony singer. Everybody in the entourage says that Bonnie is Merle's best friend. Merle says that too. So how do you figure that? You usually divorce someone you can't stand. Merle's answer is that Aries people are not easy to live with. Bonnie also got into his repertory. He wrote "I Can't Be What You Want Me to Be" for her. The subsequent Haggard marriage, I was told, is not in what you'd call a mellow groove. "She's a real ballbreaker," someone says of Bonnie's successor.

Haggard waves for Bonnie to go back on the stand. The spots, red and blue, are on, and outside, although it's not yet six, people are lining up for Merle's first show—four hours from now. Some have been there since two o'clock in the afternoon.

This is the first club date Haggard has ever played in New York. "I got nothing at all against this man's place in here," Haggard tells me, "but it's kind of cramped." And Bonnie had said, "He loves being closer to the people so he can find out what they want and what they're living like. But," she smiled to indicate she meant no offense, "we've never played in a club this small."

Haggard agreed to the one-night booking because there was a syndicated "live" radio show out of the Lone Star that covers much of the country. Also, word had been getting out to even the most renowned and picky country performers that the Lone Star was a good club to work. You get your money. All of it. And a lot of exposure. It took Mort Cooperman, the musical architect of the Lone Star, a while to break down some of the southern suspicion of Yankee traders and particularly of Jewish-Yankee entrepreneurs. But he's done it. Why, not long ago, in the middle of a negotiating conversation on the phone with a country power in Nashville, Cooperman said, "Hey, I'm the one who's supposed to be the Jew." That old southern boy laughed and laughed.

The band is really cooking. On a ballad, the fiddle player is spinning so sensuous a solo that I remember Pete Rowan—describing a mountain player whose "harmonies glowed in the dark." Haggard, rocking slightly on his heels, is smiling, and one of the guitarists is so taken with the good feeling in the air that he grins at me, one music-loving stranger to another.

Later that night, too, members of the band had plenty of solo space. Haggard has no patience with the commercial country framework in which the musicians are just there to wait on the soloist. As he recently said to a *Down Beat* reporter, "If I can't feature the instrumentalists, I just don't want to be in the business." He digs the sounds around him so much that not long ago, when his present wife, Leona Williams, wanted to give him a surprise birthday party in a remote Florida nightclub, she arranged to have the whole band come down here that evening because she knew that's what Merle most wanted to hear, night off or not.

It is just past six at the Lone Star, and Merle calls "White Line Fever." Drawing out the first two words as if he were actually tracing lines on the highway, Haggard—in that firm, slightly gritty, blues-touched voice—sings:

> *The years keep flying by like the high line poles*
> *The wrinkles in my forehead show the miles I've put behind me*
> *They continue to remind me how fast I'm growing old*
> *Guess I'll die with this fever in my soul.*

Hypnotically, in the failing light, the refrain of wh-i-i-i-te l-i-i-i-ne fever, medium-slow, with Roy Nichols's guitar keening into the far distance, immobilizes us all as Haggard comes up to the mike again, with Bonnie harmonizing on the side: "Yeah, I've been from coast to coast a hundred times or more/I ain't seen one single place where I ain't been before."

The musicians began to leave, and the Nashville publicity man came over to tell me he still didn't know if Haggard would agree to be interviewed. "He's a very private man," he said. Everybody tells me Haggard's a very private man. Bonnie said it too. "He told me no press in New York," the nervous but amiable young man went on, "but maybe he'll make a couple of exceptions.

Usually, unless I'm on a muckraking kind of story, if someone insists on being that private, I leave him to himself. The golden rule, you know. But I'm very curious about Haggard, and I don't have that many live musical heroes anymore. So I stick around. And it pays off. Haggard was not at all reticent about talking. He turns out, by the way, to be so knowledgeable about jazz that he cited—as an influence on the legendary country singer Jimmie Rodgers—a pop jazz singer out of the twenties, Emmett Miller, whom I'd never heard of. I didn't tell Haggard that I had to look Miller up afterward.

Later that night, about halfway through Haggard's first set, he introduced to the happily cramped crowd "My favorite girl singer—Bonnie Owens! She's been with us for fifteen years. And she's going to do us a song she wrote."

Bonnie, smiling, said, "I wrote this song, 'I'll Be What I Want to Be,' for all the women in New York. But," she added quickly, "it's not a women's lib song."

"You wouldn't have much of a chance with it if it was," Haggard said into the mike with somewhat excessive good humor. "Not with all the male chauvinist pigs on *this* stage."

With the band rolling behind her, Bonnie, in a crisp, pungent, pleasant voice, ran the changes on independence. "I ain't gonna do nothing I don't want to do never again!" She ended, with hands triumphantly raised, "I like *me!*"

Merle Haggard looked very proud. Later on he went into a song of his about a man whose wife had split and left him to bring up the kids. Listening, I wondered if there are any children in rock songs—aside from the children, of whatever age, doing the singing.

Toward the end there was another kind of what Jimmy Rushing used to call a he/she song. ("The foundation of all song," Rushing said.) Merle went into "Today I Started Loving You Again/And I'm Right Back Where I've Always Been." There's nobody in country music or anywhere else who can sing as tenderly as Haggard. The sound, the feeling, he gets talking to a woman are like what Michael Harper wrote for Bud Powell: "there's no rain anywhere, soft enough for you."

But then, an explosion of the blues, "Trouble in Mind," in which Haggard and the Strangers emblazoned on our very souls a fiery, exultant tribute to all the blues singers and players they have known—black, white, city, country, dead, and alive. When it was over, Haggard sighed in satisfaction: "Oh, I feel *good!*"

"You know," he had told me earlier, "this may sound corny, but when it looks like everything else is breaking up in the country and in the world, and in your own life, I keep thinking that maybe music will be the last thing to go down."

The story is that he has a spider web tattooed on his back. "He did it when he was young and felt trapped," Bonnie Owens once told southern writer Paul Hemphill, a good listener.

Merle Haggard was the child of Okies who had been farmers near Checotah, Oklahoma, not far from Muskogee. After a disastrous fire there came a drought, and so Merle's folks (he hadn't come on the scene yet) went off to California where, as Jimmie Rodgers sang, "they sleep out every night."

James Haggard had been a pretty fair fiddler and picker back in Oklahoma; but his wife, Flossie, once her soul took fire in the Church of Christ, banned him from playing the devil's music. All the more so since their child, Merle, had been born to be reared in a straight line to the Saviour. The Haggards were living in a converted refrigerator car near Bakersfield, California, by then; and James, now a carpenter with the railroad, taught the boy fishing and hunting. But when Merle was nine, his father, as Merle later put it, abandoned him. The interviewer asked if he'd be a little more specific.

"He died," said Merle.

"Mama Tried," as Haggard later titled a song, but she failed. She could not control the boy. He ran away a lot, cut school (finally dropping out in the eighth grade), and became quite familiar to the Bakersfield police. When Merle was fourteen, Flossie put him in a juvenile home, and he escaped the next day. Merle's police record grew like Pinocchio's nose—bum checks, petty thievery, stolen cars, armed robbery. Reform schools couldn't hold him. Seven times he slid out of them. But when he and some of the boys messed up a burglary of a Bakersfield bar (they got drunk waiting for the bar to close), he got sent to a place that *could* hold him: San Quentin. He was on an indeterminate sentence of six months to fifteen and a half years.

Current conventional wisdom—from hard-liners to many reformers—is that prison can't rehabilitate anybody. But Merle, unconventional as always, insists that San Quentin turned him around. Having spent his twenty-first birthday in solitary across the hall from death row—and hearing those terminal souls trying to figure out how they'd gotten there—

scared the hell out of him. "This was no movie, and I wasn't Jesse James or one of the Dalton brothers."

Haggard was in the audience when Johnny Cash came to make a recording at San Quentin, and he became part of the warden's country band. He also picked up a high school equivalency diploma. After two years and nine months, Merle Haggard was paroled; and to cut a long, hard story short, he made it very big in the music business. So now he's one happy straightened-out dude, right? Well, yes and no. ("I was born the running kind, with leaving always on my mind.")

In the band bus, as open-mouthed fans look through the window, clutching empty pages to be blessed with an autograph, we are talking about jazz and blues. I'd mentioned that one of Merle's heroes, Bob Wills, while in his teens in East Texas, used to ride fifty miles to see Bessie Smith perform.

"Sure," said Haggard. "I understand that. I go back a long way in that music myself. I go back to Louis Armstrong, Joe Venuti, Eddie Lang, Emmett Miller." (Miller, I found out when I looked him up, had a band with the Dorsey Brothers, Eddie Lang, and Jack Teagarden.)

Bonnie Owens came into the bus and soundlessly slipped into a seat diagonally across from Merle. Up front, next to where the driver would have been, nonpareil lead guitarist Roy Nichols was trying to stare some piece of electrical equipment into submission. "My big love," said Haggard, "my big jazz love was Django Reinhardt." The gypsy guitarist might have been surprised.

"What did you especially like about what he did?"

Haggard laughed. An uproarious, bus-filling laugh. "Every-thing."

"Yeah," Nichols filled out the chord. "Every note he played."

"And something else," Merle went on. "I understand they couldn't nail him down to record very often because he was such a free-will person. Django didn't give a shit about sched-ules. He just wanted to play wherever he felt like playing. That's kind of the way I am. Me and Johnny Gimble. He's that way too." (The most exultantly swinging of all country fid-dlers, Gimble, a Bob Wills alumnus, is a ubiquitous session man and a headliner too.)

"Yeah," said Haggard, "Johnny doesn't give a damn *where* he plays. He just wants to be happy, have a few beers, tell jokes, and *play!*"

"You sound envious."

"You bet that's what I'd do if I could. In fact, I've started do-ing it some on my off-time. I can't do it when I'm working. But when I'm off, I just sit in and play anywhere there's music. Anywhere somebody knows me and will tolerate me."

Roy Nichols snorts. "Come on, Merle."

"I've gone and sat in with Willie Nelson for five days at Har-rah's." Haggard ignores his guitarist. "No money. Just for the fun of the playing." He looked past me and Bonnie into some wild blue yonder.

I read Merle what Peter Guralnick had recently written about him: "He's achieved more success than he ever intended and cannot come to terms with this success."

"That's true," Haggard said softly. "Success has its benefits and its holdbacks. There are just as many in either direction, you know. It's no secret I've been in prison, and I sometimes feel that all I've done since is just secured myself in a prison I can't escape from. Everything is always committed so far ahead. Yet, you wake up one day, and you don't want to do what you're committed to do that day. Or that month. But you got to do it."

"Ever thought of giving it all up and going for freedom?"

Haggard smiled. "I did that. A couple of years ago, I went and got divorced and got married again." Bonnie leaned forward a little to hear better. "And I stopped the schedule until I decided what I wanted to do with the rest of my life. Six months went by. I was free, and all the holdbacks and problems stayed with me. And all the fun was gone. I wasn't performing. But I was still a personality that people recognized and imposed on; I never found that place I could go to and not be recognized. So I came back. And here I am, sitting in a bus in the middle of New York.

"I just kind of knocked on the door of the prison," Haggard said, "and asked to be let back in. And over the past year, I've come to accept it, give up to it, and have fun when I can. Like, when we're working, we can't play everything we want to do. We have hard-core country fans in the audience and that cuts down on the jazz we can play some places. And sometimes you have to get loud and do the old country-boy nightclub act. But somehow or another, we get in enough to please ourselves. I guess I'll stay in this prison. Where else would I go? To a foreign country and act like a man in exile?"

"When I was sixteen," Merle once told country-music chronicler Lois Lazarus, "I was picked up for a robbery I never committed. A rich kid would get a lawyer, an Okie with a record goes to jail."

In many of his songs, Merle writes about folks who have no connections that can do them any good: poor and working-class whites, migrant workers, diverse outcasts. And so too in the novel he's been at, off and on, for some time. He started writing fiction in school when he was about ten, and his grades suffered because he wasn't paying any mind to what he was supposed to be learning.

"That's what's wrong with our school system," Haggard says. "they were boring me with whatever they had to present. I couldn't get out of the classroom yet, so I just wrote. I remember an old report card my mother had: 'Sits staring out the window, scribbling.'"

Now, this novel, says Merle, is "a kind of comedy-murder mystery. Imagine John-Boy in the Waltons being an asshole, putting mirrors on his shoes in school, and still being in the fourth grade when he was sixteen years old. Only reason he kept going to school was to fuck with the girls." (The ones in the higher grades.)

"He finally winds up being arrested for rape. They think he raped and killed this girl, but they find out it wasn't him. It was the old, nasty boy at school," Haggard grins, "the rich man's son. And they proved it by the new model-A tracks at the scene of the crime. This takes place in the Depression."

Haggard is fond of imagining the Depression years. "I could find many reasons for wanting to live back there," he's told Peter Guralnick. "Such as trains was the main method of travel, the glamour of trains always appealed to me. . . . Then again, the music was young. So many things were being done in music, it was wide open back then, electronics had not yet been involved, and basically it was *real*."

But the realness of those open acoustic sounds—when it came to country musicians in the thirties and into the fourties—was distorted on recordings. Or so Merle fiercely believes.

"They made those artists sound less than they were," he says, "because the people doing the recording didn't care about this music. They didn't take time to get the full sound quality of artists like Ernest Tubb and Kitty Wells. They made the twang of country singers, for example, sound a lot more pronounced than it actually was. And a lot of other sound parts were missing. Take Bob Wills. They just farted him off. He'd come to Chicago or New York to record, and they didn't know who he was. Just a hick from Oklahoma, and they treated him that way. He was great enough so that he cut on through anyway, and so did some of the others. But the recording people sure did slight the country performers."

"Hey, Roy," Haggard looked toward Nichols who was still grappling with one of the wonders of the electronic age. "Remember the first time you ever heard Lefty Frizzell in a live appearance? He sounded four times better than he did on records, and he *was* four times better."

"Much better," Roy said reflectively. "*Much* better."

By now, country music means a lot more in profits to the record companies, and so there is no electronic slighting of current practitioners. But Haggard is not happy about much that is currently being packaged as "country." He will name no names but is manifestly disgusted by most of what's on the charts.

"There's no free will to their music," he says. "They're very strict, they're very formal, they're very pop. Yet they're being disguised and called country artists, but they don't have it. They got no heart."

"No soul," said Bonnie.

"No soul," Merle echoed.

Haggard's first huge hit, "Okie from Muskogee," started as a joke. As the band bus rolled through East Oklahoma, there was a sign with that town's name, and one of the musicians said, "I bet they don't smoke marijuana in Muskogee." The rest of the band, breaking up from time to time, fell in with more lyrics, and later Merle finished it off. He was astonished and somewhat appalled when it became the anthem of the hardhats. ("We don't burn our draft cards down on Main Street/We like livin' right and being free.") On the other hand, he still resents those who put "Okie" down for, as one critic said, its "beer-belly mentality."

According to Merle, there were at least eighteen meanings to that song when he finally got through with it, and some of them had to do with his family's roots in Muskogee. "My father came from the area," Haggard has said, "worked hard on his farm, was proud of it, and got called white trash once he took to the road as an Okie. And there were a lot of other Okies from around there, proud people whose farms and homes were foreclosed by eastern bankers. And then got treated like dirt. Listen to that line: 'I'm proud to be an Okie from Muskogee.' Nobody had ever said that before in a song."

That night at the Lone Star, Merle Haggard and the Strangers—looking like the James Younger gang with their black suits, Stetsons, and string ties—lit up "Okie" again to piercing yells from the crowd. Watching the composer, what came to my mind, like a split-screen obbligato, was the broken, desperately needful singing of "God Bless America" at the end of *The Deer Hunter*. There were yo-yos who thought that movie, too, had a beer-belly mentality.

One of Merle's numbers has a guy saying: "Someone told my story in a song. He told it all and never missed a line. He even knew I almost lost my mind."

How do you want to be remembered, Merle? "A writer, I guess," he said to Paul Hemphill. "Somebody who did some living and wrote songs about what he knew. Just like Jimmie Rodgers did."

1995

MUSIC:
A TORCHBEARER FOR
TIMELESS SWING

Bryan Shaw is not a household name, not even in jazz households. But on his first CD as a leader, "Night Owl" (Arbors Recordings, 800-299-1930), the California-based 46-year-old trumpet player recalls the flair of Bunny Berigan, the melodic romanticism of Ruby Braff and the way players in the rural South were described before the word "jazz" was in vogue. In those days, listeners called improvisers "singing horns."

Although he is a protean musician—performing in a wide variety of settings, including studio and pit orchestras—Mr. Shaw's preference is for mainstream jazz. He greatly admires Charlie Parker but finds much of postmodern jazz lacking in what he called the "heart" and deep, easeful swing of Roy Eldridge, Rex Stewart, Red Allen and Charlie Parker himself. He is turned off by music in which "you can hear their brains clicking."

Mr. Shaw's colleagues on "Night Owl" also believe that the music of the swing era is a living, evolving way of improvising that does not at all preclude having an individual voice in the present. There is a joyousness in their solos and the ensemble passages scored by trombonist Dan Barrett, whose own voice can be as lusty as a New Orleans tailgate trombonist and as intimate as a Tommy Dorsey ballad. Also in the front line is the distinctively lyrical multireed man Scott Robinson, whose own Arbors CD, "The Sound That Time Forgot," I recommended in these pages last year (Aug. 4).

Bryan Shaw says of the musicians he admires that it "just takes two notes to know who they are." He meets that standard himself. His sound is resoundingly clear, resilient and warm. And in his liner notes, jazz historian Dick Hadlock speaks of Shaw's "rich, low-register tones, his easygoing but firm leading of the ensemble and that mysterious touch of authority which could remind one of Billy Butterfield or Buck Clayton."

The authority comes from Shaw's roots in the music. As a youngster, he practiced on his father's old Conn Victor cornet—the same model Bix Beiderbecke used. In high school, Dan Barrett, his classmate, remembers, "Bryan used to practice Bix pieces and Louis Armstrong's 'Cornet Chop Suey,'" a formidable challenge for any horn player of any age. As for Shaw's jazz time, I expect that even if you were to ask him to show how not to swing, he couldn't do it.

When I asked about the musicians who have particularly moved him, Mr. Shaw, in large part, could have been speaking of his own playing. "Ruby Braff," he said, "is in love with music. He makes love to the music." Of Red Allen, Shaw said,

"He was definite, and he played with the beat, in front and behind the beat."

Charlie Parker, Shaw noted, though a primary shaper of the jazz that followed the swing era, "was still a swinger. A Kansas City swinger. He was amazing, wonderful, but he came out of the blues. He had roots in all that came before."

From Mr. Shaw's fresh conception of "Body and Soul" to Coleman Hawkin's brisk, near-bebop composition "Bean and the Boys," Mr. Shaw and his comrades exemplify on "Night Owl" what the indelibly original clarinetist, Pee Wee Russell, said when he was asked to define jazz:

"It's what you hear from a certain group of guys—I don't care where they came from—that have a heart feeling and a rhythm in their systems that you couldn't budge, a rhythm you couldn't take away from them even if they were in a symphony organization. They could feel the beat better than someone who has memorized the book."

Not being a household name, Mr. Shaw can't always play the mainstream jazz he cherishes. A musician of many parts, he plays with the two-cornet traditional High Sierra Jazz Band, as well as in local symphony and opera-company orchestras. He is heard, anonymously, on jingles for beer, Toyota cars and other products, and he performs on cruises, most recently on the Paul Gauguin ship bound for Tahiti.

Furthermore, having once, in a studio, found a recording engineer's skills and taste wanting, Mr. Shaw enrolled in a recording arts program at Golden West College and is now the master engineer at Arbors Records. "I'm the last guy," he says, "to take out notes that shouldn't be there and fix anything else that has to be fixed."

He also does master engineering for many other labels. "Anything you can think of," he says, "from choral groups to Peruvian panpipes to Vietnamese pop."

In addition to the cruises, Shaw travels a lot and once in a while does some engineering in New York; but, he adds, "I haven't gigged there in ages." I asked him about New York because I remember what Coleman Hawkins told me after he'd heard an impressive young tenor saxophonist in a Midwestern city: "I said to him, 'You've got the makings, but if you don't make it in New York, you won't make it.'"

"Night Owl" and subsequent recordings by Mr. Shaw might just make New Yorkers and others around the country sit up and listen, but he doesn't seem to spend much time thinking about it. He lives in Costa Mesa, south of Los Angeles, with his wife and two young children, both of whom study piano. He has a varied life and an abiding pleasure in keeping the swing era alive.

"It's not a matter of re-creating anything," he says. "I have no interest in that. This is beautiful music. It's American music. It's timeless."

2001

THE JAZZ PARTY

CLEARWATER BEACH, FLA.—Ken Burns's "Jazz" series on public television caused a civil war among jazz critics and musicians about the players who were omitted; and more fundamentally, about who is qualified to define what jazz is. Particularly questioned was Mr. Burns's fleeting attention to the newer players, and his very marginal mention of women improvisers, especially instrumentalists other than pianists.

In March, when a four-day Jazz Party was held in Clearwater Beach to celebrate the 74th birthday of the uncategorizable cornetist Ruby Braff, some 60 musicians gathered to honor not only him but also the scope of jazz—beyond parochial divisions of race, age, gender and country of origin.

Swinging Sessions

The sessions at the Sheraton Sand Key Resort were orchestrated by Arbors Records ("Dedicated to the Recording of

Classic Jazz"), starting in the morning and twice ending at 2 a.m. the next day. During one set, 89-year-old tenor saxophonist Jerry Jerome (an alumnus of the Benny Goodman and Artie Shaw bands) jubilantly traded choruses with swinging 72-year-old tenor Tommy Newsom (whose touring included a Russian trip with Benny Goodman). In the rhythm section, the ever cheerful 75-year-old guitarist Bucky Pizzarelli, who has recorded with a considerable percentage of the entries in "The Encyclopedia of Jazz," kept the beat flowing.

Later that night, I heard for the first time 26-year-old tenor saxophonist Anat Cohen, who was nurtured in the lively Tel Aviv jazz scene and is now a member of Take Five, an all-female combo led by drummer Sherry Maricle. Working with that group, as well as with jazzmen in other settings, Ms. Cohen filled the room with a huge, bursting sound and infectious beat—not unlike that of her influences Ben Webster, Coleman Hawkins and, currently, Joe Lovano.

Other Take Five players—notably bassist Nicki Parrott, born in Australia, and alto saxophonist Karolina Strassmayer, holder of a masters degree in jazz from the Graz Academy of Music in Austria—weren't segregated by gender wither. They moved in and out of various combos with warmth, wit and vigor. Their command of jazz time reminded me of the absence of a single full-time woman player in Wynton Marsalis's Lincoln Center Jazz Orchestra.

The birthday celebrant, Ruby Braff, first heard Louis Armstrong on the radio when he was 10, and immediately knew his calling. (In 1956, Armstrong nominated Mr. Braff as his choice for "New Star" trumpet player in a musicians' poll). The most accurately evocative description of Mr. Braff's playing is

Bobby Short's: "If Fred Astaire played cornet, he would aspire to sound like Ruby Braff."

Cornet Like a Cello

A melodist, Mr. Braff has become the most lyrical horn player in jazz. "I didn't like the brassiness of the trumpet," he told me. "So I started to think like a tenor saxophone. Then I figured why can't I think like string instruments, especially the cello? I don't play loud, so I can move up and down the horn easily. You don't play loud when you're playing chamber music."

He got his first horn when he was eight, and before there was a Victrola in his Boston home, the young Braff would play along with recordings on the radio. "That way, I learned to play in all kinds of styles and keys. I still do that with recordings. I played with Ella Fitzgerald the other night." He also performs concerts in his mind. "Two-hour concerts. I imagine different ensembles. I play and also write for them in my mind. And sometimes, also in my mind, I'm sitting in the audience, hearing what I'm doing wrong."

I've known Ruby Braff since the day when, at age 14, I was practicing clarinet by an open window at my Boston home and he invited me to a session at his home. Halfway through his soaring first chorus, as I listened to him caress the melody, I knew that although I would always be a listener, jazz would not be my vocation.

He is the most stubbornly independent person I've ever known. In Florida, I was not surprised to learn from his sister,

Susan Atran, that when his mother got him a teacher, "Ruby, he was nine, fired the teacher. He told my mother, who was furious, that the teacher didn't know what Ruby already knew."

Mr. Braff has recorded for many labels, but his home now is at Arbors Records (800-299-1930), where, he says, its owner, Mat Domber, "lets me do whatever I want to so that I can keep on learning and growing." Among his recordings on the label are: "Ruby Braff: Music for the Still of the Night"; "Being With You: Ruby Braff Remembers Louis Armstrong"; and "Ruby Braff and Strings: In the Wee, Small Hours in London and New York."

Since this was a jazz party, the four days and nights were full of surprises, such as pianist Ralph Sutton playing what sounded like three-handed stride piano with a verve that recalled Willie "The Lion" Smith and his jutting cigar. But I was wholly unprepared for Sonny LaRosa's orchestra, called America's Youngest Jazz Band: Featuring Musicians Ages 6 to 12. I thought I'd hear a number or two of these kids playing at jazz and then take a walk on the beach. But this big band hit with a "Bugle Call Rag" that had the impact of the 1950s Basie Band. They not only knew how to swing collectively, but the soloists could tell a story. A story limited by their brief experience in music and life, but nonetheless moving.

America's Youngest Jazz Band is integrated by both race and gender, and when its young members swung into the Count Basie signature "One O'Clock Jump," the brass and reed sections—in their white shirts, bow ties, red jackets and black pants—moved, in tempo, from side to side, flourishing their instruments like the big bands of yore in the stage shows between movies.

Trumpeter Sonny LaRosa started on his own horn when he was 10, and later worked with Sam Donahue's band. A teacher in Florida since 1978, he writes all the arrangements, tailoring the scores to these new jazz players' capacities. "I'm working now with a five-year-old," he says.

Always Young

Ruby Braff didn't hear the band, having played late the night before, but he was delighted when I told him about the swinging kids. There is in him too a youthful eagerness to keep learning not only about music but about learning itself. He is currently being astonished by 15th-century English poetry, Harold Bloom's book on how to read a book, and Ralph Waldo Emerson. "And now," he says, "Emerson is leading me to something else. I'm not going to go from this life until I can say I've really thoroughly learned *something*."

A musician from whom Ruby Braff learned a great deal was clarinetist Pee Wee Russell, the most continually original improviser in all of jazz. In 1958, Russell told me: "Ruby's young. He's still got a way to go, an amount of living as well as playing experience to absorb. When he gets old and gray though, the little giant will be remembered."

Ruby Braff and I were talking about Pee Wee Russell between sets. "Like Louis Armstrong," the short, indomitable cornetist said, "Pee Wee will always be contemporary."

So, of course, will Ruby.

2001

A TV Exclusive!
The Passion of
Huckleberry Dracula

"But I reckon I got to light out for the territory ahead of the rest, because Aunt Sally she's going to adopt me and sivilize me, and I can't stand it. I been there before."

—Huckleberry Finn

From now until March, 150 public television stations will be showing *The Golden Age of Television*—kinescopes of *Marty, The Days of Wine and Roses,* and six other remembrances of those years (1948–1960) when television drama was live! Showtime without the safety net of film or tape. And some of it even stayed in your mind the next morning.

In addition to Paddy Chayefsky, the writing-producing-directing credits will include Fred Coe, J. P. Miller, Delbert Mann, and John Frankenheimer. Looking over the list, I called a coordinator of *The Golden Age of Television* and asked her, "Where's something by Robert Herridge?"

There was a pause. "I'm sorry. I don't know the name. Could you clue me in?"

I told her that doing this series without a Herridge show was like producing a celebration of jazz during the same period and leaving out Charlie Parker.

"Oh," she said. "Well, in all the materials I've been reading about 'the Golden Age,' I've never come across Mr. Herridge's name."

Those of you who read obituaries may have seen the name in the August 17 *New York Times*. Within the limited space he had, C. Gerald Fraser wrote a useful obit, but there is a great deal more to be said, and since it's not likely to be written anywhere else, I am going to tell you about Huckleberry Dracula, as some used to call Robert Herridge.

In creating the single most original body of work in TV history, Herridge found for television its own forms and rhythms. He thought it was dumb "to make a small-scale motion picture and call it television." Or to shoot a play as if it were on a theater stage, the only difference on television being more close-ups. And he hated, I mean hated, the kind of naturalism represented by *Marty* and its clones of the period. Herridge called that "kitchen" writing, there usually being one or more scenes set in a kitchen which, by God, had real pots and pans. With remnants of food in them.

Herridge passionately believed that television could create its own ways of telling a story. Not only in drama, but through music. He cared and knew more about music than any other television writer or producer or director I've known, and I've met a lot of them. In his music shows, like *The Sound of Jazz* and an exhilarating hour with Eugene Ormandy and the Philadelphia Orchestra, Herridge refused to do what he called "reporting." That is, just shoot what the musicians would be doing in a concert hall or club. Instead, with no tricky camera work and without getting in the way of the musicians, he enabled you to get inside the dynamics of the making of the music. Like the way Billie Holiday was looking at Lester Young as he played their blues on *The Sound of Jazz*. It was because the cameramen were told by Herridge to improvise that we were able to see that. To see their souls, if you like, so clearly.

And when he did Dostoevski and Joyce and Faulkner and Melville, Herridge—again without the slightest distortion of the original—created each time a new theater of the imagination, a *television* theater. At first mysterious, then clear, intense, penetrating.

He not only produced but often directed and sometimes wrote. And there wasn't any part of television he had not thoroughly taught himself. Lighting, for example. Robert Carrington, a former associate producer with Herridge, told me once: "He creates a whole world—sometimes just out of light. In *Emily Dickinson* on Herridge's *Camera Three* [a series on local and then national CBS], her house was evoked by using the back wall of the studio and a piece of canvas representing the ceiling. The rest—corridors, the separate rooms, stairs—was made entirely by lighting." Herridge didn't need 20-foot scenery with wallpaper.

Herridge also found out what he needed to know about cameras, investigating their depths of focus and field. He would even push around the different kinds to get a sense of the problems a cameraman runs into with each of them when he's shooting. In addition, Herridge was involved with casting, very involved. A good many actors very much wanted to work with Herridge, even though it often meant a cut in their regular fee. (Herridge's budgets were usually sparse.)

In 1961, Nancy Wickwire said to me: "He does everything with such passion that he makes it more exciting to be part of one of his shows. Furthermore, you can trust him. I've never heard him say, 'If we can only get so-and-so, a big name, we can push up the rating.' I'm always without fear when I work with Herridge. I know that five days after rehearsals begin, an agency or network man won't come in and change everything. Herridge is in charge, and the confidence we have in him gives us more confidence in ourselves."

Oh, Herridge was always in charge, all right. In 1960, I was working with him on a prime-time folk-music show for CBS. He had insisted on including a choral group that had about the same relationship to folk music as Wonder Bread has to pumpernickel. It was one of the few times we had totally disagreed, and I had been totally overruled. Brooding, I was taking some comfort in the fact that at least Joan Baez and Cisco Houston were on the show.

From the sponsor's booth, a CBS page descended with a note for Herridge. I walked over, and Herridge showed it to me. There was still a residue of blacklisting in those days. (Pete Seeger was banished from two network programs—CBS and ABC—three years later.) The note said that someone (not named) had checked out Cisco Houston, and he was not suitable for this here folk-song show. No reason given, but it obviously didn't have anything to do with Cisco's choice of chords.

I gave the note back to Herridge. He took it and tore it up. That was the end of it. The rehearsal, including Cisco, went on, and for a while, I felt so good I could almost stand that milky chorus.

Now, to get somewhat personal. My relationship with Herridge began as a viewer. I had come to New York in 1953, at just about the time Herridge—a former poet (published), road gang worker, expert in 19th-century American literature, and dishwasher—had finally, at 39, found what he wanted to do with his life. He had just started writing, producing, and largely staging *Camera Three* on Channel 2. Every Sunday morning, even if I had closed Birdland the night before, I got up in time to watch what I had never even imagined could take place on a television screen. A six-part *Moby Dick*, for instance, in which somehow four stools, some ropes, a capstan, and a platform became the consuming world of Ahab. I didn't see the white whale, but I sure knew he was there.

The marvels never stopped. A *Ballad of Huck Finn;* and the most extraordinary show I have seen anywhere, a three-part *Notes from the Underground.* Only one actor, of course; a ladder; and an overwhelming intensity. I wasn't thinking about lighting or direction. I was just stunned that so much force was coming out of that box.

I got to know Herridge in 1957 when he asked Whitney Balliett and me to work with him on *The Sound of Jazz.* Herridge and I did a number of other shows together, and became friends. In the past couple of years, as he was trying to find a place for himself again in television—after a long absence— we were in especially frequent contact. Swapping stories, but mostly planning jazz programs that never got funded. He did have one last hurrah, *A Salute to Duke Ellington* this May on public television. But for once in his career, Herridge wasn't entirely in charge of that one; and from this experience, as I'll tell you next week, he learned that you could be a lot more inventive in commercial than in public television.

So, I do not come to this report on Robert Herridge as a dispassionate observer. I liked him enormously. In a number of ways, he was like Charles Mingus, with whom Herridge had a warm, tumultuous friendship. Both were almost ingenuous in some respects, and therefore quite vulnerable; but they could also be shrewdly realistic. Both also had a wildness in them—not mean but defiant. And, until their last years, it was a wildness that sometimes got out of control. Like a boy who gets into a state, tries to get out of it, and has forgotten how. And both, of course, were obsessed by their callings.

One of Herridge's problems in television was that he could not stand anyone, in Huck Finn's phrase, trying to "sivilize" him. Karl Genus, a director who worked often with him, said a few years before Herridge left commercial television in 1966: "He never plays it safe. He charged into television as if it were a vast, overgrown jungle, and he kept hacking away at it instead of resting in the places that had already been cleared. He's always been an enigma to the executives in this industry."

Other powers in the industry were downright furious at the very idea of Herridge. David Susskind, for whom Herridge worked briefly in the 1950s, called him "a kook." And went on to hoot at the way he dressed. "Herridge affected being a bohemian, never wore a tie," Susskind used to kvetch. "He tried to substitute nonconformity of dress for talent." Furthermore, instead of meeting with writers in the office, as responsible producers did, Herridge—Susskind told me accusatorily—met them in bars, "those *little* bars where people pose as artists. Herridge creates anarchy. That's what he creates no matter what he's doing."

Yet, while with Susskind's Talent Associates, Herridge produced, in 1958 for *Kraft Theater,* two of the most powerful shows ever associated with Susskind's name—Ernest Hemingway's *Fifty Grand* and Robert Penn Warren's *All The King's Men,* the latter a far more seizing transformation of the book than Robert Rossen's screen version. Those two productions, by the way, were the last Herridge did for Susskind. And it was on those two that Herridge demanded Susskind stay the hell out of the way until the dress rehearsal (instead of continually inflicting his artistic judgment from the top).

Maybe that's why, years ago, Susskind's final word to me on Herridge—shaking his fists and shouting—was: "The Herridge legend must be broken!"

Well, I guess it was broken. Or rather, it was forgotten. Like the PBS coordinator for *The Golden Age of Television* who'd never heard the name before. In television, it's the Susskinds who survive. The Huckleberry Draculas, being so hopelessly unsivilized, do not fit in.

That name, Huckleberry Dracula, came from S. Lee Pogostin, a writer on a number of Herridge shows. The Huckleberry part I've explained. As for Dracula, Herridge's eyes could take on a most unsettling intensity. Pogostin once told me about a discussion he and Herridge were having at the Russian Tea Room about the "kitchen" school of television writing. "Herridge let go a barrage of language in which, like Mark Twain, he cursed for 30 minutes without repeating himself. But the cursing was merely a cadenza.

"The concerto," Pogostin continued, "consisted of what seemed to be the entire classical learning of the Western world. His face got redder and redder, and he drank his whitish-green drink with such viciousness and vengeance that innocent people who just happened to be passing the table found themselves being glared at by Dracula-eyes. The women, in particular, held their necks as if: 'This is it! Imagine, in the Russian Tea Room! He's going to bite us!' Like a great storm, it was over. And there was calm. But Herridge continued to glare—with those eyes."

Once in a great while, Herridge would come up against someone as unbending and fierce as himself. In 1960, I introduced him to Joan Baez. He immediately planned a show in which she would figure significantly, but Joan had some conditions. No one else was to appear on her section of the program. She was to have a veto over the sets behind her. And *she* would decide what she would sing. Joan was not negotiating. Those were irreducible demands. She had done without national television exposure before. She could still do without it.

Herridge could not bear being without the sound of her voice on that show, though he desperately would have preferred it to be disembodied. He yielded. Later, in the control room, turning to me who had brought him this iron maiden, Herridge muttered, "The little bitch is 19 years old, and she thinks she's Thomas Mann." He growled, and then: "God, listen to that voice. Yeah, we've got to keep this show pure—but not *Partisan Review* pure, you understand.

And Huckleberry Dracula smiled through the window at the Sad-Eyed Lady of the Lowlands, who may have smiled back. It was hard to tell.

1981

PART 3

THE PERSISTENCE
OF RACE

THE INTEGRATIONIST

On May 28, 1954, Dr. Kenneth Bancroft Clark, a thirty-nine-year-old associate professor of psychology at City College, in New York, wrote out a brief statement for the press on the meaning of a unanimous Supreme Court decision, *Brown v. Board of Education of Topeka*, which had been handed down eleven days earlier. Clark himself had been mentioned in the decision, in a footnote that cited him as one representative of "modern authority" supporting the Court's conclusion that segregation in the public schools generates in Negro children "a feeling of inferiority . . . that may affect their hearts and minds in a way unlikely ever to be undone." Clark was somewhat disappointed that the Court, in citing his research, had ignored two other points he had made: that racism was as profoundly American as the Declaration of Independence, and that school segregation twisted the personality development of white as well as Negro children. Still, elated by the decision, he predicted in his statement that as a result of *Brown* white youngsters could now look to a future "in which they will not have to spend so much valuable energy apologizing for injustices which they did not invent but for which they must share the responsibility." And young Negroes, freed of the stigma of segregation, could now "be proud of the fact that they are Americans."

On a sunny morning more than a quarter of a century later, Dr. Clark was on his way to a Convocation for Competency, sponsored by the Public Education Association, at the Waldorf-Astoria Hotel, in New York. In the years since *Brown*, he had become the first black full professor at City College (he is now Distinguished Professor Emeritus of Psychology), had served on the New York State Board of Regents, had written a number of books—most notably, "Dark Ghetto"— which are widely used in colleges and universities, and had received many professional honors. Also, though he keeps insisting that he has no constituency of his own, he had become part of the inner councils of national black leadership. For a long time, moreover, Clark had been serving another function—as a source of advice and revivification for younger black activists momentarily worn down. But there are times when Clark himself seems to be fighting a losing battle with gloom. On that morning at the Waldorf-Astoria, I was with Dr. Clark as he searched for the room in which he was to be a panelist—on the subject of "Minimum Competency: A Community Strategy for Success-Based Schools?"—and I thought he seemed gloomy.

"I swear, this is the last of these educational panels I'll ever be on," he said. "I've been to so many conferences, so many symposiums, so many seminars, and all they contribute is more alibis for why the schools aren't working and why society doesn't want to deal with this problem. I get so angry at being part of the damn charade, and then I get angry at myself for being so angry. All this talk all these years, and the per-centage of black children going to segregated and inferior schools in the North is greater now than it was at the time of *Brown*. And the educational retardation gets worse and worse." Then, as almost always happens when Dr. Clark is low in spirit, a further rush of anger lifted him out of his gloom into readiness for combat. "Damn it!" he said. "The school boards and public officials in the North are *much* more subtle and persistent in defending the racial status quo than those Southerners ever were. But the damage being done to the children is precisely the same as it was in the Southern segregated schools."

Clark entered a long, narrow room filled with educators and parents. When it was his turn to speak, he began, without notes, by recalling that he had first been elected to the New York State Board of Regents thirteen years earlier. "I was told that I was the first black to be elected to that august body," he said, in a calm, rumbling voice. "I soon learned that we did more than preside over examinations. This was the body with the awesome power of responsibility for education at all lev-els, from prekindergarten to postgraduate. I decided to look particularly at the quality of elementary and secondary educa-tion in the state. And after two years I discovered that the State Education Department had been regularly giving exami-nations—Pupil Evaluation Program tests—in reading and mathematics at the third-, sixth-, and eighth-grade levels. But the scores were not publicized, because, the staff said, people wouldn't understand how to interpret the differences between schools. It took me two whole years to force the State Educa-tion Department to release those PEP scores, and when they did I found out why they had been so reluctant to do it. In the ghetto areas of New York City, from eighty to eighty-five per cent of the children were not only below the norm but *significantly* below. I asked that those scores be made available to the legislators. At the time, Charles Rangel, now a congressman, was the assemblyman from a Harlem district. When he looked at the scores in the Harlem schools, he shouted, 'My God! My district is an educational disaster area.'"

Clark lit a cigarette, gazed at the audience, and went on. "One might think that once these scores had been presented to the Regents and to the legislators there would have been an immediate demand for some kind of remedy to deal with so stark and flagrant a problem." He paused, then said, "Nothing was done. Some years later, the Regents did begin to insist that certain standards of competency be demonstrated before a high-school diploma is awarded, but that came about because of newspaper stories that suburban children were getting lower scores on the Scholastic Aptitude Tests for college. Apparently, this created greater concern in our democracy than the overwhelming evidence that many lower-class children were not even able to *take* the Scholastic Aptitude Tests, because their educational retardation was so profound. Not that I believe that competency tests given to the children are going to solve the educational genocide in our ghetto schools. We still have to deal with the competency of teachers and administrators. We have to make them accountable for what they do, and for what they fail to do. And that is not going to be easy, because it is a racist society that allows the public education system to produce hundreds of thousands of despairing, frustrated, functional illiterates each year."

A tall, lean silver-haired man at the back of the room was shaking his head in disagreement or exasperation, or both. Dr. Clark looked at him and, without breaking the even flow of his speech, said, "The most frequent criticism I receive from colleagues is that I am not sufficiently balanced when I discuss what is happening in the schools. That I am too emotional. I admit it. I am emotional. I am deeply disturbed, because I identify with the children who are being destroyed in those schools. But most middle-class educators are indeed balanced and cautious as they keep finding excuses for not educating these children. I have a hope that eventually our educational institutions will see as one of their responsibilities the training of human beings to be sensitive to what is done to human beings who are not like themselves. Until this happens, we will have one damn seminar like this after another, with no change in the status quo. I am sorry to have to say that it is really *not* a pleasure to be here."

The moderator of the panel asked for questions from the audience.

The silver-haired man rose and identified himself as a retired principal of a New York City high school. Self-assured and angry, he declared himself deeply disturbed by what he called Clark's "emotional tone," and he denied that the school system had been indifferent to children in the ghettos. Pointing a long finger at Clark, he said, "To say that the schools are both incompetent *and* racist is a slander that destroys your credibility and alienates the support you might otherwise gain from the so-called middle class. Why, every effort has been made to deal with the problems of these children most sympathetically and effectively. There have been all kinds of programs."

The moderator asked Clark if he cared to make a response.

With a slight, wintry smile, Clark said, "I first raised the question of the inferior quality of education in the schools of New York City in 1953. I had been doing research in Southern segregated schools for the N.A.A.C.P. in connection with a series of court cases that eventually led to the *Brown versus Board of Education* decision. I also testified in some of those cases, and on one such occasion a lawyer for the State of Virginia asked me during cross-examination, 'How dare you come and talk about the inferiority of our segregated schools here when you come from a city with segregated schools and you haven't done anything about them?' I was really floored by the question. I told him, to begin with, that we did not have *legally* sanctioned segregation in the New York City public schools. And the second thing I said was 'When I get back to New York, I'm going to find out whether the segregated schools in my city have the same negative educational and psychological consequences as the segregated schools in Virginia.' And that's what I did. Sure enough, the schools here had all the negative effects of the segregated schools of Virginia and the other Southern or border states. So I started trying to do something about it. I shall never forget one particular meeting at the New York City Board of Education headquarters, in Brooklyn. All the hierarchy was there, including a deputy superintendent who became very angry at me, getting so red in the face that I thought he was about to have an apoplectic fit. 'Dr. Clark,' he said, 'don't you understand that in this society we need to have hewers of wood and drawers of water, and that our schools have to be responsive to that reality?' I was terribly embarrassed, and so were his colleagues.

I got up to answer the deputy superintendent, but instead I left, and went back to the N.A.A.C.P. and the continuation of our struggle—a struggle I now know my grandchildren will have to continue after I am gone." Dr. Clark looked directly at the man who had accused him of slandering the public-school system. "Now, the gentleman back there said that the school system is providing these children with high-quality education. Therefore, their low academic achievement is a reflection of their inability to respond."

"I never said that." The silver-haired man was on his feet again. "Please do not misquote me."

"All right," Clark said, speaking very deliberately. "You said there have been all kinds of programs to achieve a very good school system. Yet this very good school system results in an intolerably high percentage of educational retardation among lower-status children. If they are *not* seen as inherently inferior, then their retardation indicates that the school system is not that good at all. It also demonstrates that these children are considered expendable, for why else would the failure of the *system* be allowed to continue year after year?"

There was no further comment from the silver-haired man.

A large middle-aged black woman rose. Gesturing toward the silver-haired man, she said in a strong, resonant voice, "Dr. Clark, the truth hurt that man over there. I am a voluntary teacher in an elementary school. And we have in there teachers who are not teachers. I say your competency tests should be given to the principals and right on down to the teachers. You would find that many teachers could not pass, because anybody who is teaching reading and writing and arithmetic— Why, when a kid gets into the sixth grade he ought to be able to make a sentence and know a period from a semicolon and a comma. But the children do not know that. I resent a teacher miseducating a child, and I resent a teacher then saying there is something wrong with the *child*."

The woman continued, "They give us—the volunteers— children supposed to be going to a psychiatrist because those teachers can't teach them.

"The teacher will say to me, 'What are you doing with that child? She seems to be doing better since you have her.'

"I say, 'Yes, she's a very intelligent child, so she's learning. I find her reading books all the day.'

"The teacher will say, 'But you don't understand. We send her to a psychiatrist because she has a mental block and they are trying to find it.'

"I say, 'When you find that block, what will you do with it?' I find that child a brilliant child—and she's not the only one. But those kids, our kids, they know when the teachers are not interested in them, and they respond accordingly."

Clark was nodding in agreement. The session ended soon afterward, and as Clark and I were making our way to the elevator he said, "What is this nation afraid of when it comes to really educating lower-status children? I don't know. I really don't know. In the entire society, this is the area most resistant to change. Of course, that woman was right about teachers, about how crucial they are. My God, they probably have the most important role in our society. I know, from my own life. Teachers certainly made a big difference in what happened to me."

Kenneth Clark went to elementary school and junior high school in Harlem. He was born, in 1914, in the Panama Canal

Zone, and his mother, Miriam Clark, brought him and his sister, Beulah, to the United States when he was four and a half. Clark's father, Arthur Bancroft Clark, who was a general superintendent of cargo for the United Fruit Company, refused to go with his wife and children. A native of the West Indies, he had been told when he applied for a transfer that he could not be appointed to a job of equal status in America. "Learning that horrified my father," Clark recalled years later. "He couldn't understand why my mother would subject us to this kind of humiliation in a strange, racist country." Miriam Clark, an indomitable woman, originally from Kingston, Jamaica, was convinced that there would nonetheless be more and better opportunities for her children in the United States, especially in terms of education. She settled herself and the children in a small apartment in a Harlem tenement and found a job as a seamstress in a garment shop downtown, where she helped organize the workers and became one of the first black shop stewards for the International Ladies' Garment Workers' Union. At home, hearing his mother tell of the troubles and triumphs of her union activities, the boy caught what he later referred to as "the excitement of people doing things together to help themselves."

The classes in the Harlem schools were not yet all black. "We had plenty of Irish and Jewish kids," Clark recalled. "And the teachers were concerned with holding *all* of us to high standards, because they were convinced that *all* of us were educable. We had not yet come to that particular breakdown in the public education of minorities which is due less to flagrant racial bigotry than to the sloppy, sentimental good intentions of certain educators, who *reduce* learning standards for low-status youngsters, because they believe that these children's home conditions are such as to make it impossible for them to learn as much as suburban children. Thus, under the guise of compassion and understanding these teachers reinforce educational disadvantage by treating the child as inherently inferior, as having real limitations of intelligence. And so each stereotyped child is denied his individuality and his potential; and the self-fulfilling prophecy of massive educational underachievement for these children is thereby perpetuated. But when I was going to public school we had teachers who did not consider themselves social workers, psychologists, and rationalizers of educational inequities. They were asked to teach reading, arithmetic, grammar, and they *did*. They understood that while there were individual differences in the children's ability to master academic subjects, these differences were not related to race or economic circumstances. I came from a broken home, but my teachers never asked me about that, or about what my mother did for a living. They were focussing on whether I was learning or not. For instance, when I went to the board in Mr. Ruprecht's algebra class, in junior high school, I had to do those equations, and if I wasn't able to do them he wanted to find out why. He didn't expect any less of me because I was black. There was an eighth-grade English teacher, Miss McGuire, who taught me to understand the beauty of an English sentence. And she didn't do it by worrying about my background. Also in the eighth grade, Mr. Mitchell, a blond, blue-eyed white Anglo-Saxon Protestant, taught us Shakespeare. Those plays came alive, right in the center of Harlem, as we took different parts. One day I was Macbeth, the next day I was Malcolm. It had nothing to do

with color—the teacher's or ours. I do believe that it was because of my experiences with those teachers that I decided to
become a teacher myself."

Not all of Clark's teachers were, as he put it, "fully developed human beings." By the time he was in the ninth grade,
there were more black children in the classes, and the guidance counsellor was advising them to go on to vocational
school, where they could learn a trade. She wrote Clark's
mother a note to that effect. The next day, Miriam Clark did
not go to work but instead showed up, with her fourteen-
year-old son in tow, at the guidance counsellor's office. "I was
mortified, because I thought that my mother's coming into
school like that would seal my doom," Dr. Clark told me. "On
the other hand, I didn't want to go to any vocational school."
He laughed. "I wasn't thinking about status—I just wasn't particularly adept at shop work. In any case, my mother marched
in, refused to sit down, and stood there looming over the
guidance counsellor. Very slowly and very distinctly, my
mother said, 'I don't give a damn where you send *your* son, but
mine isn't going to any vocational school.' That was a turning
point in my life. I went to George Washington High School
instead."

Dr. Clark continued, "At this point, I must tell you that I was
by no means the brightest person in my classes in Harlem. I
remember kids, particularly black kids—and not just in our
fast class but in other classes and on the playground—who
had minds like *that!*" He snapped his fingers. "And even though
we did have some good teachers, there were others who
shunted these black kids aside. The kids became bitter, because they were rejected. They didn't have anybody really

fighting for them, you know. They didn't have a mother who was as daring as mine, a mother saying right out, 'No, look, damn it! That's not going to happen to my son!'"

"When the child's mother does not or cannot fight for him, who can be the mother?" I asked.

He sighed. "All of us who are concerned with human beings must be the mothers, and must protect those who don't have anybody else to protect them. Does that sound corny? Well, that's what is on my mind when I go to Board of Regents meetings, when I write and talk about and work with schools. You see, the most horrible thing about Harlem—about all the ghettos—is the day-to-day destruction of human potential. In these concentration camps we build in our cities, the process of human destruction begins in the first and second grades. Back in the nineteen-sixties, I said in speeches and in papers that if there wasn't a dramatic improvement in the ghetto schools all other civil-rights gains would remain essentially empty promises. It did not require any particular brilliance to make that prediction."

Although Clark's own public-school education was quite different from what has come to be the ghetto norm, he does remember one grievous setback, at George Washington High School. He is convinced that it occurred because of his color. Though it hardly destroyed him, it may have changed the direction of his career. "In high school, I loved economics, and I read voraciously on the subject," Dr. Clark told me. "During my senior year, I was getting ninety-eights and ninety-nines on all the tests. The teacher always awarded an economics prize at the end of the year to the outstanding student, and everybody in the class was sure I was going to get that award.

But when it came time for the announcement of the prize, someone else won. There was no question that I was entitled to it on the merits, but, as it turned out, the determining factor was color. A white student got it. I've never forgotten that teacher, because he was my first big disillusionment." Clark did not question his teacher about why he had not been awarded the prize. "That sort of thing wasn't done then," he explained, "And, in any case, I certainly wouldn't have done it. I never took another course in economics. That's the way I reacted to my first major personal experience of prejudice— 'O.K., keep your prize. Keep your whole subject.' Isn't that terrible? I'm as stiff-necked as my father was, I guess. I will say one thing for that teacher, though. He taught economics in terms of the ability of human beings not to be passive victims of so-called natural laws of economics. That fascinated me. Anything concerning human interaction with and shaping of the forces that affect our lives fascinated me."

In 1931, Kenneth Clark went on to Howard University, a black institution in Washington, D.C., where, in his junior year, he became the editor of *The Hilltop*, the campus newspaper, and also organized a group of twenty Howard students to march on the Capitol—"to see if we could get them to treat us like loyal Americans, which we felt we were, by just giving us food in a public restaurant there." Food was denied, and the group was arrested.

Clark's most important experience at Howard, however, had to do with a professor of psychology. Clark had intended to go to medical school. "One day in my sophomore year," he recalled not long ago, "I was sitting, daydreaming, in Psychology I, looking out the window at two birds making love.

| 177 |

When they flew away, I started listening to my professor, and I heard some very illuminating things about human behavior. From then on, I listened very hard to what he said, and I decided, 'To hell with medical school. This is the discipline for me.' What this professor, Francis Cecil Sumner, showed me was the promise of getting some systematic understanding of the complexities of human behavior and human interaction. In the physical sciences, understanding was achieving control— up to a certain point. And in the biological sciences systematic understanding was providing the ability to manipulate the environment for the advantage of human beings. I saw no reason these kinds of possibilities should not extend to the social sciences. And although I do get depressed from time to time, I *still* believe that disciplined intelligence brought to bear on social problems can provide either the answers or the reasons we don't have the answers. The seemingly intractable nature of racism, for example, and its effects on children."

Clark continued, "Professor Sumner had *rigorous* standards for his students. And he didn't just teach psychology. He taught integrity. Once you had your facts, that was the basis on which you defended yourself. And although he led the way for other blacks in the study of psychology, Sumner would permit no nonsense about there being anything like 'black psychology'—any more than he would have allowed any nonsense about 'black astronomy.' In this and in many other ways, Sumner was a model for me. In fact, he has always been my standard when I evaluate myself."

Clark has said of Howard University, "It was the beneficiary of the idiocy of racism in American higher education. People like Sumner were not invited to teach at the University of

Chicago or Harvard. They were black." Sumner had earned his doctorate at Clark University, under the preeminent psychologist of the time, G. Stanley Hall, who was the first president of the American Psychological Association and the leading national authority on educational standards. Also on the faculty of Howard during Clark's years there were Ralph Bunche and the philosopher and cultural historian Alain Locke—"two more who were not invited to teach at white universities," Clark says. "Bunche, who had recently obtained his Ph.D. from Harvard, was chairman of the Political Science Department. He became a great influence on me: his courage, his clarity, the standards he set for himself—and for his students. We became friends, and saw each other often through the years after Howard. I especially remember one thing he said, about a year before he died: 'Kenneth, our leaders will never be taken seriously, and we will not be respected and make any really fundamental move toward equality and dignity as a people, until we learn not to settle for crumbs.'"

Clark came under another lifelong influence while he was at Howard—Mamie Phipps, the daughter of a successful physician in Hot Springs, Arkansas. She arrived on campus as a freshman when he was a senior. "I knew right away I was going to marry her," Dr. Clark says. "It was her self-assurance. Her quiet self-assurance. Mamie had come to Howard to major in mathematics, and she was very good in the subject, but eventually I persuaded her to change to psychology. I wanted her in an area in which I felt more self-assured."

Mamie Phipps Clark, a slender woman of cool dignity, remembers that her initial impression of Kenneth Clark was that "he was very, very serious." She goes on to say, "And that was

not characteristic of most of the male students on campus. I
thought they were wasting their parents' money. But Kenneth
seemed to be going someplace, and I admired that—all the
more because I had rarely seen that kind of determination.
Yes, he persuaded me to change my major. I got a C once,
rather than the grade I had expected, and he told me that the
teacher was prejudiced against women and that since the
Mathematics Department was small, I would be stuck with
that teacher unless I switched. Then he said, 'What are you interested in?'

"'Children.'

"'What are you going to do with mathematics and children?'

"'Teach it to them.'

"'If you want to work with children, you'll be able to do a lot
more for them if you know psychology.'

"So I changed, married him when I was a senior, and later we
became the first two black Ph.D.s in the history of the Psychology Department of Columbia University."

In 1936, Clark obtained an M.S. at Howard, and then he
taught psychology there for a year while Mamie finished her
undergraduate work. Then, Clark says, it was time to move
on. "Dr. Sumner, Alain Locke, and Mordecai Johnson, who
was then president of Howard, all said to me, 'Kenneth, go get
your doctorate and break the pattern. Teach at a nonsegre-
gated school.' I was part of the next generation of black acade-
mics, and I was not to come back to Howard."

As the first black Ph.D. candidate in psychology at Columbia, Clark puzzled some members of the faculty by ranking
first in the matriculation examination. "They had thought I
would need some form of compensatory enrichment, or some-

thing of the sort, and couldn't figure out how I had done so well," he says. "Then they wanted to know about Francis Cecil Sumner. Must be a pretty good teacher. All this puzzlement on their part fascinated me. Well, I went on to meet all the requirements and get a doctorate in experimental psychology. By then—1940—some of the professors who had been perplexed at my superiority to the other students were advising me to go back and share my knowledge with my people. I was to have a fine career in black colleges."

The new Ph.D. politely rejected this counsel. "I really want to teach where other Columbia Ph.D.s teach," he told his professors. Gardner Murphy, a Columbia faculty member with whom Clark had worked closely, was about to become chairman of the Psychology Department of City College, and Clark said he would like to join him there. At that time, there was no black on the regular faculty of any New York City municipal college. Clark was given a temporary appointment, for the summer and the following academic year. "I taught there that summer, but then did something stupid," Dr. Clark recalls. "Instead of staying on in the fall, I accepted an invitation to build a Department of Psychology at Hampton Institute, a black college in Virginia. I was young, and couldn't resist the chance to start something of my own." He stayed only six months at Hampton Institute. "A while after I came, the president told me he didn't want me disturbing and frustrating the students. I was to present my psychology courses in a way that would make these young black people adjust to and accept their status in the society. The president added that if I understood what he was saying, and acted accordingly, he would make me one of the best-known Negro psychologists in the

nation. I told him I certainly did understand what he was saying, but no thanks, and I left."

Ralph Bunche had meanwhile moved to the Office of Strate-
gic Services, and he arranged for Clark to get a job with the
Office of War Information, as an assistant social-science ana-
lyst on its research staff. For about a year and a half, Clark
travelled the country assessing the morale of the black citi-
zenry in time of war. In 1942, he returned to the Psychology
Department of City College. He became an assistant professor in 1949 and a professor in 1960—the first black in New
York City's history to receive a permanent appointment to a
city college. In 1970, he was named Distinguished University
Professor.

Throughout his teaching career, Clark has engaged in the
kind of research that was encouraged by his professors at
Howard—what he called "the use of disciplined intelligence
in achieving social justice." He served on Gunnar Myrdal's
staff, for example, during the preparation of "An American
Dilemma," Myrdal's study of racism in the United States,
which was sponsored by the Carnegie Corporation and was
published in 1944. In 1946, Clark and his wife set up a nonprofit organization in Harlem called the Northside Testing
and Consultation Center. (It later became the Northside Center for Child Development.) Mamie Clark was the executive
director, and Clark was in charge of research. At first, Clark
told me, the Northside staff, which was made up of psychiatrists, psychologists, and social workers, tried to help emo-
tionally disturbed children through the traditional one-to-one
therapist-patient relationship. "Over the years, however, it be-

came clear to us that, given the realities of the ghetto, we could not believe we were really helping if we ignored those realities," he said. "If, for example, we tried to get individual parents and their children to *adjust* to schools so criminally inferior that they were dehumanizing. Or if we tried to get them to *adjust* to the kind of housing to which they had been sentenced by a society that had the economic but not the moral resources to do something about that housing."

"The families we were working with were not going to respond to umpteen years of lying on a couch and talking about ego and id," Mamie Clark told me. "They needed help with housing, welfare, health, money, and all those things."

Accordingly, the emphasis at Northside shifted, Dr. Clark explained. Individual therapy continued, but "within the walls of the clinic we also had to try to develop in the parents and the children the strength to attempt to change the social pathology around them—to work at problems of injustice and inequity," he said. "We felt that this was the only way in which they could really resolve the negative self-image that a racially cruel society had imposed on them and their children."

"One of the first social issues we got involved in at Northside had to do with an educational injustice," Mamie Clark recalled. "In the public schools, a great many children had been put in classes for the intellectually retarded. We tested them at Northside and determined that most of them were not retarded. So the families protested, we protested, and the children who should not have been in those classes were taken out."

During Northside's early years, Clark became increasingly active, elsewhere in the country, as a researcher and a witness in a series of court cases aimed at what he considered the most damaging of all educational injustices—legally segregated public schools. When Mamie Clark was working toward her master's degree, she did her field work among schoolchildren in Washington. She was studying the effects of race on the way the children felt about themselves. Kenneth Clark also became absorbed in the work, and together they broadened the field of research and began publishing pioneering studies in various social-science journals on how segregation affected preschool black children's sense of self-esteem. Today, when the results of such studies are taken for granted, it's hard to imagine a time when there was a need for such studies. In one series of tests, administered to children between the ages of three and seven in, among other places, Philadelphia, Boston, Worcester, and several cities in Arkansas, the children were asked to choose between otherwise identical brown and white dolls in response to such instructions as

> Give me the doll that you like to play with.
> Give me the doll that is the nice doll.
> Give me the doll that looks bad.
> Give me the doll that is a nice color.

The Clarks reported that the majority of the children "indicated an unmistakable preference for the white doll and a rejection of the brown doll," and concluded, "The fact that young Negro children would prefer to be white reflects their knowledge that society prefers white people."

In 1950, Clark wrote a monograph for the Midcentury White House Conference on Children and Youth, in which he summarized not only his and his wife's research but also the rest of the existing literature on the effects of racial segregation on black children. The monograph came to the attention of Robert Carter, a young lawyer with the National Association for the Advancement of Colored People. An N.A.A.C.P. legal team, headed by Thurgood Marshall, had decided to make an all-out attack on the constitutionality of state laws mandating or permitting segregation of the schools. Such statutes, the N.A.A.C.P. claimed, violated the equal-protection clause of the Fourteenth Amendment ("No state shall . . . deny to any person within its jurisdiction the equal protection of the laws"). Carter thought that Clark might be a useful witness in some of the pending cases; he also wanted to explore with Clark the possibility of enlisting other social scientists to buttress the N.A.A.C.P. argument that "separate but equal" schooling not only was inherently unequal but also inflicted psychological damage on the segregated black children.

The "separate but equal" doctrine had been established by the Supreme Court in Plessy v. Ferguson (1896). During a train trip in Louisiana, Homer Plessy, a "seven-eighths Caucasian"—he had had one Negro great-grandparent—refused to move to a car for "colored" passengers, as a recently passed state law required. A New Orleans judge ruled that, contrary to Plessy's argument, the segregation statute did not violate the Fourteenth Amendment. On appeal, the Supreme Court, by a seven-to-one vote, affirmed the lower court's decision. Justice Henry Billings Brown, speaking for the majority, declared that laws requiring racial separation "do not necessarily imply the inferiority of either race to the other." Indeed, he said, "we consider the underlying fallacy of the plaintiff's argument to consist in the assumption that the enforced separation of the two races stamps the colored race with a badge of inferiority," and he continued, "If this be so, it is not by reason of anything found in the act, but solely because the colored race chooses to put that construction upon it." As long as they were equal, separate facilities—based on "the established usages, customs and traditions of the people"—were constitutional. And, to give further support to that conclusion, Justice Brown noted that "the most common instance" of lawful segregation "is connected with the establishment of separate schools for white and colored children, which have been held to be a valid exercise of the legislative power even by courts of states where the political rights of the colored race have been longest and most earnestly enforced."

In 1951, when the N.A.A.C.P. was organizing its legal strategy for getting Plessy overturned, racial segregation of children was in force in more than eleven thousand school districts in the United States. (Seventeen states and the District of Columbia had passed laws establishing school segregation, and four other states allowed school segregation where it was the wish of a local community.) The year before, N.A.A.C.P. lawyers had scored partial victories in two cases dealing with segregation at the state-university level. One, *Sweatt v. Painter*, concerned a black student who had tried to enroll in the University of Texas Law School, whereupon state authorities created a separate black law school. Here the Supreme Court ruled in favor of the black plaintiff, Herman Sweatt, but not on the ground that separate but equal facilities were unconstitutional. In this case, the Court said, the State of Texas had manifestly not made the separate facilities equal, and so it was ordered that Herman Sweatt be admitted to the white law school to which he had applied. It was not necessary, said Chief Justice Fred M. Vinson, that "we reach petitioner's contention that Plessy v. Ferguson should be reexamined in the light of contemporary knowledge respecting the purposes of the Fourteenth Amendment and the effects of racial segregation."

The other case, *McLaurin v. Oklahoma State Regents*, which was decided on the same day as Sweatt, was more difficult for the Court to resolve without considering the validity of *Plessy*. Under federal court order, George McLaurin had been admitted to the graduate School of Education at the University of Oklahoma, because the courses he wanted to take were not available in the state's Negro college. But within the university McLaurin had been segregated from his classmates. His desk was separated from all the others by a rail, to which a sign reading "Reserved for Colored" was attached. He also had a segregated desk in the library, and he was compelled to eat by himself in the cafeteria. Everything else was "equal"—professors, books, and physical facilities. The Supreme Court, deciding unanimously for McLaurin, said that "the conditions under which this appellant is required to receive his education deprive him of his personal and present right to the equal protection of the laws," because "such restrictions impair and inhibit his ability to study, to engage in discussion and exchange of views with other students." What particularly encouraged the N.A.A.C.P.'s legal team was the Court's further judgment: "We hold that under these circumstances the Fourteenth Amendment precludes differences in treatment by the state based upon race." Nonetheless, *Plessy v. Ferguson* had not been struck down. Had the State of Oklahoma provided a separate graduate school for McLaurin with truly equal facilities, that maneuver would conceivably have been lawful, according to the decision reached in *Sweatt* the same day. But once McLaurin had been enrolled in the University of Oklahoma there could be no "differences in treatment . . . based on race" in that newly biracial environment. This appeared to mean that certain forms of segregation were unconstitutional but not all. Furthermore, these two cases were restricted to graduate education. For millions of young black children, the N.A.A.C.P. maintained, the harm done by segregated schools began in the first grade.

One approach to combatting racial separation in elementary and secondary schools was to keep bringing lawsuits on the basis that a particular black educational facility was unequal to its white counterpart. Since this was indeed the case in most segregated school districts, the N.A.A.C.P. figured that it could win discrete victories on these grounds, but to break down the racial walls on a case-by-case basis might take a half century or more. The alternative was to launch a direct assault on the *Plessy* doctrine by arguing that even if all facilities were "equal" the very nature of segregation made separate education profoundly unequal for black children, and profoundly damaging to their sense of self-worth.

In February, 1951, Kenneth Clark began to work with N.A.A.C.P. lawyers on the preparation of three of the four cases—from Kansas, South Carolina, Virginia, and Delaware—that, three years later, were to be grouped by the Supreme Court in its *Brown v. Board of Education* decision. In all but the Kansas suit (the title case), Clark testified and helped recruit other social scientists as witnesses. The N.A.A.C.P. had used social-science testimony before. In *Sweatt*, for instance, an anthropologist had testified on scientific interpretations of racial differences. But now the legal strategy was to include a systematic analysis—by psychologists, sociologists, anthropologists, and a variety of experts on education—of the nature of segregation itself, and of its effects on children. As a witness in one of the four test cases, *Briggs v. Elliott*, Clark testified before the federal District Court in Charleston, South Carolina, in May, 1951, saying, "I have reached the conclusion from the examination of my own results and from an examination of the literature in the entire field that discrimination, prejudice, and segregation have definitely detrimental effects on the personality development of the Negro child. The essence of this detrimental effect is a confusion in the child's concept of his own self-esteem—basic feelings of inferiority, conflict, confusion in his self-image, resentment, hostility toward himself, hostility toward whites, intensification of . . . a desire to resolve his basic conflict by sometimes escaping or withdrawing."

In February, 1952, testifying in Richmond, Virginia, in another of the cases, *Davis v. County School Board*, Clark was asked on cross-examination by T. Justin Moore, chief counsel for the Prince Edward County school board, if it was not true that the Negroes of Virginia, as long as they were provided with equal facilities and equipment, could indeed get an equal education. "Why can't the Negro have pride of race?" Moore asked. "Why does he want, I suggest, to be in the category of what I believe someone has described as a 'sun-tanned white man'?"

Clark answered coolly, "I don't think it is the desire of a Negro to be a 'sun-tanned white man.' I think it is the desire of a Negro to be a human being and to be treated as a human being without regard to skin color. He can only have pride in race—and a healthy and mature pride in race—when his own government does not constantly and continuously tell him, 'Have no pride in race,' by constantly segregating him, constantly relegating him to a second-class status."

In three of the four N.A.A.C.P. cases, the lower courts held firm to *Plessy*. In the fourth, *Gebhart v. Belton*, Judge Collins J. Seitz, of the Delaware Court of Chancery, said that while he himself believed that "the 'separate but equal' doctrine of education should be rejected," it was up to the Supreme Court, rather than to him, to make that decision.

As part of the appeal of the four cases to the Supreme Court, the N.A.A.C.P. legal strategists decided to present all the social-science data for the Court's consideration in a special appendix to the formal briefs. This appendix was prepared by Kenneth Clark; Stuart Cook, chairman of the graduate Psychology Department of New York University; and Isidor Chein, director of research for the Commission on Community Interrelations of the American Jewish Congress. Titled "The Effects of Segregation and the Consequences of Desegregation: A Social Science Statement," the appendix summarized and documented the testimony that had been presented at the trials by the N.A.A.C.P.'s expert witnesses. It was signed by thirty-two prominent social scientists and psychiatrists who had done extensive research in race relations. Dr. Clark has since noted that "while there was some precedent for inclusion of social-science data in legal briefs, this was probably the first time that a separate nonlegal brief dealing with the social and psychological aspects of a constitutional issue was submitted to and accepted by the United States Supreme Court."

On May 17, 1954, the Court, in a unanimous decision delivered by Chief Justice Earl Warren, overturned *Plessy v. Ferguson.* To separate black children "from others of similar age and qualifications solely because of their race generates a feeling of inferiority as to their status in the community that may affect their hearts and minds in a way unlikely ever to be undone," the Court declared. "Whatever may have been the extent of psychological knowledge at the time of *Plessy v. Ferguson,* this finding is amply supported by modern authority." At that point in the decision, there was a footnote, No. 11, consisting of a list of sources exemplifying "modern authority," the first of which was "K. B. Clark, Effect of Prejudice and Discrimination on Personality Development (Midcentury White House Conference on Children and Youth, 1950)." The Court continued, "We conclude that in the field of public education the doctrine of 'separate but equal' has no place. Separate educational facilities are inherently unequal. Therefore, we hold that the plaintiffs and others similarly situated for whom the actions have been brought are, by reason of the segregation complained of, deprived of the equal protection of the laws guaranteed by the Fourteenth Amendment."

Kenneth Clark was, of course, jubilant—the more so because it appeared that the Supreme Court had taken "judicial notice," as he put it, of that unusual social-science appendix. As his professors at Howard University had taught him, disciplined intelligence *could* achieve social justice, and the social sciences were surely going to be as effective in their fields as the biological sciences were in theirs.

Despite the unanimity of the Supreme Court in *Brown*, and despite its acknowledgment of "modern authority," racism has, of course, proved much more intransigent than Clark anticipated in the immediate aftermath of the striking down of Plessy. But long after it had become clear that the expectations of that May day might not be fulfilled until the end of the century, if then, Dr. Clark was still emphasizing the historic impact of the 1954 decision. In 1976, speaking in Munich on "The Status of American Minorities in the Bicentennial Year of the American Revolution," he noted, "Within three years after the Brown decision, Martin Luther King, Jr., Roy Wilkins, Whitney Young, and Malcolm X emerged as the significant leaders of the modern civil-rights movement, which then became in effect a mass movement. American . . . blacks who seemed to have accepted compliantly racial segregation since the latter part of the nineteenth century now openly defied institutionalized racism. They refused to sit in the back of the bus. They boycotted all public accommodations that sought to impose racial humiliation upon them." And in the wake of Brown, Clark added, Congress passed the Civil Rights Act of 1964 and the Voting Rights Act of 1965.

That said, Clark, in his Bicentennial lecture, turned to the "distinction between appearance and substance." After all the marches, demonstrations, and new laws, the majority of blacks "are still to be found in menial positions, are underemployed, or are unemployed," he pointed out. And he continued, "Most black children, twenty-two years after the Brown decision, are still required by various evasive devices to attend racially segregated and inferior schools. This problem is particularly exacerbated in northern urban communities, such as Boston, New York, Chicago, Philadelphia, Los Angeles. These so-called cosmopolitan centers of America are now the bastions of sustained resistance to . . . the desegregation of their schools. Racially segregated communities remain the norm in American cities. White suburbs remain predominantly white *bantustans*, with only occasional Negroes being permitted to purchase homes within these compounds of privilege. Urban ghettos are expanding and proliferating and the pathologies of the ghettos—crime, drugs, defeatism of the young, reinforced by inferior education—remain unsolved problems which threaten the viability if not the survival of major American cities." *Brown* had indeed made history, but not enough.

In the decades since *Brown*, Kenneth Clark has become more and more firmly convinced that the primary way to regenerate the hopes and energies ignited by the *Brown* decision is to transform the schools. In speeches and seminars, he has said, "One cannot expect a group to attain the full status of equality of citizenship if the masses of the children of that group are being denied adequate education in their elementary and secondary schools, if the abilities of these children are not being developed to the maximum at these crucial states of their development, and if these children are being subjected to educational experiences which deprive them of the ability to compete successfully with others."

Even before the *Brown* decision, Dr. Clark had been pressing for change in the New York City school system, and throughout the nineteen-fifties he continued to accuse the

Board of Education of permitting significant increases in de-
facto segregated education that was decidedly unequal. His
indictments were rejected, and in the late fifties, to document
further the damage done to black children in the city's public
schools, Clark assigned a number of white students of his at
City College to interview white elementary and secondary-
school teachers. In "Dark Ghetto," Clark reported that many
of the teachers told the interviewers "that Negro children are
inherently inferior in intelligence and therefore cannot be expected to learn as much or as readily as white children; and
that all one would do, if one tried to teach them as if they
could learn, would be to develop in them serious emotional
disturbances, frustrations and anxieties." Obviously, Clark
continued, "children who are treated as if they are uneducable
almost invariably become uneducable." Furthermore, it is the
"negative influence" of such teachers—more than the influence
of home and community—that causes the negative self-image
of so many minority schoolchildren.

To any who asked, and to the many who did not ask, Clark
provided his own answer to teaching "the disadvantaged." It is
"embarrassingly simple," he wrote. "Teach them with the same
expectations, the same acceptance of their humanity and their
educability and, therefore, with the same effectiveness as one
would teach the more privileged child. In other words, teach
them the way you would the kids in Scarsdale, or in any other
upper-middle-class community." In 1955, to prove that this
embarrassingly simple approach would work, Kenneth and
Mamie Clark began a "crash program" in remedial reading at
the Northside Center. It had long been evident to the Clarks
that, as he puts it, "the most frequently stated concern of the

parents of Northside children is not their economic status, not their housing, not their family problems, but the inefficient education of their children." And so, for four or five weeks in the summer, one-hour classes in reading were given five days a week at the Center. Each summer, over a period of five years, the average gain in reading level for each child who took the course turned out to be about a year. "These children were woefully retarded academically," Clark points out. "So much so that their schools had said they couldn't do anything with them, because they could not learn. And they were poor. Their parents suffered from all the disadvantages that are supposed to cripple the learning abilities of children from such homes. Most were on welfare. But in this place these children were being taught to read by people who believed they could learn to read, and who related to them with warmth and acceptance. Under these conditions, they learned. And, what's more, they sustained what they had learned during the regular school year. But they did not increase those gains during the regular school year. In the public schools, their progress stopped. But their home environment had remained constant. They had been just as poor in the summer, with us, as they were for the rest of the year in school. The difference was in the learning environment." Despite what Northside kept proving about black children's ability to learn, achievement levels in the ghetto classrooms of the city continued to fall; indeed, the longer most poor children stayed in school the more steeply their rate of learning declined.

In 1962, Kenneth Clark thought he might finally have the chance to demonstrate—in a much, much larger setting that Northside—that black children are as educable as any others.

The Kennedy Administration had set up an interdepartmental President's Committee on Juvenile Delinquency and Youth Crime, with Attorney General Robert Kennedy as chairman. The Committee provided funds to Harlem Youth Opportunities Unlimited, or HARYOU, for a two-year study of how best to control juvenile delinquency in central Harlem. The study was also to include a specific plan that, if it was approved, would get large-scale funding for its realization. Clark was appointed acting chairman of HARYOU.

"From the beginning," Clark told me, "we recognized that we could not deal seriously with the problem of delinquency in Harlem without identifying and remedying those pervasive problems in the community which stunted and dehumanized Harlem's youth." One of those problems was education. Accordingly, the eventual plan, which was presented in a six-hundred-and-twenty-page report entitled "Youth in the Ghetto: A Study of the Consequences of Powerlessness and a Blueprint for Change," included a carefully detailed design for "thorough reorganization of the schools." Along with rezoning, open enrollment, and other strategies to increase the number of racially heterogeneous schools, Clark called for the selection of teachers and administrators solely on the basis of their "special competence," with "extra pay tied to superior skill." The promotion of these educators would depend on how well the children in their classrooms learned.

On the basis of the Northside experience in intensive summer reading, Clark, in a written proposal, recommended a Reading Mobilization Year. Since "all studies of the problem of education in deprived communities agree on the fact that the central pathology in these schools is the fact that the children in these schools are woefully deficient in reading," he wrote, the central Board of Education would drop its normal curriculum in the Harlem area for half a year or a year, and during that time "the total school program . . . would be geared toward the improvement of reading." (There would be a different curriculum during that year for children not retarded in reading.) This vast "crash program" in reading, Clark declared, would significantly decrease juvenile delinquency by reducing the dropout rate and giving thousands of children some realistic hope for their future. In addition, Clark's plan included extensive preschool education. To start with, at least four thousand children between the ages of three and five would be enrolled in Pre-School Academies, which would also instruct parents in how to "participate fully in the education of their children." As might have been expected from Clark, the focus in these early classes would be not on "the conventional play approach of most day-care-center and nursery-school programs" but, rather, on "linguistic and conceptual skills," because such skills "are necessary preparation for learning to read, write, and handle numerical relationships."

Still another part of the HARYOU plan envisaged After-School Study Centers, which would "compensate for the past failures of the public schools." And, along with a variety of continually monitored job-training programs, there was to be a counselling service for high-school dropouts which would either get them back into school or train them in work skills. Furthermore, Clark had devised a plan for a Community Service Corps, for those "so severely damaged" that they were not yet ready for advanced job training.

Pervading the entire "Youth in the Ghetto" report was an insistence on the continuing participation of the residents of Harlem, including the young, in the development of each part of the design. They would act as recruiters, research aides, and teaching aides, among other capacities. This, Clark pointed out, was to be a break with "the traditional social service, welfare, dole approach" to the poor—an approach that continually increased the dependency and stigmatization of "the clients." If Harlem was not to continue to be "a powerless colony," its citizens would have to learn the skills—including those of confrontation, if necessary—to bring about lasting social change on their own. HARYOU, if it worked, was to be Harlem's declaration of independence. "The program must work," said Clark in his proposal. "It is the city's last hope to save these children from a wasted life."

"Youth in the Ghetto" was presented to the review panel of the President's Committee on Juvenile Delinquency in April, 1964 (the Committee was continuing its work under President Lyndon Johnson), and the panel recommended an initial allocation of a million dollars to begin to make the blueprint real. An additional three and a half million dollars was provided by the City of New York, and the Department of Labor made a grant of five hundred thousand dollars to begin the job-training and job-placement programs. Over a period of three years, there would be a total of some hundred and ten million in federal funds for all the intersecting programs. At this point, as the two years of research and planning appeared to be moving toward realization, Clark resigned from HARYOU. There had been a struggle between him and Representative Adam Clayton Powell, Jr., over its independence, and Clark had lost.

Clark later explained, "Powell was the first major political figure to understand the political dynamite inherent in the
community-action components of the HARYOU planning
document. Seeing this, he insisted that if it was going to operate in his district, it would have to be under his control." Powell already controlled an existing "action program"—ACT,
which had set up Associated Community Teams to provide
work for Harlem youth, and which was being financed in part
by the President's Committee on Juvenile Delinquency. Under
pressure from Powell, HARYOU and ACT were merged, and
a former Powell assistant became the executive director of the
new organization. Powell controlled the board of directors.

Clark had resisted the merger, knowing that if his plan became subject to Powell's political patronage and political direction it would surely fail. For a time, feeling that all the
moral weight was on his side, he had believed he could successfully force Powell to back off. "Adam kept trying to win
me over," Clark recalled. "He'd say, 'Kenneth, don't be such a
baby.' I must admit I liked him very much. He was a charming
man. And he was honest. That is, he was honestly corrupt. He
had undertaken the most difficult civil-rights challenge—the
integration of corruption. He knew exactly what he was doing, and he enjoyed doing it. Adam had no sense of guilt that I
was ever aware of, and he was very shrewd. He had read the
HARYOU report carefully, and he knew that, for him to survive, the ghetto must survive as it was. If the ghetto were
transformed so that its residents took power for themselves,
his power would be destroyed. Adam kept telling me that I
couldn't win this battle, because he had too much power. But I
was naïve and refused to believe him. Until the very end,

moreover, I was trying to persuade Adam that if he did not contaminate HARYOU, if he insulated it from pork-barrel politics, it would become a monument to him."

Clark finally realized that he had been defeated when he went to see Powell in his Washington office in the summer of 1964. "I was in the city for a board meeting at Howard University, and I wanted to try once more to convince Adam that he should leave us alone," Clark told me. "I still did not believe I was entirely powerless, because Robert Kennedy agreed with me, and he still chaired President Johnson's Committee on Juvenile Delinquency, the chief funding source." Powell, Clark recalled, began by saying amiably, "You know, you have nobody on your side, Kenneth. I am chairman of the House Education and Labor Committee, through which all anti-poverty legislation must go, and so Lyndon has to keep me satisfied. So does Bob Wagner, because, as Mayor of New York, he needs Lyndon. As for Bobby Kennedy, he's going to run for the Senate in New York, so he can't afford to antagonize me, either. He needs the votes I can deliver."

The telephone rang at that point. It was not an ordinary phone but, rather, an instrument that allowed Powell to carry on a conversation without having to speak directly into a receiver. He could move freely about the room as he talked, and the amplified voice of the caller could be heard throughout the room. Powell had first seen such a telephone on Lyndon Johnson's desk, and when he expressed admiration for it the President had given one to him. On the phone was a close associate of Robert Kennedy's. The associate was on the staff of the President's Committee on Juvenile Delinquency. During the previous weeks, he had been assuring Clark that he was right to continue battling Powell, and that the Committee would support him. "But here was the man's voice floating in the room," Clark recalled. "'Mr. Congressman,' he said, 'I want you to know that I've got the Puerto Ricans lined up behind us, and they will attack Clark on this HARYOU thing.' He ended the phone conversation by saying, 'Keep up the good work. And tell the Attorney General I sent my best.' Adam hung up, and said, 'See, that's politics. You've got to grow up, Kenneth.'"

Clark resigned from HARYOU immediately after this postgraduate lesson in politics. "I really was naïve," he said. "Roy Wilkins had tried to warn me. He had told me that a tough-minded, competent, independent HARYOU would not be permitted by Adam. As for Bobby Kennedy, when reports began to appear in the press that Adam was about to exploit HARYOU, Bobby was quoted as saying, 'I have no fault to find with Adam Clayton Powell.' So Adam won, and his victory effectively blocked any systematic and serious realization of the plan. Once more, the poor had been fought *about*, not for. They remained hostages, instruments of other people's profit and power. As it turned out, all we did at HARYOU was to produce a document. Oh, it had some influence. When President Johnson appointed Sargent Shriver the director of his War on Poverty, Shriver talked with me a number of times, and it was clear that he and his staff had read 'Youth in the Ghetto.' That's where they got the idea for their 'community-action programs' and for having the 'maximum feasible participation' of the poor in the planning stages. But, despite those slogans, the actual takeover pattern set by Adam Powell was repeated throughout the country. The poor just didn't have the training, let alone the power, to cope with the established political bureaucracy in terms of who was to control the so-called community-action programs. Middle-class bureaucrats took them over, and while some of the indigenous poor did learn to become anti-poverty hustlers, the masses pretty much remained as they were—except that their frustrations grew deeper, because of what these anti-poverty programs had promised. It is probably not coincidental that the urban riots of the middle and late nineteen-sixties came in the wake of all the false talk about 'maximum feasible participation' of the poor."

Clark added that mistakes were also made by those planners who were not part of the old political apparatus but earnestly regarded themselves as allies of the poor. "The most important mistake," he said, "was that we did not take into sufficient account the debilitating, inhibiting effect of the most persistent and stark factor in American poverty—the quality of education in the public schools in the low-income areas of our cities." With so much damage being created by those schools, Clark said, it was difficult to find enough people with the analytic skills, the disciplined, sustained energy, and the hope required to engage in the long, complex battles necessary to overcome white political power, on the one hand, and the Adam Clayton Powells, on the other. Nonetheless, Clark still does not believe the War on Poverty was a total failure. "For all the pork-barrelling," he said, "many individuals in the ghettos did get a sense that they have certain rights and that community action *is* the way to proceed—if they could ever become strong enough politically to control that action."

After losing the HARYOU battle, Dr. Clark continued teaching at City College and, in 1967, also became the president of a nonprofit corporation known as MARC—the Metropolitan Applied Research Center. Staffed by specialists in the social sciences, law, and municipal affairs, MARC described its work as "an attempt to determine by systematic exploration whether trained intelligence can be mobilized as an effective form of power for positive social change." Through research, to be followed sometimes by intervention, MARC intended to address itself to specific problems of the poor, and through fellowships and student-internship programs it would create cadres of experienced, disciplined activists who could function anywhere in the country. MARC was housed near Fifth Avenue in an attractive three-story building on East Eighty-sixth Street. The rooms were airy, the furnishings were imaginative and crisply coordinated, and Clark himself occupied a spacious third-floor office that opened onto a plant-lined terrace. "If the Ford Foundation can have a place with class and taste, why shouldn't a black think tank?" he said at the time. Actually, the staff was integrated—as all of Clark's research teams have been. "Racial separatism is a blind alley," he says. "It means the abandonment of hope. Furthermore, just as there are white idiots, so there are black idiots." Although MARC explored a considerable range of urban issues, Clark, characteristically, was most concerned with finding ways to make the public schools work for the poor. In 1970, it looked as if he, and MARC, would finally get a chance to demonstrate in the school system of an entire city what he had been prevented from demonstrating through HARYOU—that low-income black children are as educable as any other children. In Washington, D.C., a newly elected school board, headed by Anita Ford Allen, a graduate of Howard University who had become an administrator in the United States Office of Education, invited Dr. Clark to design an educational program for the hundred and fifty thousand children then attending school in the District of Columbia. More than ninety per cent were black, and many were poor. (Many middle-class residents of Washington, black and white, were sending their children to private schools.) Mrs. Allen had come to Clark because for years District of Columbia students had been scoring considerably below national norms in reading and mathematics, and the longer they stayed in school the further they fell behind. By the end of the sixth grade, a majority of the children were at least two years behind their peers in other school systems, and many of those who finally graduated from high school were clearly deficient in basic skills. Dr. Clark accepted the challenge, saying at the time, "This is an opportunity to show that it is possible to raise the academic achievement of minority-group children by accepting them, by respecting them, and by teaching them with the same efficiency as one would educate more privileged children. These educationally retarded children are human beings. They are not expendable. We simply cannot allow another generation of black youngsters to be sentenced to lives of failure and futility." Clark and his associates at MARC designed an Academic Achievement Project for Washington. (It appeared as a book in 1972, with the title "A Possible Reality: A Design for the Attainment of High Academic Achievement for Inner-City Students.") In his design, Clark called, as he had in Harlem, for a Reading Mobilization Year for all the students in the first through the ninth grades in the District of Columbia school system. Intensive instruction by teams of teachers would raise the reading levels of all children to their grade level, and higher. Teachers and administrators would be held accountable for the success or failure of their students. Their rank and salary level would depend on the achievement of the children in their charge. And, to find out just how much, or how little, was being achieved, standardized testing and other assessments of reading progress would take place throughout the year.

Clark's "possible reality" did not have a chance to prove or disprove itself. From the beginning, as one academic observer of the experiment has explained, "Clark and his plan were seen as a threat by the educational professionals." Hugh Scott, a new superintendent of schools—and the first black to hold that post in the District—felt that Clark, as an outsider, would weaken his own control of the system. And the largely black teachers' union, led by William Simons, objected strenuously to the idea of having teachers monitored and evaluated on the basis of the academic progress of their students. Implicit in such a plan, the union felt, was the eventual erosion of tenure protections. If the students of a particular teacher consistently failed, the time might come when the teacher could be fired, tenure or not. Simons said at one point, "What is good for children is not going to be purchased at the price of dignity for adults."

Furthermore, there was much disagreement about whether the Clark plan was realistic, considering the nature and quality of the District's students. Dr. Clark had said that normal children, of whatever color, could learn, but both the superintendent of schools and the head of the teachers' union questioned

whether the term "normal" could be applied to the black children of Washington. "Let's face the facts," Scott said in a
speech to a group of Young Republicans. "A goodly number of
the black kids in this district were not raised in a normal social, political, and economic environment, and it may not be
an accurate thing to use that terminology—normal—without
taking in the full consequences of these other factors." In sum,
his position was that the District's black children, though they
were born with the potential to participate effectively in society, might have been so handicapped in their intellectual
growth and development by "the historic grievances and limitations of an abnormal environment" that they could not function normally in school. If this was so, Scott said in subsequent
statements, it would be unfair to hold schools and teachers responsible for the failure of students, since it was the society
that had stunted their development.

Clark responded sharply to Scott's line of reasoning. "I used
to think that a man could only talk that way because he is not
black," he said. "These are the same things I've heard from
white segregationists and white liberals and condescending
whites. It's crossed the color line." He went on to say, "The
fact that Dr. Scott is black does not grant him immunity from
assessment of his performance. I believe Dr. Scott cannot be
an effective implementer of any academic design."

Another black man attacked the "possible reality" in a different way, Clark recalls. "On television one night, a teachers'-
union official said that if my plan turned out to be successful it
would merely store up frustrations for black youth, because
once they were able to read and compete they would still be
discriminated against on account of their color and would be-

come even more bitter. When I heard it, I did not believe that a teachers'-union official could really be saying such a thing."

Scott and Simons joined forces against Clark and his reading plan, and it failed: it had been stripped of a crucial element—the ranking of teachers according to the progress of their students. This concession by the Board of Education came after the union had threatened that its members would simply refuse to administer that standardized tests—and some had refused. To avoid further confrontations, the Board agreed that under no circumstances would test results be used to evaluate teachers. In 1971, Clark's firmest supporter, Anita Ford Allen, was defeated in her attempt to be reelected president of the Board of Education, and the Academic Achievement Project essentially came to an end. "The most terrible thing about the Washington experience was the passivity of the community," Clark has said. "Once the teachers' union, the superintendent, and the rest of the educational hierarchy had decided to dismantle the plan, we couldn't get any significant number of parents to fight for their own children. Nor did such community organizations as the local chapter of the N.A.A.C.P. and the Washington Urban League publicly support us. Certain officials in those groups cheered us on privately, but they did not want to become involved in the politics of the conflict. The politics of adult power. In this case, black adult power. The children did not count."

One day in early July, 1970, as Clark was outlining his Academic Achievement Project to the District of Columbia Board of Education, one of its members heatedly objected to the proposal that standard English be used exclusively in the teaching of the almost entirely black school population. Arguing for an emphasis on what had come to be called Black English—the language used by many of the children at home and on the streets—the critic insisted that rejecting a child's speech patterns was equivalent to rejecting the child. "Here was this black man, speaking impeccable English—he was a graduate of Harvard, I believe, and he really used the language impressively," Clark recalls. "I could not resist saying to him, 'Look, I would like these youngsters to speak the way you do, so that people will pay attention to them—even when they're speaking nonsense, as you are now.' And while this was going on I remembered reading that Harold Laski once said, 'You know, the class system in England will never really be improved until someone finds a way of teaching the Cockneys to speak middle-class English.'" Clark won his point at that meeting, but not before his antagonist on the school board had called him a racist for insisting that black children be held to the same standards of language as white children.

Racial separatism of any kind, whether in the teaching of English or in the setting up of exclusively black departments or facilities on a college campus, has always been vehemently opposed by Dr. Clark. "I do not believe that the purpose of education is to reinforce parochialism," he has said. "What I try to help my own students understand is the commonality of man. As for the supposed justifications for black separatism in any form, I do not believe that genuine pride in oneself can be based on anything as external as color. I do not accept the pride argument from Black Power people any more than I do from white supremacists. In both cases, It's racism."

In 1968, Edward H. Levi, then provost of the University of Chicago, asked Dr. Clark for advice when a group of black students demanded an all-black dormitory on campus. Clark responded in a letter. "The university's involvement in the setting up of an all-black or an all-white dormitory for its students would be a profound violation of academic freedom," he wrote Levi. "It would be a mockery of the goals of education and could only occur in a society which was so severely ill with the disease of racism and its symptoms of guilt, hostility, and ambivalence as to be in severe crises of survival." Though he was not an expert in constitutional law, Clark added, he was convinced that "any university or college which sets up an all-Negro dormitory violates the letter and the spirit of the *McLaurin* decision and also the *Brown* decision of the United States Supreme Court." He explained, "In the McLaurin decision, the Court was quite clear that the University of Oklahoma and its governing board could not segregate or isolate Negro students on the arbitrary basis of race without violating the equal-protection clause of the United States Constitution. I do not believe that this basic principle is inoperative merely because the victims ask for the segregated facilities." He went on to say, "For all of the above reasons—and others which are much too visceral for me to express with any pretense of coherence—I am personally unalterably opposed to any educational or other public or quasi-public institution classifying, or in any way categorizing, its students or personnel on the basis of the irrelevant and arbitrary factor of race or color. I am opposed to all-Negro or all-white classes, dormitories, schools or colleges." Clark ended the letter by saying, "those of us who still believe in the positive potential of human beings, and that educational institutions must reinforce these positives, cannot contribute to the disease but must try to cure the patient even when such cure might require the painful remedies of courage and clarity."

The year before, Clark had antagonized some of the Black Power advocates at his own alma mater by proposing that Howard University become a nonracial institution. "I had tended to idealize my all-black college experience," he said then. "But as I grew older I came to believe that the very fact of a segregated college is an abomination. It's institutionalized psychosis, and is possible only in a crazy society."

In 1969, Clark was attacked as a "moderate," and even as an "Uncle Tom," by a number of black militants around the country when he resigned from the board of directors of Antioch College because the college had supported the creation on its campus of a racially exclusive Afro-American Institute. In his letter of resignation, after citing the arguments against all forms of segregation which were based on psychology and constitutional law, Clark said, "I do not believe that Antioch, in permitting some of the more hostile Negro students to coerce and intimidate other Negroes and whites . . . has showed the courage necessary to maintain that type of academic climate which permits man that freedom of inquiry, freedom of thought, and freedom of dissent which are essential to the life of the intellect." He also made the rather mordant point that precisely those "who need a black studies program most of all"—the whites—were, with the full cooperation of the college, being barred from this Afro-American Institute.

The vogue for black separatism intensified in the early nineteen-seventies. During that period, Dr. Clark was sometimes confronted personally by its advocates. "I was once stopped on my way to class at City College by a well-dressed black man in his late thirties," he recalled recently. "'You're Dr. Clark?' this man asked. I nodded, thinking he was going to compliment me, and he said, 'We're going to get you, you son of a bitch!' I just looked at him and asked when this was going to happen. He walked away, and that turned out to be the end of it. But that was the climate of those years." Not long after that encounter, Clark was walking to class during a time when some black and Puerto Rican students were trying to close down City College by way of enforcing their demands for more Third World courses and faculty members. "I saw a group of those on strike physically keeping one of my students from going to class," he told me. "I was so furious I walked over and yelled, 'Damn it! Leave him alone!' They were so shocked at the spontaneous force of my rage that they let the student go. We went in to class, and there were only a couple of others there. But I would have conducted that class if there had been only one student. A class is sacred. It should never be interfered with."

Mamie Clark thoroughly understood her husband's uncharacteristically loud public rage at the assault on his classroom. "His first love is teaching," she said not long ago. "It always has been. He has given a great deal to his students, not only by teaching them how to think but also by impressing on them the possibilities of using their education to affect the society they live in. And, of course, his impact as a teacher has reached far beyond those who have actually been in a classroom with him. Most well-known black people are not in the academic field—they're in the theatre or in sports or, increasingly, in politics—and so the renown and the great amount of respect that Kenneth has achieved have been of a rather rare kind. And I think that by achieving them he has given psychic sustenance to many blacks, whether or not they themselves have gone into teaching on the college level."

Dr. Clark retired from City College in 1975, intending to concentrate on research and writing. He couldn't bear to give up teaching entirely, however, so he leads a weekly seminar for adult students at Mercy College, in Dobbs Ferry, New York, some two miles from where he lives—in a Tudor-style house, in Hastings-on-Hudson. He describes the seminar as dealing with "contemporary social issues from the perspective of a psychologist." Although the seminar is now his only regular academic commitment, Dr. Clark has more than filled the hours he used to spend as a professor at City College: he still complains that he can't find enough time for writing. But he recognizes that this chronic conflict is of his own making.

"Kenneth is more restless than ever," his wife says. "He feels there's so much to be done, and there's not enough time in which to do it all. I keep saying, 'Why don't you rest a little bit and be an elder statesman, which is such a nice comfortable thing to be?'" She adds, smiling, "But that's only my opinion."

"I came to realize that I just couldn't devote myself solely to a life of leisurely scholarship and writing," Clark says. "And Mamie, for all that she talks about the comforts of my becoming an elder statesman, knew that before I did. A year or so before I retired from City College, she said very calmly one day, 'Kenneth, do you realize that you've never been able to write anything without competing commitments?' Well, she's a psychologist, you know, and I said, 'I'd like to try. I'd like to see what it's like to have nothing to do but write.' Even more calmly, she said, 'I hope you succeed.' I kept thinking of that conversation, and it bothered me increasingly as the retirement date came closer. It might well be that if all my time were free for writing I wouldn't write at all."

Lest he have to put that possibility to the test, Dr. Clark, before he left City College, figured out a way to get involved in an abundance of projects, which would set up a ceaseless round of competing deadlines. He formed a consulting firm, Clark, Phipps, Clark & Harris, Inc.: Dr. Kenneth B. Clark, president; Dr. Mamie Phipps Clark, treasurer; Hilton B. Clark, vice-president; Kate Clark Harris, secretary. The vice-president and the secretary are the son and daughter of the president and the treasurer. Hilton Clark, who is thirty-eight, is a graduate of the Kent School, in Connecticut ("I wanted him to understand power and the training of people who wield power," his father says), and Columbia College, where he earned a degree in political science. He lives in Harlem ("There is no place in the world where I feel more comfortable," he says), and he has been a Democratic district leader there since 1979, having defeated the incumbent, whose home base was the Adam Clayton Powell Club. Kate Clark Harris, who is forty-two, went to public school in Hastings-on-Hudson. Her father, who has been criticized for not sending his children to Harlem schools, says, "I've always fought to improve those schools, but each child of mine has one life and I could not risk that." Kate went on to earn a B.A. from Oberlin (her major was psychology) and a master's degree from the Smith College School for Social work. Before she began to work with the family consulting firm, in 1980, she was the director of the scholarship program of National Medical Fellowships, which helps minority students in medical schools.

Much of the day-to-day work of the firm is handled by Kenneth, Mamie, and Hilton Clark. There is a staff of about twenty people, some of whom worked with Clark at MARC, and the firm occupies the building that MARC occupied; MARC itself dissolved in 1976. The new firm quickly attracted clients from both government and business who needed help in designing and monitoring affirmative-action programs and in solving other problems in race relations. Business has increased faster than Clark anticipated, so it is all the more difficult for him to get his writing done. "Every now and then, I still wonder whether I shouldn't have opted for the life of a scholarly recluse for whatever years I have left," Clark said recently. "But, damn it, I like what I'm doing. It's challenging, because I'm really testing whether it's possible for someone who has been an academic and a social activist all his life to be successful in business—a business that has to do with social change."

Among Clark, Phipps, Clark & Harris's clients are Chemical Bank (affirmative-action programs) and Con Edison (diagnosing racial problem areas). Projects have been completed for American Telephone & Telegraph (one was a study of minority students in college who are majoring in the disciplines from which the corporation does its hiring) and an international engineering consulting firm. "On the basis of our selection process," Clark said, "they are hiring as draftsmen and designers youngsters who would not ordinarily be employed by them but who have potential. We turn the young people over to the consulting firm for training, but during that period we provide them with support and counselling—on any kind of problem, personal or professional—and also monitor the training program. Included are blacks, Hispanics, Asians, and some whites. As you can see, this is not what you'd call an ordinary business."

In a brochure describing its terms of employment to prospective clients, Dr. Clark's firm makes clear that it "reserves the right to terminate its services should its senior staff conclude that the client is not seriously committed to achieving the agreed upon objectives."

I asked Vice-President Hilton Clark, who is solidly built and self-assured but tends to look rather guarded, if that clause had ever been invoked.

"Yes," he said. "Not often, but we've dropped some clients. For an example of how that can happen, a top executive might be trying to get a government contract, but complaints to the government by some disgruntled minority employees about how they're being treated might lose the contract for the firm. So this executive figures, 'Maybe if we hire Kenneth Clark's organization it'll look as if we were really doing something about our minority problems.' He does that; we come in, identify what the problem really is, and make certain recommendations. But the firm keeps coming up with alibis, and putting roadblock after roadblock in the way of those recommendations. It becomes obvious that it's not going to move on them. We see that there's no sense in our being there, and we leave."

For all the broadening of his activities in recent years, Dr. Clark's primary focus is still on education. "I continue to be an extremist," he says. "An extremist in persisting in believing that black kids can learn, and that segregation is one way in which they are prevented from learning. I remain an incorrigible integrationist. Or, if you prefer, I remain a rigid, hard-line integrationist. Some of my black friends urge me to be more 'realistic,' more 'pragmatic'—to accept the fact that the *Brown* decision has just not worked in the big cities, especially those outside the South, and that we should therefore go for separate but 'quality' schools."

That is the position that Robert Carter, who, as an N.A.A.C.P. lawyer, initially recruited Clark to the research team that helped bring about the victory in the Brown decision, has reluctantly adopted. In the *Harvard Civil Rights—Civil Liberties Law Review,* Carter, a longtime battler for school integration (he is now a federal district judge in New York), wrote that the main requirement of the *Brown* decision was "equal educational opportunity." The Court, in 1954, equated that goal with integration. But, Carter now maintains, if equal educational opportunity can be achieved without integration "Brown has been satisfied." Carter wrote, "I am certain that a racially integrated America is best for all of us, but I also know that quality education is essential to the survival of hundreds of thousands of black children who now seem destined for the dunghill in our society. There are solutions, I believe, which can readily achieve integration and deliver equal education at the same time: state systems, metropolitan school districts combining the central city and suburbs, or clusters of schools outside districts on large campuses (much like colleges). The hope of getting approval of such remedies today through litigation or legislation is, I think you will agree, minimal." Therefore, although it would be a "disaster" to abandon integration "as the ultimate solution," Carter wrote, to focus on it for the present "is a luxury only the black middle class can afford." He concluded, "The immediate and urgent need of the black urban poor is the attainment, in real terms and in settings of virtually total black-white school separation, of at least some of the benefits and protection of the constitutional guarantee of equal educational opportunity that Brown requires. The only way to insure that thousands of the black urban poor will have even a remote chance of obtaining the tools needed to compete in the marketplace for a decent job and its accompanying benefits is to concentrate on having quality education delivered to the schools these blacks are attending, and in all likelihood will be attending for at least another generation."

Clark's response to Carter and to others who have come to this conclusion is "I don't doubt they now find this position more practical, but what they are advocating will intensify and further rigidify segregation." He says, "Under the guise of what they call realism, they are willing to concede defeat, as they mask that defeat with various euphemisms. Those who propose to raise the achievement level in segregated schools instead of renewing their efforts to integrate those schools are actually renewing the myth of 'separate but equal.' They are resurrecting *Plessy versus Ferguson*. And, even aside from the fact that their proposal is unconstitutional, they provide no evidence that 'separate but equal' will work educational wonders in any school, in any system, when it has not done so anywhere in these United States for over a hundred years. As Robert Carter says, there *are* ways to achieve integration. And, yes, one approach is to form metropolitan school districts, combining the central city and the suburbs. Another is for states to finance regional schools that would cut across urban-suburban boundaries. There could also be prestige regional schools, financed by the federal government, that could cut through *state* boundaries and provide facilities for resident students. There is indeed enormous opposition to any workable attempts to integrate the public schools, but there always has been. I remain convinced that there is no choice but to keep fighting for integration. The accuracy of the Supreme Court's language in Brown has not changed: 'To separate [children] from others of similar age and qualifications solely because of their race generates a feeling of inferiority as to their status in the community that may affect their hearts and minds in a way unlikely ever to be undone.' The act of segregation itself damages the personality. This is as true now as it has ever been. If necessary, I am prepared to stand alone as an integrationist. Oh, attempts have been made to move me backward. Some years ago, Barbara Jordan, who was then in Congress, called a meeting of some black legislators and educators to gain recruits to her position that the best way to get more federal aid for all the public schools was to lessen the pressure to integrate all the public schools. I raised hell. I told her, 'This is "separate but equal." You're trying to equalize the separateness, and I will not be a party to that.' She looked at me and said, 'Your unrealism is passé.' So there I was, my old-fashioned extremism once more supposedly getting in the way of progress."

In her office, on the first floor of Clark, Phipps, Clark & Harris, Mamie Clark talked about the schools as they are, and about the children who are not learning in those schools. "If children don't learn, teachers and administrators should be fired," she said softly. "At least, if a sizable number of them were fired the rest might start doing what they're paid to do. There has to be a war. A war with the teachers' unions. A war with the whole system. A war for the children. But you have to get the parents to fight that war, and there has not been any force to move them, to help them develop strategies."

She paused, and her voice was even softer when she resumed. "You know, things are *worse* than they were when we started Northside. They really are worse. More people are without hope now. But thirty years ago there *was* hope. People got excited when things happened to their children. They tried harder to change things for their children. And they tried harder still in the nineteen-sixties. But now—well, now they know that nothing has changed. I'm depressed about it. So is Kenneth. We talk about it all the time." She laughed—a short, dry laugh. "We say the same things over and over. I don't know what the answer is."

Her voice now was barely audible. "I really don't know." There was another silence, and she smiled. "But he won't stop looking for the answer. Oh, sometimes Kenneth is very down, but he bounces back. He always bounces back. It's quite marvelous to watch, because, when you consider the issues he's always dealing with, he could become so depressed he'd commit suicide. But there are always new battles."

"That's it," another voice said. Kate Clark Harris, a woman of vibrant energy and an easy, informal manner, had come into the room. "It's all those challenges, all those battles, that keep him continuing. My father has a lot of anger. He's often angrier than he'll say, or show. But this way, battling all the time, he's found a way to express that anger so that it's constructive for him and—if people would listen—for society. For all the despair, he really enjoys his life."

"We have a place on the Cape," Mamie Clark said. "In West Hyannisport. He has never spent a whole lot of time there. Oh, he always announces that he's going to take the whole summer, but at best he manages three or four long weekends, because there's always a new project or problem here. Just about all he does when he's there is read and sleep. He has nothing to do with any physical activity. Kenneth has no aptitude for any sport. He even had a hard time getting out of physical education in college. But he does have one avocation." She smiled. "He's very fond of raising cactuses. They're tough plants, and somehow survive against all odds."

A few days later, I paid another visit to Dr. Clark's office. He was wearing a pin-striped gray suit, a button-down blue shirt, and a gray-and-red striped tie. It occurred to me that although I had known him for more than twenty years, I had never seen him without a tie—or, for that matter, without a button-down shirt. His office held shelves of books and reports, pictures of his grandchildren, and a portrait of W. E. B. Du Bois. "One of my heroes," Clark said. "Such a tough mind. Such courage, clarity, and persistence." In a *Times* Op-Ed article written two years ago with Lawrence Plotkin, Clark had quoted from Du Bois's "The Souls of Black Folk": "One ever feels his two-ness— an American, a Negro; two souls, two thoughts, two unreconciled strivings; two warring ideals in one dark body, whose dogged strength keeps it from being torn asunder."

I spoke of what his wife had said about the worsening state of children in Harlem, in all the Harlems.

"Things *are* worse," Dr. Clark said. "In the schools, although scores are going up in some places, more black kids are being put on the dung heap every year. But it's not just the schools. Residential segregation is worse. Not only the increase and proliferation of ghettos but the pathology of ghetto life. The closest I can find to something positive is that more blacks are now in positions in the private sector from which they were previously excluded. Also, there is the fact that more blacks are being elected to office. There are more black mayors, for example. But I'm stymied when I try to tie that to observable positive changes in the lives of black people who live where there are black mayors. Maybe it's too early for a connection to be made, or maybe this development will just contribute to further political disillusionment among blacks. Yet there must be options that will work. My job is to keep looking for those options. Honest options. That's what I've had to do all my life—differentiate between the evidence and my wishes. That's what my new book, 'Beyond the Ghetto,' is about. I've been at it for ten years now. I've *got* to take some time off to finish it."

Russia Hughes, a thin, auburn-haired women in her sixties who has been an associate of Dr. Clark's since 1968, came in with some checks for him to sign. Then he had several phone conversations. When he finished with the phone calls, he lit a cigarette and said, "There are times when I feel that all I've done with my life is produce documents—reports, memorandums, books—and that as for actually helping produce social change my life has been one big failure. It's as if I were a physician, and the disease had metastasized."

"Then what keeps you going?" I asked.

"When I was in high school, my biology teacher made his subject real by having us look at living cells through a microscope. And what I took out of that ninth-grade class was that the cell is constantly in a state of struggle. Looking at the amoeba and the paramecium, I saw they were continually active. The irritability of protoplasm, as it's called, is the essential difference between protoplasm and other forms of matter. As I grew up and went through college and graduate school, and later, when I was teaching, it became all the more evident to me that, while there are gradations of intensity, life really is a continuous struggle. And when the irritability of protoplasm stops, life stops. On our level of the biogenetic scale, that struggle takes on different forms—struggle for comfort, struggle for status. But the highest form of life, in terms of evolutionary development, involves struggling for such abstractions as justice and decency. And always there has been a minority of human beings engaged in that kind of struggle—people who insist on being unrealistic, people who won't give up when everything seems to indicate that they should. If you're one of those people, it's just something you have to keep on doing. You have no more choice than the amoeba has in whether to be active or not. In other words, I can't stop. There are times when, for instance, I just don't feel like going up to Albany for yet another meeting of the Board of Regents, where the majority of my colleagues are going to be on one side and I'll be one of the few, sometimes the only one, on the other. But I have to get up and go. Why? Because if I didn't go

I'd feel ashamed. There's so much that needs doing there, and, like everywhere else, it's getting much harder to do. In the nineteen-sixties, the struggle was so much more clearcut. You could see the dogs and the hoses on television. It was not un-like the newsreels from Germany showing the Storm Troopers forcing Jews to scrub the sidewalks. And the *Times* would put pictures of the civil-rights demonstrators in the South on the front page. They'd also be on the network news. So people got immediate, visceral reactions to visible atrocities. But that's not what we're dealing with now. These years, children are be-ing destroyed silently, in the first and second grades."

As I was about to leave the building, I saw Russia Hughes again. Before coming to work for Dr. Clark, she had been a teacher, and, indeed, had taught his daughter at the Horace Mann–Lincoln School. We talked about Dr. Clark's unwavering focus on education, and she said, "My very first memory of him has to do with a classroom. He and Mamie brought Kate to school on her first day in the first grade. Mamie made the more striking impression on me. She had on a little, many-colored knit hat, with bits of metal dangling from it. She looked terribly elegant, terribly beautiful. And there, also, was her husband. From that day on, he came all the time, to observe the class. I'm a terribly involved kind of person, who doesn't really notice things going on outside of what I'm doing, and all of a sudden— I didn't even know *when* he first came in—I'd see Dr. Clark standing quietly in the corner. He'd stay there quite a long time. He was utterly absorbed. Not only in what Kate was doing but in the other children, too. He wanted to see children learning."

1982

LOUIS ARMSTRONG AND
RECONSTRUCTION

It was around midnight backstage at Symphony Hall in
Boston. I was about to record a radio interview with Louis
Armstrong, who had just finished a long concert. He was
tired, very tired. Louis, like Duke Ellington, always believed in
putting out everything he had for those who had paid to see
and hear him.

So all night he had grinned, and he had sung like the mel-
lowest of horns. And played with such passionate authority
that as Edmond Hall—who was Louis's clarinetist for a long
time—told me, "I still get goose pimples when Louis's sound
just gets *cracking*. Even when it's a number we've played so
often."

That night, I felt guilty taking Louis's time when he was so
beat, but he said it was okay. He talked for a long time. He
didn't grin once. He talked about race in America, what he
himself had been through, was still going through, and what
he saw ahead—which wasn't much different from now.

I lost the acetate on which the interview was recorded.
That is, I didn't remember fast enough to steal it from the sta-

tion before it got erased to use again for a wrestling match. It was a big loss because Louis seldom talked about blackness in public.

Anyway, I was not surprised when Louis did explode in public—on race—in 1957. Most people were astonished because all they knew of Louis were his grin and his big handkerchief as he sang "When It's Sleepy Time Down South" on the Ed Sullivan show. Some of the younger jazz players, the boppers, were also startled because they saw Louis as a kind of Uncle Tom. Sure, he had turned the jazz world upside down in the 1920s, but this was another age and he was a relic. A useless relic, they said, so far as fighting racism was concerned.

Orville Faubus, governor of Arkansas, had defied the Supreme Court of the United States, which had ruled in *Brown* v. *Board of Education* (1954) that all segregated public schools were inherently unequal and therefore unconstitutional. Accordingly, the Little Rock School Board had drawn up a plan to desegregate the public schools—beginning with Central High School. Faubus sent Arkansas National Guard units to block that plan and to block nine black students from entering that high school. For three weeks, the students kept coming and for three weeks the soldiers, standing shoulder to shoulder, kept them out of the schools. Meanwhile, every day, white mobs were screaming and trying to get at the kids.

In Washington, President Dwight David Eisenhower, not wishing to give in to what some called the "extremists on both sides," did nothing.

Louis Armstrong was on tour, and during a press conference—the first to my knowledge in which Louis had ever said anything that made the front pages around the country—he snapped, "The way they are treating my people in the South, the government can go to hell." As for Ike, the beloved Ike, Louis added, "The President has no guts!"

In New York, Louis Armstrong's manager, the late, terrible-tempered Joe Glaser, started roaring like one of his prize dogs. There are some who say that Glaser was "good" to Louis, sending him a sizable regular check and taking care of his other needs. There are others who have some doubts about the bookkeeping.

Nearly everyone agrees that Glaser was fond of Louis—but I'm not sure how Glaser saw that relationship. I do remember—the one time I was given an audience with Glaser, who booked a lot of other artists, many of them black—I kept looking at a decoration on his wall. It was made out of black velvet on which was superimposed a scene of antebellum plantation life. The darkies were grinning, some were strumming banjoes, and massah was basking in their sweet sounds of gratitude which, clearly, he richly deserved.

One explanation for that scene of darkies celebrating their place on Glaser's wall might have been that he had a sardonic streak. But Joe Glaser's dogs had a much more developed sense of humor than he did. And he wouldn't know sardonic from existential.

(A suggestion for Randall Kennedy, editor of *Reconstruction* magazine, about which I wrote last week: commission a piece on the economics of jazz, from the beginning to now. How much has actually changed? Do the musicians and composers get what they're due in recording royalties? What about publishing royalties for the original compositions? Do some of the players still *have* to publish in certain firms connected with the a&r man or the record company? And now that blacks are doing some of the booking into clubs, concerts, and festivals, is the playing field substantially more level for black artists these days?)

Anyway, when Joe Glaser heard what Louis Armstrong had said—in public, about the President of the United States, for Godsakes!—he sent a troubleshooter to shut Louis up. The emissary came into Louis's dressing room, relayed the orders from headquarters, and was kicked out of the dressing room by Louis.

Eight years later, when a march led by Martin Luther King in Selma, Alabama, was brutally assaulted by local and state police, Louis Armstrong, in Copenhagen, saw what had happened in Selma. Said Louis—in public—"They would beat Jesus if he was black and marched."

There were no press conferences when Louis himself was jumped by Jim Crow. In the second issue of *Reconstruction*, photographer Herb Snitzer tells of being on the road with Louis in 1960. They weren't going through Alabama or Mississippi. They were in Connecticut:

"We set out on a bright, warm Saturday afternoon, headed north, with everyone in a good mood. The bus did not have a toilet. So somewhere in Connecticut we stopped in order for Louis to go to the bathroom.

"I was stunned when the owner of a restaurant, clearly on the basis of race, refused him use of otherwise available facilities. I will never forget the look on Louis's face. Here he was, world-famous, a favorite to millions of people, America's single most identifiable entertainer, and yet excluded in the most humiliating fashion from a common convenience."

Yeah, but think of all the black people, not world-famous, who were excluded from that common convenience all over the United States and, in some places, still are.

Reconstruction magazine, in its third issue, had an essay on a writer and thinker (the two are not necessarily synonymous) who is blessedly—and bristlingly—free of orthodoxies whether he's writing about jazz or race or the politics of both, and everything else.

Stanley Crouch, when he was at this paper, was, I thought, the most challenging writer we have ever had. And the challenging didn't stop when the paper went to bed. Stanley used to stand in the newsroom dismantling some barracks of political correctness or a Spike Lee movie. Gradually, more and more people would gather around, and it was, I suppose, like the agora in ancient Athens. A marketplace of ideas. Or rather, a tournament of ideas. To win your point, you'd have to unhorse the large, gravel-throated man riding a steed of relentless reason.

In his article on Crouch, Randall Kennedy quotes from Stanley's essay on Jesse Jackson in *Notes of a Hanging Judge: Essays and Reviews, 1979–1989* (Oxford University Press). By the way, I saw Jesse Jackson recently on a train out of Washington. We had a long talk, and I was left with reactions much like these by Crouch:

"Given all the accusations made about Jackson, mixed with his handsomeness, his wit, his seductive arrogance, and his ability to lift the hearts of his listeners, the radiant reverend stands before us all as a man besmirched by his own conduct, his willingness to make pretzels of the truth, but also a figure who symbolizes American potential in his better moments and who has more populist appeal than anyone since the Kennedys and King."

Randall Kennedy notes that Stanley demands Jesse should be accorded fair play. As for the albatross of "Hymietown" and the embrace of Arafat that Jackson can't get off his neck—although he has surely tried—Crouch notes:

"Jackson is in process, and, like Lyndon Johnson, the ex-segregationist; Hugo Black, the ex-Klansman; and a bevy of others whom we must see as men who walked side by side with the Devil at times and left him later, [Jackson] should not be counted out and forced to remain in the lesser ditches of his spirit. . . . If white men can grow, so can black men."

On April 21 in Las Vegas, Jackson was speaking to the Service Employees International Union Convention:

"Ultimately it is not about black and brown and white. It's about wrong and right. It's about ethics and character. You know, when the plants close and the lights go out, you cannot use color or gender or religion for a crutch because we all look amazingly similar in the dark."

Jackson, as Stanley Crouch points out, can, from time to time, dismay those who see his potential. But he also does grow. And as Crouch says in his book, "If this man cannot be used in some way by this country, through fusing his colossal ambition to the appropriate tasks, then there is a problem of political immaturity within us much greater than any we have faced thus far. . . .

"When he spoke to over 5000 black churchgoers in Milwaukee's Mecca Auditorium, the reverend challenged his audience by going on at length about his participation in the Gay

Rights March. Jackson knew well, as could anyone watching, that most of them did not want to hear that. When he talked of embracing homosexuals who are dying and who weren't addressed in person by *one* elected official, the feeling of recoil was in the air.

"It is not right, [Jackson] said, it is not right. America can be better than that."

On the train, Jackson talked to me about the vengeance taken on Jerry Brown in New York for having said he would offer the vice-presidency to Jackson. The albatross, the immovable albatross. What more can he do, Jackson asked, to shrive himself of "Hymietown"? I had no slick answer to give him. I said—as I later did at the B'nai B'rith Hillel forum on multiculturalism in Washington—that I wondered how many of those who will not forgive Jackson nonetheless use the term *schvartze* every day or every week or every month?

Rabbi Abraham Heschel, who marched with Martin Luther King in Selma, said: "The gravest sin for a Jew is to forget what he represents."

Is that what we represent—the kind of permanent hatred against Jesse Jackson that anti-Semites direct at us?

1992

MULTICULTURAL MYTHS
ABOUT JEWS

In June, on CNN, Minister Farrakhan, no longer smiling, lashed out at Jews, adding that he had no reason to apologize to them for what they are. Long before Farrakhan was named by *Time* magazine, also in June, as one of the 25 most influential Americans, I asked a friend, Bayard Rustin—a strategist for Martin Luther King—why there was such bitter anti-Semitism among some blacks.

"It's not theological," Bayard said. "You're not being accused of killing Christ."

He was concerned, but had no further answer. Recently, I read an analysis by Clarence Page—a continually illuminating syndicated black columnist—in the *Forward*, a lively New York Jewish weekly. Page cited James Baldwin, who wrote that "Blacks are anti-Semitic because they're anti-white." Moreover, says Page, "Baldwin explained that blacks have watched Jews assimilate into mainstream white America quite rapidly compared to black folks, and many of us feel left behind, resentful."

Obviously, nothing in the American experience compares in any way to the holocaust of the Middle Passage and the terrors of slavery. But for Jews, there were certain badges of exclusion.

As a child in Boston, a cradle of abolitionism, it was foolish of me to go out alone after dark and become prey to violent, roving bands of Christian youngsters whose most satisfying sport was to break the faces of Jews. One boy on my street got an ice pick in his head and was never the same afterward. I received only a busted nose ("You Jewish, kid?") and a lot of blood on my clothes.

One of my more vivid boyhood memories is that of an old, bony Jew grabbed by his beard and thrown into the gutter by an invading hooligan—like the newsreels from Berlin.

Assimilation of Jews was not as rapid as James Baldwin thought. For a long time, there were areas of work largely closed to Jews—engineering, architecture, insurance companies, mainstream banks and corporate law firms. And there were jobs where Jews had to change their names because their own names were too Jewish. Some public schools and radio stations, for instance.

In any case, if, as James Baldwin said, blacks are anti-Semitic because they're anti-white, why the continuing obsession with only Jews? The Irish have come a long way from the rental signs in Boston: "No Dogs or Irish Need Apply." Why are Wasps given a pass? They were markedly less involved in working with blacks for justice than Jews and Catholics.

I think I may have finally come to an understanding of black anti-Semitism. As Bayard Rustin said, it is not based in theology. But, revealingly, copies of The Protocols of the Elders of Zion—a classic 19th-century tract about a worldwide Jewish conspiracy—were sold, years ago, at a Harlem mosque of the Nation of Islam. And the shadowy Protocols have also been referred to with enthusiasm in some black college newspapers.

Moreover, there are strong resemblances between the historic anti-Semitism of Father Charles E. Coughlin and that of Minister Louis Farrakhan. Coughlin had a weekly paper, Social Justice, which gave preferred space to the Protocols. It also printed Coughlin's own homilies of hate, which he included in his very popular national radio programs.

Along with my parents, I listened to those broadcasts every Sunday. We did not feel assimilated. The mellifluous priest from the Shrine of the Little Flower in Royal Oak, Mich., said he had discovered that the international Communists—and the international bankers depriving widows of their mites—had one vicious thing in common. They were all Jews.

In a remarkable multi-dimensional April profile of Minister Farrakhan in The New Yorker, Henry Louis Gates tells of Farrakhan's speeches "in which he has talked about a centuries-old conspiracy of international bankers—with names like Rothschild and Warburg—who have captured control over the central banks in many countries and who incite wars to increase the indebtedness of others and maximize their own wealth. . . . Farrakhan really does believe that a cabal of Jews secretly controls the world."

Gates adds that Farrakhan also believes that "there is a small group of Jews who meet in a Park Avenue apartment or in Hollywood to plan the course of [this] nation."

Minister Farrakhan has cemented the Nation of Islam's hatred of Jews into deeply traditional white anti-Semitism. He has, at last, found a common ground with many whites.

1996

A Racial Incident
on a Train

J ust as the New Haven, Conn., train was leaving New York's Grand Central terminal, a white woman sitting next to me turned around sharply to listen to a conversation. The black conductor, who had been genially collecting tickets, was standing next to a middle-aged white woman who looked confused.

The conductor was trying to explain to her that if she didn't have a ticket, or didn't have the money to buy one, he'd have to put her off at the next station—125th Street. That thoroughfare is in the center of Harlem. "It's the rule," the conductor said. "I have no choice."

The white woman beside me put down the romance novel she had been reading and said, to no one in particular, "He can't put her off on 125th Street!"

She rose and strode to where the conductor was still talking to the white woman who—now that I looked more carefully—appeared to have had a couple of drinks too many while waiting for the train.

My seatmate said loudly, "You cannot put her off at 125th Street! You cannot! She's in no condition to be put off the train!"

The conductor looked up, and said indignantly, "What's wrong with 125th Street? I put people off at that station all the time."

"Tell me," the conductor said to the woman, who saw herself as a good samaritan, "would you be saying this if I were letting a black woman off at 125th Street?"

In the crowded car, passengers had been talking or reading, but now everyone's attention was focused on the exchange taking place next to the seated woman, apparently without a ticket, who didn't seem aware of the controversy going on over her head.

"Would you," the conductor said again to the good samaritan, "have any objection if I were to put a black woman off at 125th Street? Why don't you answer that?"

The concerned passenger snapped back, "Yes, I would!"

"Really?" the conductor said derisively. "What you are really saying is that because 125th Street is in a black neighborhood, it's a dangerous neighborhood."

Without answering that question, the samaritan, looking down at the woman at the center of the discussion, asked the conductor, "How much is her ticket?"

He asked the woman at issue, "What's your stop?"

She looked up. "Darien," she mumbled. Darien is an upscale, predominantly white Connecticut town.

"Twelve dollars," the conductor said.

The samaritan hurried back to her seat, opened her purse, rummaged through it, and took out seven dollars. She leaned over to several white passengers across the aisle with whom she had been talking before the train started.

They were paying close attention to the dispute and looked uncomfortable when the woman beside me asked them, "Any of you got a five? I must have left my other bag at the office."

Frowning, one of them handed her, without a word, a five-dollar bill. I hadn't noticed anyone else, including me, volunteering. It was as if we were all paralyzed in acute embarrassment.

The samaritan marched over to the conductor and thrust the fare at him. He punched out a ticket and handed it to the woman from Darien, who let it fall in her lap.

Just before my stop, I was standing next to the conductor. In front of us, an infant in a stroller was fiercely wailing. "At that age," the conductor, smiling, said to me, "you can't reason with them."

"I know," I, also smiling, said. "I've had four."

Getting off the train, I asked myself why I hadn't stood and backed up the sole samaritan. Well, because I knew why the conductor had been so angry. He felt that his entire community, his family and his friends, were being stereotyped. But the good samaritan didn't understand that.

And that was why the conductor wasn't able to acknowledge that the samaritan's fear of what might happen to the woman from Darien—wandering drunk in Harlem—wasn't necessarily due to racism, though it could have been. He, because of his life experiences, believed that it surely was.

But why had I been silent? Because I didn't want to think that I was a racist?

2000

INVISIBLE MURDERS

Some 20 years ago, a friend of mine, one of the very few African-American reporters then at the *New York Post,* told me of a call he had received the day before at the paper. It was a tip on a murder on Park Avenue. The reporter told his editor, "I'm going right up."

"Wait a minute," said the editor. "What's the address?"

It was uptown. Harlem.

"No," the editor said, "we're not covering that."

Not much has changed since then. In the April 13 New York *Daily News,* Stanley Crouch, a columnist who is black, noted that "for all the reduction in homicide" under Mayor Rudolph W. Giuliani, "50% of those murdered in this city" are African Americans and Latinos. Crouch added that these so-called "minorities"—though half the population in the city—"suffer 75% of the violent crime."

Nationally—as Rod Dreher reported in the April 9 New York *Daily News*—"according to most recent [U.S.] Justice Department statistics, in 1998, blacks were seven times more likely to commit homicide, and six times more likely to be . . . murder victim[s]" than whites.

There is some coverage of black-on-black crime, particularly when a given act is stunningly vicious and gruesome. But, in terms of the less-than-startling run of common muggings, rapes, and murders, white readers know very little of individual black victims of crime.

One of the few who consistently reports on these victims in the nation's capital is Colbert I. King, whose column appears every Saturday morning at the top of the Op-Ed page of *The Washington Post.* I've always seen stories on African-American victims of crime in the black press, but King's continued prominence in a white newspaper is very rare.

On April 1, King wrote, not for the first time, about the murder of 16-year-old Tia Mitchell, shot in the head and neck as she rode her bicycle in her own neighborhood, within sight of the Capitol dome. The gang member charged with her killing, David Reginald Johnson (a k a "Stinka"), allegedly shot her because he believed she was associated with a member of another gang. Johnson was 15 at the time.

How did King first come to focus on this murder that happened four years ago? "It earned a place in my mind," he wrote this April, "by the insignificance . . . it was assigned" at the time in *The Washington Post:* "a two-inch item on Page D5 simply headlined, 'Girl, 16, Slain While Cycling in NW Alley.' No name, no motive, nothing."

Only King kept digging into the story, as he has with other ignored crimes against blacks—those human beings, he said in one column, "with whom we don't identify or think much about." At the end of another column, he noted that Tia Mitchell's mother had called him to see if he could help her find out what was happening to her daughter's alleged killer.

"She said," King wrote, "no one downtown would return her calls."

Because too many newspapers treat such crimes as so "routine" as to be not worth the space to report on them—except occasionally for stories based on generalized crime statistics—readers have no sense of who the victims were or who their families are.

Making diversity in newsrooms a priority in more substantive ways than in speeches at conferences should not result in assigning African-American reporters solely—or even primarily—to black news. As many nonminority journalists have shown again and again, no beat should have a color line. But it is reasonable to expect that many journalists of color would be as aware as King of the stories of black crime victims that are routinely downplayed, if reported at all. And as more nonmajority readers find there are reporters who want to know about these cases, they will call—just as King keeps getting calls from people who live in neighborhoods where white reporters easily get lost, as I have in Washington.

In November 1996, King wrote of "a world of people who are treated by the rest of us as so worthless that a Southeast Washington man could be shot at a gas station last Sunday night, pursued by his attacker to the hospital, and then be shot once again outside the emergency room—this time fatally—by the same gunman, and then have his name mentioned only briefly on Page B8 of the *Post*. Hell, if he'd been a Capitol Hill staffer or a downtown lobbyist, he would at least have made [the] 'Style' [section]."

King also wrote in that column about another call from Tia Mitchell's mother, who said of her daughter's alleged killer—at the time still on the loose—"I don't want him dead. Dying is too easy. That's been proven to me."

She wanted—and still wants—"just a little bit of justice and peace," King wrote. "In that part of the world, they need that, too: So I keep coming back to the pain."

Nothing should stop white reporters and editors from coming back to the pain, but the presence of more black colleagues might awaken them to that pain.

2000

ONE BOY'S
"SENSITIVITY TRAINING"

D awn Letus lives in a largely integrated neighborhood—Ulster County in upstate New York. Her 13-
year-old son, Vincent, who is white, is in the eighth
grade at Accord Middle School. His best friend, who is black,
sits next to him in social studies class.

Recently Vincent's mother told me of a lesson her son had
learned in race relations in that class. The teacher was dis-
cussing what happened when black people, freed from slavery,
came north. They were willing, she said, to work for as little as
50 cents a day. Vincent jokingly asked his black friend if he
would work for 50 cents a day. The girl at the desk behind
Vincent said, "That was rude!"

"What was rude?" the teacher asked. Another student told
her what Vincent had said. The teacher, feeling that this was
too important to wait until she could speak to the two boys after class, decided to talk to all the kids about racism. The
teacher told Vincent she knew he was only joking, and his
black friend said it hadn't bothered him; he knew Vinnie. But

then, with racism as the topic of the day, some of his class-mates attacked Vincent in class for his racism.

News of the incident spread to other classrooms—and to the cafeteria. Vincent, within hours, was known throughout the school as a racist. Back in class, he cried in front of the other students. He was so embarrassed that it took him awhile to tell his parents what had happened. "Vincent," his mother, Dawn Letus, told me, "was horrified at the idea that anyone would consider him a racist. Like me, he has always taken one person at a time."

Vincent's teacher explained that this social issue had to be dealt with in the marketplace of ideas that is her classroom. Dawn Letus replied that her son had been involved in a pri-vate conversation. "I understand," Mrs. Letus says, "that the teacher believes that racial issues ought to be discussed openly, but she didn't have to do that by making my son the center of the discussion when he hadn't said anything racist."

When I spoke to the principal, Peter Beckwith, he said brusquely, "that matter has been settled internally." I asked him if he had anything more to say. Mr. Beckwith said he would get back to me. He has not.

Vincent has had a lesson in sensitivity training. It takes place, one way or another, in many classrooms—from elemen-tary grades through graduate school classes. In Brooklyn re-cently, a white first-year teacher, Ruth Sherman, had sudden sensitivity training. As reported in *The Washington Post* Dec. 3, she was having her mostly black and Hispanic third-grade class at PS75 read a book, "Nappy Hair," written by Carolivia Herron, an assistant professor of English at California State University in Chico.

Herron's grandfather had told her to be proud of her nappy hair, and she wrote the book to celebrate diversity and help children be proud of who they are.

Armed with out-of-sequence photocopies of some pages from the book, a number of black parents bitterly condemned Ruth Sherman at a school board meeting. Some of them threatened her.

"Here was a teacher," Carolivia Herron told the New York newspapers, "doing what many don't have the nerve to do— giving black children, especially little girls, self-esteem."

Most of the parents at PS75 eventually rallied around Ruth Sherman, but she's afraid to return. "Nappy Hair" will not be banned at PS75. Meanwhile, the children are confused. They burst into tears when they found out the teacher wasn't coming back.

The reading scores at PS75 are low, too low. Ruth Sherman, while still in college, was a volunteer reading tutor at PS75. Now, she says, "My children lost two days of instruction at a very important time of the year."

She has now decided she will never again assign an "offensive" book.

1999

BREAKING THROUGH
RACIAL BARRIERS

On Jan. 19, 1994, Janice Camarena Ingraham, a student at San Bernardino Community College in California, began her first day of English 101. A widowed mother of three small children, she was eager to absorb as much education as she could because she expected to have to support her family for a long time to come. She was 24.

In front of the class, the instructor told Ms. Ingraham that she had to leave the room because the class was reserved for only African-American students. As she went out the door, the laughter of the students followed her.

The class was part of the Black Bridge Program that is geared to enabling black students to go on to four-year colleges. And it is largely successful in that goal. Those students receive special academic counseling and seminars, black mentors who advise on career development, and other targeted services.

The Black Bridge project exists on several dozen campuses in the community college system, as does the Puente Project that provides Latinos with special academic support. Ingraham also tried to enter the Puente Project but was informed that because she is white, there was no place for her.

Ingraham told me that the double-rejection made her realize that while one of her three children could in time enter the Puente Project, the other two would, like their mother, be excluded. Her eligible child is half Mexican-American.

As she said to the *Crestline Courier-News* at the time, "I have told my daughters they'd be treated fairly, regardless of race, but now they couldn't even attend the same college class together."

Furthermore, Ingraham discovered that there were black students in the Black Bridge project who came out of a background that was more economically advantaged than her own. By contrast to those students, she could be defined as disadvantaged.

Janice Ingraham decided to break down the racial and ethnic barriers in the California community colleges. She found the right lawyer, Robert Corry, who is on the staff of the Pacific Legal Foundation, a conservative outfit. Corry is particularly interested in free speech cases and in countering the separation of college students "into ethnic enclaves and telling them they can only succeed in an atmosphere restricted to other members of their race and mentors of their race."

I first knew Corry when, as a recent graduate of Stanford Law School, he succeeded in having its speech code overturned even though he was faced in court by the university's high-priced attorneys. It was like Paul Newman v. James Mason in "The Verdict."

Ingraham's lawsuit wound up in the Federal District Court for the Eastern district of California. It resulted in a settlement that affects the nation's largest community college system—with its 106 campuses—and it may influence colleges in other states.

Ingraham did not ask for compensatory damages. She wanted all students to be treated fairly. This is what she won, as summarized by the *Chronicle of Higher Education*:

"Course catalogues and other marketing tools produced by the system may no longer describe certain offerings as 'designed' for black or Hispanic students. The system also cannot choose mentors or counselors for students on the basis of race."

That is, the system cannot mandate that students of one race choose mentors or counselors of the same race. But the students themselves can choose the mentors they want.

At the core of the settlement is that "all academic and educational programs at the California community colleges shall be open equally to students regardless of race, color, national origin or ethnicity."

Programs to help black and Mexican-American students move on to four-year colleges will continue, and those students will be able to tell clearly from the description of the course content what it's about. But now, no students will be told to leave the room because of their color.

A considerable number of signatures supporting Janice Ingraham were circulated by students. The petition said: "We do not feel that anyone has the right to tell students that we do not belong together because we are of different races. In 1954, the Supreme Court outlawed racial segregation in public schools. We feel that it is time that the public education system acknowledge the laws of the United States of America."

Among the signers were a number of black and Mexican-American students.

Recently, Janice Ingraham enrolled her children at a school in Lake Arrowhead, where she lives. A clerk reminded her she had neglected to check the box that declared the race of her children.

"I told her," says Ingraham, "that they're human."

1996

PART 4

THE BEAST OF
POLITICS

THE MARK OF THE BEAST

From *Speaking Freely*, Knopf (1997)

While we often disagree—as on abortion—Margot and I were as one in our opposition to the Vietnam War, though she went further than I did; for example, she committed civil disobedience, alongside A. J. Muste, in the entrance to an Atomic Energy Commission office.

We also shared disgust at those prestigious antiwar liberals who supported an end to violence in Vietnam while simultaneously nodding in approval at violence committed at home by antiwar activists. Some of these whited sepulchers, for instance, appeared at a sentencing hearing for a student who—in his zeal to show how opposed he was to the war in Vietnam—had bombed a University of Wisconsin building, killing a researcher inside.

This was the revolting underside of the antiwar movement.

On August 24, 1970, the University of Wisconsin's Army Mathematics Research Center was bombed. It happened at around four o'clock in the morning, and resulted in the death

| 251 |

of thirty-three-year-old Robert Fassnacht, a physicist, who, unfortunately for him and his family, was working very late.

After the bombing and death, the Marion Delgado Collective—who "accepted the terrible responsibility" for the act—declared in an unsigned pronunciamento: "While the major pure research center of the Army was demolished, a man was killed and others injured when the blast went off four minutes early. For this death, there can be no rationalization. But while we mourn an unnecessary death, we celebrate the blow to U.S. imperialism. . . . "

In the September 10, 1970, *Voice,* I wrote the following:

These young men—having grown up during a time when the normative public speech in America has been newspeak (antihuman speech that has caused so many deaths)—have themselves become so infected by this murderous corruption of meaning that they too are executioners.

"We accept the terrible responsibility"—What does that *mean?* In what fundamental sense does it differ from all those statements by all those American spokesmen who also accept "the terrible responsibility" for all those deaths in Vietnam but then go on—in each next sentence—to "celebrate" each new blow to what they call "Communist aggression"?

A man has been killed. What do his executioners have to say to his wife and children? We goofed. The blast went off four minutes early. But we will not rationalize. We mourn. We mourn and yet we celebrate.

How easy. How terribly easy. Our official leaders have always been expert at mourning in the abstract. They also do what they have to do for the greater good of some other abstraction. But because of them, specific people die. Now, because of a set of "revolutionary" abstractions, one more man has died. In the name of humankind, of course.

Lyndon Johnson and Richard Nixon, meet the members of the Marion Delgado Collective.

More than three years later, Karl Armstrong, one of the bombers for peace, was in court in Madison, Wisconsin. He had pleaded guilty to reduced state charges of second-degree murder and arson. And he pleaded guilty to several federal charges.

For some days, a mitigation hearing, based on Armstrong's character, was held before a circuit judge in Madison. On the basis of that hearing, Armstrong's sentence would be determined.

In the mail I received exculpatory literature from the Karl Armstrong Defense Fund. Its thrust was that the Math Center bombing, in a year that had witnessed the American invasion of Cambodia, came about because "we had been protesting against this war for so long and it seemed then that the government just wasn't able to listen to its own citizens, to those of the world."

What about citizen Fassnacht? The Karl Armstrong Defense Committee said: "A life was lost in the attack. An action carried out in the name of humanity inadvertently killed a man."

Sorry about that.

"The bombing," the Karl Armstrong Defense Committee further clarified the issue, "was a political act in which the government is the victim."

But the government survived. The committee's justification continued:

In Madison, on September 28 [1973], Karleton Armstrong assumed the responsibility for the bombing: he has acknowledged that it was, in fact, he who attacked the building," the Defense Committee continued. "He does not by himself assume the responsibility for the death of Robert Fassnacht. Though sorrowful, Karl, with other anti-war activists here, realizes that the loss must be shared by those who carried out the war in Indochina, setting the context and the imperative for acts of resistance against their policies. . . . Far from being a criminal, we feel Karl to be just one of many who took actions when they saw the results of our acts.

A gentle and courageous man, Karl is admitting the facts to avert the example he feels that the government would make of the case and, most importantly, he is doing it so that at his hearing to determine sentence, the facts of the war will themselves be put on trial.

And the facts of the war were put on trial. On October 16, John F. Naveau, a thirty-eight-year-old former Marine Corps sergeant, testified that he had been responsible for the deaths of twenty-four Vietnamese schoolchildren. A former army man, after testifying that brutality against Vietnamese civilians had been commonplace, pointed toward Karl Armstrong and said, "I feel a lot more criminal than him."

On October 19, former Senator Ernest Gruening of Alaska, who, with Wayne Morse, had been alone in the Senate against the war for a long time, testified for Karl Armstrong. Gruening, now seventy-six, told the judge that war resisters deserved not "castigation, but an accolate. . . . All acts of resistance to this war are fully justified—in whatever form they take."

Or, as the Karl Armstrong Defense Committee put it, "Karl deserves your continuing support not only because his actions were motivated by deep feelings of love and sorrow, but because he is continuing to resist the government now and in the coming weeks and years."

On the day of Gruening's appearance, Professor Richard Falk of Princeton, also a longtime and knowledgeable opponent of the war, cited, according to the *New York Times*, "the Nuremberg trials as precedent for defense assertions that private American citizens had 'a right, and perhaps a duty' to actively oppose the war by any means. . . . Scientists who worked at the mathematics center are 'indictable for war crimes conspiracy, depending on the extent of their knowledge and involvement.'" Professor Falk's authority for that statement was the Nuremberg code, which, he said, "was formulated with the assistance of the United States government."

Robert Fassnacht, it turned out, was not working on anything to do with the war. But what if he was?

On October 22, six former students who had become radical activists at the University of Wisconsin in the late 1960s agreed (as one of them, Billy Kaplan, said tearfully) that the bombing of the Math Center came from the "highest motivation." The bombing, he explained, was intended as an "affirmation of life" to "hinder" the Vietnam War.

Philip Berrigan, the former priest, said that "Robert Fassnacht's death is mourned but I believe very profoundly that it was accidental and has to be balanced by the calculated deaths of millions."

Is that the profundity we have as a legacy from this branch of the peace movement? That you can "balance" one death against those of millions? And that you can do this balancing in the name of humanity?

The corpse of Robert Fassnacht ought not to be explained away so glibly on the thesis that because the United States government criminally took life wholesale, an individual American had the right—and perhaps the duty (according to Professor Falk)—to oppose that war actively by any means, even if his actions resulted, however accidentally, in one retail death.

The taking of a life—any life, on any side—should not be so glancingly dismissed as the death of Robert Fassnacht has been dismissed (with routine expressions of regret) by those who consider themselves to be affirmers of life.

The literature of the Karl Armstrong Defense Fund, for instance, said that the bombing took place "between semesters at 4 a.m. on a Monday morning, with a warning telephoned into the police."

The Karl Armstrong Defense Committee somehow neglected to mention that the warning was telephoned just *three minutes* before the explosion. Obviously that gesture of "warning" was perfunctory, as perfunctory as Philip Berrigan's fleeting reference to such "sad happenings" as the death of Robert Fassnacht.

Then there is the primary excuse by Armstrong and his supporters for this unfortunate accident. Peaceful demonstrations had not worked. The destruction of draft-board records had not worked. Nearly every witness at the Madison hearing implied or stated explicitly that Karl Armstrong had been driven to bomb the building because he felt so keenly the frustration of the continuing war and the continuing research-for-death at the Army Mathematics Research Center.

In his frustration, Armstrong fulfilled the prophecy of Father Daniel Berrigan: "The mark of inhuman treatment of humans is . . . the mark of the beast, whether its insignia is the military or the movement."

And:

"A revolution is interesting insofar as it avoids like the plague the plague it promised to heal."

Consider, by contrast, Cesar Chavez and his long, hard march—in the context of the "revolutionary" act of Karl Armstrong. Chavez wrote:

I was talking to a teamster in Coachella. He said, "Don't be such a coward. Take the women and kids out of there and you men stand up and let's fight it out." And I said, "Why? Do you want to beat us up? We're game. Beat the women and kids too. What's the difference?" And he started complaining, "Ah, we don't even know who in the hell we're fighting when we fight you guys. If we fight the worker, we've got to fight with his wife and his kids and his grandmother and his grandfather and the first, second, third, fourth, and fifth cousins!"

And I said, "That's right! Plus millions of other brothers and sisters throughout the country in the labor movement, the religious communities, the blacks, the whites. You'll have to fight everybody. And we make it that way. . . .

"Farmworkers everywhere are angry and worried, but we are not going to fall into the trap that you have fallen into. We do not need to kill or destroy to win. We are a movement that builds and not destroys."

Chavez and the United Farm Workers, of course, never did anything quite as exciting as blowing up buildings, with or without people in them, but Chavez and the UFW certainly avoided like the plague the mark of the beast.

The killing act of Karl Armstrong did not particularly surprise me. I have known a number of people who have believed in the necessity of violence—for personal revenge, for historical revenge, to shock the populace into recognition of a horrifying injustice that must be paid for.

What did somewhat surprise me was the testimony at Armstrong's sentencing hearing of such self-satisfied liberals as Daniel Ellsberg, Professor Richard Falk, Senator Ernest Gruening, and Philip Berrigan. I wondered if any of them had read Arthur Koestler's novel *Darkness at Noon*, a chillingly illuminating exploration of ends so infected by means that they bore the mark of the beast. It was based on fact, on Stalin's facts on the ground.

I knew, and interviewed, Daniel Ellsberg during those years, and respected him for his liberation of the Pentagon Papers. I never doubted the seriousness of his commitment to finding a way to end the war in Vietnam. But, at Karl Armstrong's sentencing hearing, Ellsberg—as reported in Tom Bates's valuable book *Reds* (HarperCollins)—said, "However misguided, the bombing by Karl was a conscientious action."

To which the prosecutor, Michael Zeleski—a Wisconsin assistant attorney general—replied:

"Let's look at his act. He saw cars parked there. He saw bikes parked in the rack. He saw lights on. What did he do? He lit the fuse and walked away."

1997

RESCUING HIV INFANTS
FROM ACLU DOGMA

In recent years, several New York newspapers and magazines have reported the rage and hopelessness of women, many of them black and Latina, who have discovered for the first time that their very young children are infected with the HIV virus.

"They should have told me," said one furious woman, "so I could have taken care of myself—and him."

These women were subject to the state's strict confidentiality law that was part of the epidemiological test of all infants to track the geographical spread of the infection leading to AIDS. If an infant tested positive for HIV, the results were not routinely given to the mother or her doctor because of discrimination against people with AIDS. The information shouldn't get out. But the results of tests for other diseases were revealed.

Every year, some 1,200 to 1,400 infants test positive in New York state. Seventy-five percent are simply carrying their infected mothers' antibodies and are not truly infected. But 25 percent are leaving the hospital without treatment; these chil-

dren, their infection undisclosed, are prey to devastating op-
portunistic attacks on their immune systems.

And although the 75 percent are healthy when they get
home, the mothers are infected, and in their lack of knowledge, they can infect the child through breast feeding.

Since May of this year, New York hospitals have been required to at least ask new mothers if they want to be told the
test results. Of 18,150 mothers surveyed in the month of May,
11,200 never answered the question and 1,038 did not want to
know.

As the number of dead and dying infants increased, a state
assemblywoman, Nettie Mayersohn tried for three years to
get a bill passed requiring mandatory testing of all newborns—with the results given to their mothers. And to their
physicians.

Mayersohn is a Democrat, a feminist, and in 1989, the National Organization for Women named her Legislator of the
Year.

Since she started to spread the word of these careless
deaths, Mayersohn has been bitterly opposed by the National
Organization for Women, gay groups, AIDS activists, some
medical organizations and the American Civil Liberties
Union.

They charge that mandatory testing of infants—which reveals the fact that the mothers are infected—is a violation of
privacy. Also, they say, forced testing would lead mothers to
flee the health care system. There is no evidence of that, but
there is growing evidence of mothers cursing the ignorance in
which they were kept for their "protection."

The ACLU and others demand that mothers be counseled to take the test voluntarily. That approach has had only scattered success in New York's hospitals. Moreover, many poor women do not get to a hospital before giving birth. So they get no prenatal counseling of any kind at all.

Nettie Mayersohn never gave up. (This lethal secrecy, it should be noted, has also been going on in many other states, but the story made news only in New York because of Mayersohn.) "I got up with it in the morning," she told me, "and I went to sleep with it."

At last, in June, Nettie Mayersohn's bill passed both houses and was signed by Gov. George Pataki. In the assembly, she was given a standing ovation.

The new law was the first in the country to require mandatory testing of all newborns—and disclosure of the results to the mothers. (A bill passed by Congress earlier this year had many preliminary stages and did not kick in until 2000.)

"Every infected HIV baby," Nettie Mayersohn says, "will finally be able to access health care and treatment that really can prolong and enhance their lives. And under my law, infants who are not infected will be protected from getting infected through breast feeding." And if treatment is early enough, an infant with the virus may be able to escape AIDS.

Since infected newborns will now qualify for the quality of treatment that adults with AIDS rightfully demand, one would think that AIDS activists would have fought for the infected infants all along. But they have not.

At the end of June this year, the American Medical Association endorsed mandatory testing throughout the country of all newborns for the AIDS virus—as well as all pregnant women because it has been established that pregnant women who are tested and treated can cut the risk to the unborn child by two-thirds.

Meanwhile, the ACLU has expressed no regrets to certain grieving mothers. As one of them put it, "We should not have been protected to death."

1996

THE AWFUL PRIVACY OF
BABY DOE

Eighteen months had passed since the Indiana baby, born with Down's syndrome and a defective digestive system, had been allowed to die of starvation and dehydration. But Linda McCabe, a registered nurse in the special-care nursery of Bloomington Hospital, was still mourning both the infant and her inability to save him.

"At least I wasn't part of the killing," she told me when I asked her to talk about it. "The other nurses in special care and I told the hospital administration we would not help starve that child. So the baby was moved to another part of the hospital, and the parents had to hire private nurses."

Linda McCabe, remembering the evening the orders came to give the baby nothing by mouth and no intravenous feeding, became angry all over again. "Who did they think they were—asking me to do something like that? By the fourth day it go so bad, thinking about that baby just lying there, crying, that some of us nurses started checking in law books to see if we could find some legal arguments to stop the killing of that baby. But as it turned out he only had two more days to live."

I had found Linda McCabe through a Bloomington pediatrician, James Schaffer, who when the baby was born had strongly recommended routine surgery to correct the infant's deformed esophagus, so that he could eat normally. The parents rejected Dr. Schaffer's advice. They did not want a retarded child.

It is impossible to tell so soon after birth whether a child with Down's syndrome will be mildly, moderately, or severely retarded. The coroner wrote later: "The potential for mental function and social integration of this child, as of all infants with Down's syndrome, is unknown."

Nonetheless, the parents had agreed with their obstetrician, Dr. Walter Owens, that a child with Down's syndrome cannot attain what Dr. Owens called "a minimally adequate quality of life." On the baby's last day Dr. Schaffer and two colleagues, despite the wishes of the parents, went, bearing intravenous equipment, to feed the baby. They were too late. The process of dying could not be reversed.

The baby died on April 15, 1982. Two days later *The Evansville* [Indiana] *Courier* printed a letter from Sherry McDonald: "The night before little Infant Doe died, I called the Indiana Supreme Court and told them I wanted the baby saved. Then my 16-year-old called and said, 'I am a Down's syndrome child and I want the baby boy saved.'"

I had come to Dr. Schaffer and Linda McCabe while trying to learn more about this form of infanticide—the decision by parents and physicians to deny lifesaving medical treatment (and sometimes nourishment) to handicapped babies. I had started looking into the subject because of conversations I'd had, in New York and elsewhere, with nurses and pediatric surgeons who felt that unless more public attention were paid to quiet killings, they would continue and perhaps increase, as if these newborns were still unborn, and therefore subject to the summary judgment of abortion.

One specialist in the treatment of newborns has terminated so many brief lives that, as he told B. D. Colen, the science editor for *Newsday,* he has a recurring dream: "I've died and I'm going to Heaven, and as I go through the gates, I see what looks like this field of gently waving grass. When I look closely, it's babies, slowly undulating back and forth—the babies I've shut off."

A good many of those lives could not have been saved, because the infants were born dying. Even doctors and nurses who are critical of the ways in which irreversible decisions are made in neonatal intensive-care units would not want heroic measures to be taken in these and certain other cases: babies born with only a brainstem, for instance, or with Lesch-Nyhan syndrome, an incurable hereditary disorder that leads to mental retardation, uncontrollable spasms, and self-mutilation.

At issue are lives that could be saved, the lives of infants with such handicaps as Down's syndrome, cerebral palsy, and spina bifida. Spina bifida involves a lesion in the spinal column that can be repaired through surgery, the sooner after birth the better. Without surgery there is considerable likelihood of infection, which can lead to permanent brain damage. Nearly all children with spina bifida also have an accumulation of spinal fluid within the brain. Unless a shunt is inserted to drain the fluid, the pressure on the brain can and often does lead to mental retardation.

As a result of these medical procedures, however, along with knowledgeable follow-up treatment, children with spina bifida can grow up to be bright, productive adults, who may need braces in order to walk. Yet death is the prescription some doctors give for newborns with spina bifida. The prediction is that the child will never walk, will be severely retarded, and will suffer progressively worse bladder and bowel problems. In one highly publicized case, that of Baby Jane Doe on Long Island, the physician chosen by the parents added that the child would be in constant pain throughout her dismal life.

The leading medical expert on spina bifida is Dr. David McLone, the chief of neurosurgery at Children's Memorial Hospital, in Chicago. McLone has successfully operated on hundreds of infants with spina bifida, and he and his staff follow the children for several years and perform indicated surgery and other therapy. He asserts that physicians who do not know enough about spina bifida leave infants with that handicap untreated in hospitals throughout the country. In an interview on CBS-TV's *Sunday Morning* last August, McLone said, "Physicians are making decisions not to treat certain numbers of these children on the basis of criteria that are invalid. They are assuming that by examining a newborn child they can predict the quality of life or how independent or how productive that child is going to be, how much stress that child is going to be on the family, how much of a burden on society. They make all of these judgments based on that initial exam, and almost every one of the criteria that they use to make that judgment is invalid."

Invalid or not, as a result of those judgments many infants with spina bifida and other handicaps are allowed to die. It is as if we were already living in that ideal special-care nursery envisioned (in the context of a discussion of quality-of-life issues) by Francis Crick, the 1962 Nobel laureate in medicine and physiology: "No newborn infant should be declared human until it has passed certain tests regarding its genetic endowment and . . . if it fails these tests, it forfeits the right to live."

No one knows exactly how many Baby Does forfeit their right to live each year. No death certificate is going to declare infanticide as the cause of an infant's departure. With regard to babies with Down's syndrome, Dr. Norman Fost, a professor of pediatrics at the University of Wisconsin, noted in the December, 1982, issue of *Archives of Internal Medicine*: "It is common in the United States to withhold routine surgery and medical care from infants with Down's syndrome for the explicit purpose of hastening death." With regard to infants otherwise handicapped, the President's Commission for the Study of Ethical Problems in Medicine declared in its March, 1983, report, "Deciding to Forego Life-Sustaining Treatment": "Decisions to forego therapy are part of everyday life in the neonatal intensive care unit; *with rare exceptions, these choices have been made by parents and physicians without review by courts or any other body*" (emphasis added).

In consideration of the shock and grief of parents, such decisions must be private, the American Medical Association and most physicians insist. The American Civil Liberties Union tacitly agrees. In Baby Doe cases, after the whistle has been blown by a nurse or a right-to-life organization, not once has an ACLU affiliate spoken for the infant's right to due process and equal protection under the law. Indeed, when the ACLU has become involved, it has fought resolutely for the parents' right to privacy. Baby Doe's own awful privacy, as he or she lies dying, is also thereby protected.

Along with my fellow civil libertarians, most liberals strongly support parents, and only parents, in these situations. It is hard to imagine anyone more powerless than a handicapped baby who has just been given the black spot, but to my knowledge no organization of liberals or civil-rights group has ever said a word about the rights of Baby Does. Nor has any feminist group, even though the civil rights and liberties being violated in these infanticides are not only those of males.

I have discovered, moreover, that most members of these groups do not take kindly to questions on the subject. Some liberals and feminists, for instance, have told me sharply that if I were to look more closely at the kinds of people trying to save those Baby Does, I would understand that such rescue efforts are a way to make women subservient again to those who would tell them what they can and cannot do with their own bodies.

It is true that the most prominent defenders of the Baby Does are such conservative hobgoblins as Ronald Reagan, the right-to-life squadrons, and the Reverend Jerry Falwell. Having picked up bad companions so early in life, the Baby Does indeed bear out the adage that people are judged by the company they keep.

After mighty internal struggles, a few liberals have decided that handicapped infants might, after all, have some constitutional rights independent of their parents' wishes for them. One such heretic, a professor of education with a history of

At the end of their article Duff and Campbell, having discussed the ethical and legal implications of decisions (including ones in which they participated) to let infants die, wrote: "If working out these dilemmas in ways such as those we suggest is in violation of the law, we believe the law should be changed."

An authoritative guide in these particular legal matters is John A. Robertson, a professor of law at the University of Texas and the author of *The Rights of the Critically Ill*. Robertson asserts that an infant born with severe mental and physical disabilities has the same right to be treated as anyone else, new or old. That right, Robertson says, "does not depend on his IQ, physical abilities, or social potential." The only exceptions are "a few very extreme cases in which . . . the burdens of treatment outweigh the benefits," as when the treatment inflicts severe pain and only delays death briefly. Otherwise, even though certain handicapped infants "appear from the perspective of 'normal' people to face a meaningless or greatly limited life," that is no justification "for denying them essential medical treatments."

Accordingly, Robertson says, parents who refuse treatment for infants with such handicaps as Down's syndrome and spina bifida "with the intent and result that they die" can be prosecuted for murder or manslaughter, not to mention child abuse and neglect. Physicians in these cases can also be prosecuted, for homicide, child neglect, and violation of child-abuse reporting laws (the parents should have been reported).

Yet Drs. Duff and Campbell, and the parents who agreed to the denial of treatment for their children, were not charged with any crime. Actually, Robertson says, "while parents of retarded children have been convicted for directly killing them, there has been only one prosecution of parents and doctors for nontreatment of defective newborns." In that case the charges were dismissed, because no one would testify at a preliminary hearing that the parents and doctors had ordered that the Baby Does—Siamese twins joined at the waist—be starved to death.

That prosecutions have been so rare is traceable to a widespread belief that decisions about the welfare of newborn infants should be made only by the parents and physicians. A more proximate factor is the infrequency with which these infant deaths become known outside the nursery. On occasion the refusal of treatment to a handicapped infant does become news—as with the Bloomington baby and, in 1983, with Baby Jane Doe on Long Island. But in neither of these cases were the parents prosecuted.

Very occasionally a court's attention is drawn to a Baby Doe who seems about to die. The hospital, unsure of its legal ground, may initiate the court action lest it be sued later for complicity in the killing of the infant. Or an outsider, learning of the imminent death from a nurse or someone else in the hospital, may try to bring a court action to save the child. No consistent pattern of court decisions has emerged, although treatment has been ordered more often than not in the relatively few cases that have come before a judge.

In one such case an infant was born with only one eye, no ear canals, a deformed esophagus, and almost certain brain damage. He soon developed convulsive seizures of unknown cause. The parents wanted him starved to death, and their doctor agreed. But Justice David Roberts, of the superior court in Cumberland County, Maine, ruled in February, 1974, that "at the moment of live birth, there does exist a human being entitled to the fullest protection of the law. The most basic right enjoyed by every human being is the right to life itself."

The doctor in the case had predicted that should the infant live, he would not have a life worth living. Said Justice Roberts: "The doctor's qualitative evaluation of the value of the life to be preserved is not legally within the scope of his expertise." The baby died soon after the ruling, but Justice Roberts told me ten years later that he had no regrets about his decision, because the infant had been entitled to his chance to live.

But Justice Roberts would not have known about this Baby Doe if the hospital and, initially, the parents' doctor had not asked for a hearing because they wanted to treat the child (the doctor later changed his mind). No court intervened, however, in any of the forty-three infant deaths described by Drs. Duff and Campbell in their *New England Journal* article. No court knew about any of the cases. Indeed, no one except doctors reading that medical journal might have learned about the killings if *Newsweek* had not picked up the story.

In its coverage of death as a management option at Yale–New Haven Hospital, *Newsweek* used the term *vegetables* to describe some severely handicapped newborns who eventually died. Sondra Diamond wrote a letter to the magazine, and here is some of what she said:

I'll wager my entire root system and as much fertilizer as it would take to fill Yale University that you have never received a letter from a vegetable before this one, but, much as I resent the term, I must confess that I fit the description of a "vegetable" as defined in the article. . . .

Due to severe brain damage incurred at birth, I am unable to dress myself, toilet myself, or write; my secretary is typing this letter. Many thousands of dollars had to be spent on my rehabilitation and education in order for me to reach my present professional status as a Counseling Psychologist. My parents were also told, 35 years ago, that there was "little or no hope of achieving meaningful 'humanhood'" for their daughter [afflicted with cerebral palsy].

Have I reached "humanhood"? Compared with Doctors Duff and Campbell, I believe I have surpassed it!

Instead of changing the law to make it legal to weed out us "vegetables," let us change the laws so that we may receive quality medical care, education, and freedom to live as full and productive lives as our potentials allow.

Four years later, in 1977, Sondra Diamond wrote an afterword in *Human Life Review*. She told of being taken to the hospital with third-degree burns over 60 percent of her body when she was in her early twenties. "The doctors felt that there was no point in treating me because I was disabled anyway, and could not lead a normal life," she reported. "They wanted to let me die. My parents, after a great deal of arguing, convinced the doctors that I was a junior in college and had been leading a normal life. However, they had to bring in pictures of me swimming and playing the piano."

The doctors were still reluctant to treat her, but Sondra Diamond's parents insisted. Once she was again living what she considered a normal life, Diamond observed: "To take the time and effort to expend medical expertise on a person who is physically disabled seems futile to many members of the medical profession. Their handiwork will come to naught, they think." Even so, she said, "I would not give up one moment of life in which I could have another cup of coffee, another cigarette, or another interaction with someone I love."

Some physicians' prophecies about imperfect babies are shown to be startlingly wrong when the child has a chance to live long enough to confound the prediction. A particularly vivid illustration of auguries turned upside down appeared as part of *Death in the Nursery*, a 1983 series on the Boston television station WNEV-TV. The segment focused on two classmates in a West Haven, Connecticut, elementary school, Jimmy Arria and Kimberly Mekdeci. The boy, born prematurely, had weighed only four and a half pounds at birth, contracted pneumonia a day later, and suffered seizures. The girl was born with spina bifida.

A pediatrician suggested to the parents of both infants that they choose death as the preferred management option. Kimberly Mekdeci's father remembers that doctor saying that his daughter would probably grow up to be a vegetable. The quality of Jimmy Arria's life, the doctor predicted, would be very poor.

Jimmy Arria is a good student; Kim is also bright. According to the parents of both children, the physician who counseled death back in the nursery was Dr. Raymond Duff.

Not all physicians approve of withholding treatment for the parents' and the baby's own good. *The New England Journal of*

Medicine, shortly after the Duff-Campbell report had appeared, published a letter from Dr. Joan L. Venes and Dr. Peter R. Huttenlocher, of the Yale University School of Medicine:

> As consultants to the newborn special-care unit, we wish to disassociate ourselves from the opinions expressed by [Duff and Campbell]. The "growing tendency to seek early death as a management option" that the authors referred to has been repeatedly called to the attention of those involved and has caused us deep concern. It is troubling to us to hear young pediatric interns ask first, "should we treat?" rather than "how do we treat?"
>
> We are fearful that this feeling of nihilism may not remain restricted to the newborn special-care unit. To suggest that the financial and psychological stresses imposed upon a family with the birth of a handicapped child constitute sufficient justification for such a therapy of nihilism is untenable and allows us to escape what perhaps after all are the real issues— i.e., the obligation of an affluent society to provide financial support and the opportunity for a gainful life to its less fortunate citizens.

After months of talking to parents, doctors, judges, and a number of the severely handicapped, I thought I had a reasonably clear sense of the scope of deliberate death in the nursery. But then I discovered a new frontier: a death row for infants in Oklahoma.

As Drs. Duff and Campbell had done, the physicians themselves told of the deaths they had caused, and once again they spoke not in confession but in pride. The article, "Early Management and Decision Making for the Treatment of Myelomeningocele," appeared in the October, 1983, issue of *Pediatrics*, a publication of the American Academy of Pediatrics. Among the authors were Drs. Richard H. Gross, Alan Cox, and Michael Pollay.

Over a five-year period an experiment had been conducted at the University of Oklahoma Health Sciences Center. The subjects of the experiment were newborn infants with spina bifida. Each was evaluated by a team of physicians, nurses, physical and occupational therapists, a social worker, and a psychologist. The team decided, in each case, whether to recommend "active vigorous treatment" or to inform the parents that they did not consider them obligated to have the baby treated; the family could choose "supportive care only." Each infant in the first group was given all medically indicated treatment, including an operation to close the spinal lesion and the implanting of a shunt to drain spinal fluid from the brain. The unfortunate infants relegated to supportive care received no active medical treatment: no surgery, no antibiotics to treat infection, and no routinely administered sedation during the dying process that began inexorably with only supportive care.

Of the twenty-four infants who did not get active, vigorous treatment, none survived. The mean age at death was thirty-seven days. As the babies' physicians wrote in *Pediatrics*, "The 'untreated survivor' has not been a significant problem in our experience."

All but one of the infants who received active, vigorous treatment survived. The exception was killed in an auto accident.

To determine which infants were to be given death tickets, the medical team relied in substantial part on a "quality of life" formula: $QL = NE \times (H + S)$.

QL is the quality of life the child is likely to have if he is allowed to live. NE is the child's natural endowment (physical and intellectual). H is the contribution the child can expect from his home and family. S is the probable contribution to that handicapped child from society.

Since under this formula the patient's natural endowment is not the sole determinant of the medical treatment he gets, his chances of being permitted to stay alive can be greatly reduced if his parents are on the lower rungs of poverty. If, moreover, he is poor and has been born during the Reagan Administration—which prefers missiles to funding for the handicapped—the baby has been hit with a double whammy.

The creator of this powerful formula, which has influenced physicians around the country, is Dr. Anthony Shaw, the director of the Department of Pediatric Surgery at the City of Hope National Medical Center, in Duarte, California, and a clinical professor of surgery at the UCLA School of Medicine. He is also the chairman of the Ethics Committee of the American Pediatric Surgical Association. When I charged Dr. Shaw, during a television debate, with having created a means test for deciding which infants shall continue to live, he said he had intended no such thing. I asked him how else one could read his formula, and he said that its purpose was to help the parents. And, of course, the baby.

The last two elements of the formula, plainly, have nothing to do with medical judgments. Yet Martin Gerry, a civil-rights lawyer who was the director of the Office for Civil Rights of the Department of Health, Education and Welfare from 1975 to 1977, and who investigated the Oklahoma experiment, found that the parents of the infants involved "were told by representatives of the [medical] team that the proposed treatment/non-treatment alternative represented a medical judgment made by the team. The quality-of-life formula used was neither discussed with nor revealed to the parents."

An appalled reader of the article in *Pediatrics* was Dr. John M. Freeman, of the Birth Defects Treatment Center at Johns Hopkins Hospital, in Baltimore. Writing to *Pediatrics*, Freeman observed that while the Oklahoma medical team did prove that it "can get the infants to die quickly," such skill hardly qualifies as "the best available alternative" for the management of babies with spina bifida. Dr. Freeman added that the twenty-four infants who died "might also have done well and might have . . . walked with assistive devices, gone to regular school, been of normal intelligence, and achieved bowel and bladder control."

Should anyone be charged with criminal responsibility for their deaths? "The facts, just as written by the doctors themselves in the article, clearly demonstrate violation of both state and federal law," Martin Gerry says. "I think there are clearly violations of state child-abuse laws; there are violations of state criminal laws. I think what you have here is a conspiracy to commit murder." So far, however, no prosecutors have been interested in going after indictments. The Reagan Administration says it is unsure that it has sufficient legal basis—given the laws in force at the time of the Oklahoma experiment—for moving against doctors who withheld treatment.

Two years ago, however, after the death by starvation of the baby with Down's syndrome in Bloomington, Indiana, President Reagan angrily ordered the secretary of the Department of Health and Human Services to apply Section 504 of the Rehabilitation Act of 1973 to handicapped infants. Section 504 says that under any program receiving federal assistance a handicapped person cannot be discriminated against because he or she is handicapped. Accordingly, handicapped infants must—like all other infants in the nursery—be fed and given appropriate medical treatment.

Regulations came down from Washington to enforce the application of 504 to handicapped babies. A hotline was set up so that anyone hearing that treatment or food was being denied a Baby Doe could report the details to federal investigators. And the Justice Department claimed that because of Section 504 it had the authority to review a Baby Doe's medical records in order to determine whether the baby was being discriminated against.

So it was that the Justice Department demanded the records of Baby Jane Doe, the Long Island child born with spina bifida whose parents, acting on the advice of their doctors, had refused operations to close the spine and to insert a shunt in order to drain the fluid pressing on her brain. (Months later a shunt was implanted.)

The privacy of Baby Jane Doe was protected against the federal government by the attorney general of the State of New York, the New York Civil Liberties Union, the American Hospital Association, the American Academy of Pediatrics, and other medical groups. Supporting the Administration's position were the American Coalition of Citizens with Disabilities, the Association for Retarded Citizens, the Association for the Severely Handicapped, the Disability Rights Education and Defense Fund, Disabled in Action of Metropolitan New York, and the Disability Rights Union. They said they were on the side of Baby Jane Doe.

The federal government lost all the way, up to and including the United States Court of Appeals for the Second Circuit, where, on February 23, 1984, a panel decided 2 to 1 that if Congress meant Section 504 of the 1973 Rehabilitation Act to apply to Baby Does, it ought to say so loud and clear. Until then the privacy of the parents and of the infant must not be violated.

In a strong dissent, overlooked by much of the press, Judge Ralph Winter wrote that the question wasn't even arguable. He drew an analogy to race. "A judgment not to perform certain surgery because a person is black is not a *bona fide* medical judgment. So too, a decision not to correct a life-threatening digestive problem because an infant has Down's syndrome is not a *bona fide* medical judgment." Both decisions are acts of discrimination. Buttressing the logic of this analysis, Winter added, was the fact that Section 504 of the Rehabilitation Act of 1973 had been patterned after, and is almost identical to, the anti-discrimination language of Section 601 of the Civil Rights Act of 1964.

No major newspapers that I know of published editorials lauding Judge Winter's dissent. Practically all of the nation's leading and lesser newspapers had claimed throughout the odyssey of Baby Jane Doe that the infant and her parents were being persecuted by a grossly intrusive and insensitive federal government.

Baby Jane Doe had been saved from Big Brother. "The federal government," said Richard Rifkin, a spokesman for the attorney general of the State of New York, "is now barred from conducting any investigation of medical decisions regarding defective newborns."

Liberals and civil libertarians cheered. This had been one of their few victories over Ronald Reagan.

Signs persisted, however, that Congress might come to the aid of Baby Does. On February 2, 1984, the House debated with much passion a bill to extend the Child Abuse Prevention and Treatment Act. The amendments to one section broadened the definition of child abuse to include the denial of medical treatment or nutrition to infants born with life-threatening conditions. The section also mandated that each state, to keep getting funds for child-abuse programs, would have to put in place a reporting system that could be alerted whenever a handicapped infant was being abused by denial of treatment or food.

Liberals led the debate against those provisions on the House floor, and conservatives, by and large, supported the measure. Particularly eloquent was Henry Hyde, an unabashed Tory, whose history of implacable opposition to abortion reinforced the view of many liberals, in and out of the House, that all of this compassion for Baby Does was actually propaganda to gain sympathy for the unborn.

"The fact is," Hyde said during the debate, "that . . . many children . . . are permitted to die because minimal routine medical care is withheld from them. And the parents who have the emotional trauma of being confronted with this horrendous decision, and seeing ahead a bleak prospect, may well not be, in that time and at that place, the best people to decide. . . . I suggest that a question of life or death for a born person ought to belong to nobody, whether they are parents or not. The Constitution ought to protect that child. . . . Because they are handicapped, they are not to be treated differently than if they were women or Hispanics or American Indians or black. [Their handicap] is a mental condition or a physical condition; but by God, they are human, and nobody has the right to kill them by passive starvation or anything else."

On the key vote concerning this section of the bill Congresswoman Geraldine Ferraro joined other renowned liberals in the House in voting against protections for handicapped babies, though most, to be sure, said they were supporting the right of parents to make life-or-death decisions about their infants and opposing government interference in that process. Among the others in opposition were such normally fierce defenders of the powerless as Peter Rodino, Henry Waxman, Don Edwards, Barney Frank, John Conyers, Thomas Downey, Charles Rangel, Robert Kastenmeier, Gerry Studds, George Crockett, and Barbara Mikulski.

The vote on expanding the definition of child abuse to include the neglect of handicapped infants was 231 to 182 in favor. Not until July, however, did the Senate pass a bill protecting the lives of Baby Does. An unusually ecumenical team of senators sponsored the bill: Orrin Hatch, Alan Cranston, Christopher Dodd, Jeremiah Denton, Don Nickles, and Nancy Kassebaum. Edward M. Kennedy was involved until nearly the end.

Handling the day-to-day maneuvering were members of the staffs of various senators. They were continually fearful that the fractious coalition of medical, right-to-life, and disability-rights organizations that had to agree on the language of the bill would fall apart. Yet at the end the AMA was the only medical group to walk out. Its representative had kept insisting on the need to allow physicians to make "quality of life" decisions as to whether an infant should live or die. Staying behind and signing the agreement were, among other medical organizations, the American Academy of Pediatrics, the American College of Obstetricians and Gynecologists, the American College of Physicians, and the American Nurses Association.

As finally passed, the Senate bill (which, with a few modifications, was accepted by the House in conference) redefines child abuse and neglect, for purposes of this federal statute, to include "the withholding of medically indicated treatment from disabled infants with life-threatening conditions." No heroic measures are required, however, if treatment would merely prolong dying and would be "virtually futile in terms of the survival of the infant," or if the baby "is chronically and irreversibly comatose."

Under this Child Abuse Prevention and Treatment Act each state, in order to get federal child abuse and neglect grants, is required to create a system for reporting to state child-protection agencies cases in which infants are being denied treatment. As a last resort these agencies have the authority to "initiate any legal remedies" needed to prevent such a child from being killed. In effect, this means that Baby Does have rights independent of the rights of their parents. If they are not born dying or irreversibly comatose, handicapped infants, as persons under the Constitution, are entitled by federal statute to due process and equal protection under the law.

Meanwhile, the American Medical Association is likely to test all this in court, having already indicated its preferred approach to the Baby Doe question. On June 20 delegates to the AMA's 133rd annual convention, in Chicago, voted to support the concept of "local option" for Baby Does. That is, they wish communities and hospitals to have the legal right to set their own life-or-death standards for handicapped infants. Baby Does to come are not out of danger. Parents as well as doctors will be trying to get the new law struck down.

One of the first things I did when the bill passed was to send the news to a woman in Mount Airy, Maryland, who has been much dismayed at the infanticides in the nurseries in her county. She told me of going to a hospital seminar on the subject a couple of years ago and listening to the head of a neonatal nursery staff complain that it was awfully hard on her nurses when a baby deprived of treatment took fifteen days to die. Other infants, she felt the lecturer had implied, were more accommodating.

This woman in Mount Airy had written to me last summer: "As a social studies teacher of ancient civilizations, I conducted classroom discussions covering the topic 'Ideals of Sparta vs. Ideals of Athens.' It was always . . . a shock for my students to learn that the Spartans, who valued 'body' over 'mind,' could be as callous and cruel as to leave their deformed newborns on the rocky hillsides to die.

"In this matter, it would seem, we have not come very far. What shall be written of us in years hence? That we merely brought this barbaric practice indoors?"

1985

SOMETHING TO HIDE IN
THE NURSERY?

I n 1984 Congress, after bitter debate, passed the Child
Abuse Prevention and Treatment Act. When it became law,
child abuse and neglect were redefined to include "withholding medically indicated treatment from disabled infants
with life-threatening conditions."

Part of the impetus for this child-saving law had been the
widely reported death by starvation of a Down's Syndrome
baby in Bloomington, Ind., in 1980. The parents had agreed
with their obstetrician that this child could not attain "a minimally adequate quality of life" because it would be mentally
retarded. A horrified pediatrician at Bloomington Hospital
tried to bring intravenous equipment to feed the baby, but he
was too late.

In 1982 an article in the Archives of Internal Medicine reported, "It is common in the United States to withhold routine
surgery and medical care from infants with Down's Syndrome
for the explicit purpose of hastening death." The requests
sometimes came from the parents.

Additional cases of summarily dispatching infants with other defects had surfaced in the news. These decisions ending life were made on behalf of born children, not fetuses. Though handicapped, they were entitled, at birth, to equal protection of the laws.

During the 1984 debate in the House, I was dismayed to see some of the most prominent Democratic liberals—Henry Waxman, Barney Frank, Charles Rangel, Geraldine Ferraro, among them—oppose these protections for handicapped infants. It should be up to the parents and their doctors, these humanists said, to make such life-or-death decisions. Children, therefore, were chattel, with no rights of their own.

The new law required each state—in order to get federal child-abuse and neglect grants—to create a system that would report to state child protection agencies whenever damaged infants were being denied treatment. No action would be taken by the state, however, if treatment would merely prolong dying or if the infant was "chronically or irreversibly comatose."

After the law went into effect, there was much anger from physicians writing in some of the medical journals. Their professionalism was being interfered with, they said. There were pledges that the statute would be resisted.

What actually has been happening to disabled infants since then has been very difficult to determine. Not all records of the reasons for ending treatment are thorough or painstakingly honest. The hostility of many physicians to the 1984 law continues, and some have pointed out that since no doctor has been held responsible under that statute for civil or criminal liability, the law should be ignored because it is irrelevant.

Recently, in the prestigious journal *Pediatrics* (January 1997), the first detailed study of the consequences of the 1984 law has appeared. Drs. Stephen Wall and John Colin Partridge are the authors of "Death in the Intensive Care Nursery: Physician Practice of Withdrawing and Withholding Life Support." Over three years, they have reviewed the medical records of all 165 infants who have died in the Intensive Care Nursery at the University of California, San Francisco.

"Most deaths among hospitalized newborns," they write, "result from neonatologists' decisions to limit [life-sustaining] treatment. . . . [S]uch decisions are not infrequently based on the physicians' concerns about the infant's quality of life."

I have known a number of adults born disabled whose parents were advised by physicians to end their children's lives because of the future quality of those lives. One is now a lawyer; another is a psychotherapist. Yet in this study in *Pediatrics* the only reason physicians had for discontinuing treatment in 23 percent of the cases was the infant's future quality of life. And it was a contributing factor in marking other infants for death.

Moreover, "physician notes indicated that parents initiated the discussion of limiting treatment in only a few [13 percent] of these deaths." Parents were eventually drawn into the discussions, but the fact that a neonatologist—with all of his or her authority—was the first to recommend death had to change the infant's prospects.

During House floor debate in 1984, Rep. Henry Hyde (R-Ill.) said: "The Constitution ought to protect that child." It did not save many of those children before 1984, and it has not since. This time Congress should make sure that the Constitution does protect these born children.

As it is, say the authors of the *Pediatrics* article, since the 1984 debate "no extensive United States studies have as yet reported on actual physician practices of limiting neonatal life support—how frequently and for whom?" Why haven't there been such studies, except for this one hospital? Is there something to hide in the intensive care nursery?

1997

PRESS SWOONS FOR A
BUNCO ARTIST

On April 29, I attended—for the first time—the allegedly prestigious White House Correspondents' Association dinner. The stars were two stand-up comics: Jay Leno and the president of the United States.

The audience at the Washington Hilton included about 2,000 renowned print and television journalists, as well as celebrities from Hollywood and network television. I am grateful to *The Washington Times* for the invitation, because the evening changed my view of many in the Washington press corps—and not for the better.

In his May 3 *Washington Times* column, Tony Blankley wrote that "almost alone" among the guests, he was "appalled both by President Clinton's performance and by the positive response of the audience."

He was not alone. During several standing ovations for the president, I remained seated. And although many laughed at his jokes until there were tears in their eyes, I was disgusted, not amused. I have greatly enjoyed Richard Pryor, Dick Gregory, Moms Mabley and Lenny Bruce (who was a friend); but they did not memorize someone else's script. They improvised and they boldly and hilariously skewered the hypocrisies of the powerful—in and out of politics. They did not—as the president always does—focus on the way one's ability to rise from adversity increases one's own glory.

Clinton's performance was written by Mark Katz of the Soundbite Institute. Katz also ghosts for Al Gore and Hillary Rodham Clinton, who is not notable for her wit. Video clips assembled by Phil Rosenthal, the creator and producer of "Everybody Loves Raymond," were shown during the president's monologue. For some reason the president neglected to acknowledge his helpers. I wonder if they did this pro bono, as a patriotic service.

The president's stamp was on every line. The jokes that continually broke up the sophisticated diners were intended to cloak the ways he has dishonored his office by enabling him to be seen as "the poor soul" who is, after all, only human.

Now that he has survived, partly by making people laugh at his bumbling misadventures (his routine that night has been widely televised), he shows what good sports we all are. And the president—after all the mortification he has endured from Ken Starr and other prudish, malicious "right-wing zealots"— shows that he is the best sport of all.

As Tony Blankley astutely put it, "By gaining the laughter of the political and media elite in the room [and the American viewing audience], he implicates them as after-the-fact co-conspirators with him."

During the evening, Clinton made a joke about Travelgate. Amid the laughter, I wondered if Billy Dale, who ran the White House travel office, was watching C-Span. Clinton ruined the man's life by falsely accusing him of misuse of funds.

I guess writer Mark Katz couldn't come up with a joke about the president's tampering with witnesses involved in the impeachment proceedings. Nor could he find any humor in the way Clinton deliberately denied due process—elemental fairness—to another citizen, Paula Jones, by deliberately lying during a deposition in her case. White House Special Counsel Lanny Davis might have spun it if he had been asked to work on the script.

But the correspondents who orchestrated the event much preferred Jay Leno, who poked at some sore spots in what will be the Clinton legacy, but never really darkened the overall tribute to The Comeback Kid. And Leno practically genuflected in praise of the president's comic timing.

That night, I ran into a couple of journalists who also declined to join the ovations for the president. Particularly outraged was Matt Drudge, the "lonely pamphleteer" who is looked down upon by his more establishment colleagues.

Drudge railed at what has become of the press, which used to bask in its critical independence but now cheers a bunco artist. Drudge told me that Deputy Attorney General Eric Holder—fresh from his role in orchestrating the commando raid that extracted Elian Gonzalez—chided such criticism of the merry correspondents' dinner. "It's all in good humor," Holder told Drudge.

As the laughter of the audience rolled on, I thought of my mentors in journalism: George Seldes, I. F. Stone and Murray Kempton. I don't think they would have joined the standing ovations for this president. And I remembered my first editor,

William Harrison, whom I worked for when I was 19 years old. He ran a weekly newspaper for black readers, *The Boston Chronicle*.

"There are three rules here," he told me. "Accuracy, clarity, and don't let the people you cover con you."

At last I know who the inveterate Washington insiders are. They're the press corps.

2000

LIFE OF THE PARTY

R obert Casey, who died on May 30 at age 68, was a Democrat fiercely committed to his party's tradition of
protecting society's most vulnerable. And, for that, his
party made him a pariah.

As governor of Pennsylvania from 1987 to 1994, Casey created model school-based child-care programs that offered infants and preschoolers—including poor children—full-day
services and before- and after-school programs. That way,
teenage parents could stay in school and poor adults could go
to work knowing their children were safe. He lobbied unsuccessfully for universal health care in his state, but, failing that,
as *The New York Times* reported in its May 31 obituary, "he did
sign a bill providing health insurance for children whose families were too poor to pay for it but whose incomes were too
high to be eligible for public assistance." Before breast cancer
became a political cliché, Casey invested $1 million in aware-
ness and screening for the disease and required HMOs to pay
for annual mammograms for women over 40. Harvard University pediatrician T. Berry Brazelton described Casey's multidi-

mensional health care programs for women and children as "a model for the rest of the country."

The son of a coal-miner-turned-lawyer, Casey believed in the party of Franklin D. Roosevelt, and he doggedly rebuilt it in Pennsylvania. In 1991, he personally raised more than $1 million to help underdog Harris Wofford defeat Dick Thornburgh, then-President Bush's former attorney general, for a United States Senate seat. At the time, Paul Begala, who worked for Casey and later for President Clinton, told Mary McGrory of *The Washington Post*: "Save for Bob Casey, Harris Wofford would have lost. Casey rebuilt the party from ashes, and made it a better organization than the Republicans'."

Nonetheless, Casey's party treated him with disdain. As the 1992 Democratic Convention in New York approached, Casey told me he expected, in light of his policy accomplishments and political loyalty, to be a speaker, maybe even the keynote speaker. But he wasn't the keynote speaker. The honor of nominating Clinton went to New York Governor Mario Cuomo, who ignited the crowd by declaring, "Bill Clinton believes, as we all here do, in the first principle of our Democratic commitment: the politics of inclusion."

Casey was not asked to speak. In fact, he and his Pennsylvania delegation were exiled to the farthest reaches of Madison Square Garden—because Casey was pro-life. It didn't matter that, under his leadership, state contracts to minority- and women-owned firms had increased more than 1,500 percent in five years, or that he had appointed more female Cabinet members than any Democratic governor in the country, or that he had appointed the first black woman ever to sit on a state Supreme Court. Ron Brown, chief convention organizer and the

Democratic Party's symbol of minority inclusion, told Casey, "Your views are out of line with those of most Americans."

Casey had the misfortune of being present during a great shift in the Democratic Party. A mere six years earlier, on September 26, 1986, then-Governor Bill Clinton of Arkansas had assured the head of his state's chapter of the National Right to Life Committee, "I am opposed to abortion and to government funding of abortion." But, by the early '90s, the Democrats, seeking the votes of upper-middle-class Republican women, were de-emphasizing economic protection and stressing cultural libertarianism. And, just to make sure everyone got the message, Democratic strategists invited Kathy Taylor, a pro-choice Pennsylvania Republican who had helped defeat Casey's progressive tax reforms, to the New York convention. She appeared onstage pledging the National Abortion Rights Action League's allegiance to the Clinton-Gore team. Then DNC officials sent Taylor, with a camera crew in tow, to find Casey in "Outer Mongolia," as he put it, to further humiliate him. Tipped off, he declined the national exposure. Shortly before Casey left the convention, Al Gore called him to apologize for any embarrassment. The governor told me dryly that he doubted Gore was speaking from the heart.

"What has become of the Democratic Party I once knew?" Casey asked when he returned home. But he didn't leave the party, even though, in his view, "it ha[d] become a wholly owned subsidiary of the National Abortion Rights Action League." The GOP would have been delighted to gather him in, but Casey said, "The pro-life Republicans drop the children at birth and do nothing for them after that." He added, in an interview with the *Pittsburgh Post-Gazette* not long before he left office in 1994, that "as far as the Republican Party is concerned, the business of government is business." Casey's politics were simple, but they were so heretical that in the language of '90s American politics they quite literally didn't have a name. And so last week, in a final slap, the *Washington Post*, *New York Times*, and CNN obituaries identified the former governor as a "conservative Democrat."

James Carville worked on Casey's 1986 and 1990 reelection campaigns. In a June 1 interview with *National Review Online*, Carville said of his former boss: "You have no idea what a deep sense of probity he had. . . . He was just the kind of person that made the whole Washington establishment completely uncomfortable. . . . They could never understand him." Carville also noted his former partner, Begala, was also "a Casey protégé." I wonder how they felt, and what they did, while Casey was being humiliated in 1992. As Bob Casey was being driven from the Democratic Party because he refused to sacrifice his beliefs, they ascended further up the party ladder, going to work for a politician who didn't have such problems. And, when Casey died, President Clinton said he admired the governor's "commitment to principle."

2000

My Friend the Cardinal

There's no point in simply talking to people about filling their souls if you don't fill their bellies.

—John Cardinal O'Connor, Christmas 1986

Even before John O'Connor left his post as the bishop of Scranton, Pennsylvania, in 1984 to become archbishop of New York, he ignited a firestorm of controversy. In a Sunday morning interview on WNBC-TV, O'Connor compared the killing of 4000 babies a day in the United States to the holocaust.

"Hitler tried to solve a problem, the Jewish question," he said. "So kill them, shove them into ovens, burn them. To me [abortion] is precisely the same."

Supporters of abortion rights were furious, and many Jews charged the newcomer with diminishing the horror of Hitler.

I was on the staff of *The New Yorker* then, as well as being a columnist for the *Voice*, and decided to find out if O'Connor was worth a profile in that magazine. If he was just a rigid, orthodox conservative, it wouldn't be worth the extraordinary time and trouble those pieces took. So I went to the Catholic Center on First Avenue to see for myself.

Waiting in the anterooom of his office, I heard him shouting in the corridor. In all the time I spent with O'Connor in the years since, I never again heard him raise his voice. But on this day of a citywide hospital strike, including the Catholic hospitals, called by District 1199, the man in charge of labor relations for all the hospitals had decided to hire strikebreakers.

"Over my dead body," the archbishop was yelling, "will any person be fired because he or she belongs to a union and is exercising the right of collective bargaining. I will not stand for union busting."

Three years later, in 1987, he held a press conference with Jesse Jackson in New York to call indignant attention to the indecent wages being paid to the largely black and Hispanic home-care health service workers. He told reporters that 51 percent were earning less than $7000 annually, and that 80 percent were living below the poverty level.

I remember Francis Cardinal Spellman's reaction in 1942, when the United Cemetery Workers, Local 93—earning $59 for a six-day, 48-hour week—went on strike. Spellman commanded a large number of seminarians from St. Joseph's Seminary in Yonkers to go to Calvary Cemetery in Queens and break the strike by digging the graves themselves. Cardinal Spellman was the first to dig.

The new cardinal turned out to be much more difficult to stereotype than I had first thought. But some New Yorkers still found him repellent. O'Connor knew, for instance, that Gloria

Steinem had said that the two worst things to happen to New York in years had been "AIDS and Cardinal O'Connor."

I asked him about this tribute, and he said, laughing, "She's not the only one who thinks I'm the Genghis Khan of the Church."

There were others, however, who were convinced that the purportedly conservative prelate had dangerous socialist leanings.

One evening, the cardinal was the guest of dishonor at a dinner held by a group of prominent conservative and neo-conservative intellectuals in a private dining room of a university club on the East Side. Because I was writing about him for *The New Yorker*, I was asked to come along.

The National Conference of Catholic Bishops had recently issued the first draft of a pastoral letter on the economy. It called for economic justice for the poor in this land of rampant free-market inequality. O'Connor had signed and strongly supported this speaking of truth to the powerful.

I knew that at least one of the men at the table was a big contributor to Catholic charities. He and the others accusingly asked the cardinal what business it was of the church to get involved in political, secular advocacy that undermined the future economic growth of the nation. "It's a socialist document," one of them said.

Firmly, O'Connor looked at his inquisitors and said, "About 900,000 individuals in New York live in substandard conditions not fit for pigs, including overcrowding, with all the attendant evils of that kind of life. I would be failing my religious and moral responsibilities if all I did was to say Mass and carry out the customary religious duties of my office."

Later that night, sitting across from him, I whispered, "Maybe you now have a keener appreciation of some of the economic thinking on the Left than before you came into this plush place with those hunting prints on the walls." The cardinal laughed and kept laughing for quite a while—to the puzzlement of the stern critics around the table.

At another time, a man dying of AIDS wanted to renew the civil-marriage vows he had made to his wife three years before. A Protestant, he had been gay in the past, and desperately hoped for a religious marriage ceremony in St. Patrick's Cathedral because his wife, a Catholic, regarded St. Patrick's as her "dream church."

The cardinal was in Israel, where he was characteristically creating controversy by saying that since "the Palestinians don't have a land they can call their own, they can hardly be called a people who yet have the right to self-determination."

The rector of St. Patrick's refused to allow the marriage ceremony. On his return, the Genghis Khan of the church reversed that decision. On Valentine's Day, the cardinal welcomed the couple to the cathedral, kissed the bride, shook hands with the groom, and blessed the couple.

"There are many who would question my very presence at such a marriage," O'Connor told the press, "but every human life is sacred."

2000

INDEX